Fluid Gender, Fluid Love

At the Interface/Probing the Boundaries

VOLUME 108

The titles published in this series are listed at *brill.com/aipb*

Fluid Gender, Fluid Love

Edited by

Deirdre C. Byrne and Wernmei Yong Ade

BRILL
RODOPI

LEIDEN | BOSTON

Cover illustration: "Jenny-Anne and Elen get married". Photograph by Sara Davidmann. Used with permission.

Library of Congress Cataloging-in-Publication Data

Names: Byrne, D. C. (Deirdre C.), editor.
Title: Fluid gender, fluid love / edited by Deirdre C. Byrne and Wernmei Yong Ade.
Description: Boston : Brill, 2019. | Series: At the interface/probing the boundaries, ISSN 1570-7113 ; VOLUME 108 | Includes bibliographical references and index.
Identifiers: LCCN 2018039500 (print) | LCCN 2018043151 (ebook) | ISBN 9789004380233 (ebook) | ISBN 9789004378285 (alk. paper)
Subjects: LCSH: Religion and culture. | Toleration–Religious aspects.
Classification: LCC BL65.C8 (ebook) | LCC BL65.C8 F58 2018 (print) | DDC 201/.7–dc23
LC record available at https://lccn.loc.gov/2018039500

Typeface for the Latin, Greek, and Cyrillic scripts: "Brill". See and download: brill.com/brill-typeface.

ISSN 1570-7113
ISBN 978-90-04-37828-5 (hardback)
ISBN 978-90-04-38023-3 (e-book)

This book is printed on acid-free paper and produced in a sustainable manner.

Contents

PART 3
Aspects of Love and Gender for Transgender People

PART 4
Fluid Gender, Fluid Love in Postmodernity

Notes on Contributors

Wernmei Yong Ade
is Assistant Professor with the English Programme at Nanyang Technological University, where she lectures and researches in the areas of feminist studies, contemporary women's writing, critical theory, and love. Her main research addresses ideological and ethical dimensions of love, and their representations in literature, philosophy and film. In recent years, this research has converged with her long-standing interest in women's issues and feminism. She is currently working on a monograph on the topic of love in the fiction of British writer Angela Carter.

Deirdre C. Byrne
is a full Professor of English Studies and the Head of the Institute for Gender Studies at the University of South Africa. She is the editor-in-chief of two academic journals: *Scrutiny: Issues in English Studies in Southern Africa* and *Gender Questions.* She holds a C2 rating from the National Research Foundation of South Africa as an established researcher. She is engaged in research on the writing of Ursula K. le Guin and on South African women's poetry. She belongs to the steering groups of the International Association for the Study of Gender and Love and also of ZAPP, the South African poetry project.

Dikmen Yakali-Çamoglu
received her PhD in cultural studies from the University of Birmingham, UK. She is an Associate Professor of Communication Studies and teaches courses on communication theories, cultural theory and popular culture. Her current research and writing interest is the construction of narrative identities in the family and in popular culture.

Tuija Saresma
is an adjunct professor and senior researcher at the Research Centre for Contemporary Culture, Department of Music, Art and Culture Research, University of Jyväskylä. She has published widely on the areas of gender studies and cultural studies. Recently, she co-edited a volume *Populism on the Loose* with Urpo Kovala, Emilia Palonen, and Maria Ruotsalainen (Nykykulttuuri 2018, free access e-book). Besides populism, her research interests include affects, gender and other intersecting differences, performativity of writing, hate speech, social media, and mobility and migration. She is former chair of

Kulttuurintutkimuksen seura [Finnish Association of Cultural Studies] and former editor in chief of journal *Kulttuurintutkimus*.

Marianne Schleicher
is Associate Professor in Jewish Studies, Department for the Study of Religion, Aarhus University, Denmark. As part of her research on the role of scripture in Judaism, Marianne has published on the function of Biblical and Talmudic imagery in Jewish mysticism (*Intertextuality in the Tales of Rabbi Nahman of Bratslav*, Brill 2007), which led to her development of a systematic distinction between "Artifactual and Hermeneutical Use of Scripture in Jewish Tradition" (in ed. Evans: *Jewish and Christian Scripture as Artifact and Canon*. T & T Clark 2009), to capture the material and sensory aspects of such uses, also among lay people ("Engaging All the Senses: On Multi-sensory Stimulation in the Process of Making and Inaugurating a Torah Scroll", *Postscripts* 2017). Marianne has worked for several years on tracing developments in gender norms in Israelite-Jewish religion from antiquity until today ("Constructions of Sex and Gender: Attending to Androgynes and *Tumtumim* Through Jewish Scriptural Use", *Literature & Theology* 2011) to reflect on the premises for cultural tolerance of deviating genders and practices of love in the face of embodied resistance to conformity ("Androgyny/Hermaphroditism: Early Judaism", *Oxford Biblical Studies Online* 2017).

Bridget Sandhoff
is assistant professor of art history at the University of Nebraska Omaha, USA. She specializes in the art of the ancient Mediterranean, especially Etruria. She has published on a variety of topics on Etruscan art including gender ambiguity, feminine beauty, representations of love, and engraved bronze mirrors.

Kelly Gardiner
is a lecturer in creative writing at La Trobe University, Australia, and an award-winning novelist. She has published eight books, including *1917: Australia's Great War*, *Goddess*, and the young adult novels *Act of Faith* and *The Sultan's Eyes*.

Andrea Mathews
has been a teacher for over 20 years and is currently a teacher in a Catholic sixth form college. Having taught a number of transgender students over recent years, Andrea decided to conduct this research to find out if the religious ethos of a school had any impact on the transitioning experience of transgender students.

Veenu Kakkar
is an independent consultant with 18 years of experience in programme implementation and training with varied stakeholders such as young people and government functionaries on gender issues. Previously, she led Breakthrough India's programme on gender-biased sex selection and gender based discrimination in Haryana.

Aanchal Kapur
is a gender and development specialist with 28 years of experience. Major publications: 'Women Workers Rights: Issues and Strategies', ILO, Geneva/ India, 1999; 'From Thought to Action: Building Strategies on Violence against Women', Oxfam/ Kriti team, India, 2004.

Angela Tumini
is an Associate Professor of Film at Columbia College Hollywood. Her various publications include a book on Danish filmmaker Lars von Trier and several articles and volume chapters concerning women and film. She is also the co-editor of an interdisciplinary volume on the subject of making sense of pain, published by Inter-disciplinary Press.

Sylvia Tidey
is Assistant Professor in the Department of Anthropology and the Global Studies Program at the University of Virginia. She is a cultural anthropologist who focuses on (trans)genderism, sexuality, corruption, bureaucracy, and the state in Indonesia. In her ongoing research, she attends to possibilities for selves, care, and happiness as they develop within the nexus of Indonesian transgender family intimacies, in relation to broader local, national, and global contexts, in which ideas of living happily for gender nonconforming persons is increasingly gets framed in activist and medical terms. In 2006, she produced an HIV/AIDS prevention film, *Sonia's Story*, in collaboration with and targeted at transgender women in Yogyakarta, Java.

Illustrations

Introduction

Deirdre C. Byrne and Wernmei Yong Ade

Fluid Gender, Fluid Love is a thoroughgoing academic investigation into two concepts that are so broad that they seem to invade all areas of cultural and scholarly life. Love, in particular, is endlessly thought, re-thought, re-represented and reconfigured in the popular and cultural imagination. There are indubitably as many variants of love as there are individual lovers. Gender is a similarly encompassing concept, which touches on personal identity, intersubjective relationships, communal and cultural practices. Indeed, as Andrea Mathews notes in her chapter, "What Would Jesus Do? Transgender and Transsexual Narratives of the Relationships between Religion and Education," the fact that the social media website, Facebook, offers 50 options for the user to customize their identity points to the increasing fluidity of gender in the twenty-first century. This, in turn, derives from the fact that gender identities are not given, but constructed, usually along ideological lines that serve the goals of social reproduction. As constructs, both gender and love can be interrogated, subverted, and even negated. The chapters in this book turn these constructs upside down and inside out from different angles at various points.

This book is divided into four sections. The first section, "Historical Insights into Norms for Gender and Love," consists of three chapters. The first chapter by Marianne Schleicher, entitled "Attitudes to Deviation from Gender Norms in Israelite and Early Jewish Religion," explores the Jewish view of gender and love relationships, to suggest a way forward towards the intelligibility of complex and deviant identities, and what this could bode for the survival of culture. Through an analysis of the way Israelite and early Jewish texts seemingly promote gender norms to secure cultural survival, this chapter argues that gender deviation was tolerated if the deviation contributed to preventing the loss of land and the weakening of cultural boundaries. Based on these insights from Jewish history, Schleicher's chapter contends that scholars should continue to gather knowledge about complex, liminal and marginal identities, paying attention to how these have contributed in the course of history to the success and survival of culture. The next chapter in this section is Bridget Sandhoff's "The Art of Etruscan Love." Sandhoff's discussion pays close attention to the way married love in ancient Rome and Etruria between the third century BC and the second century AD is represented in funerary art, murals and other visual art forms. Surprisingly, she finds that these artefacts demonstrate how a significant number of ancient Etrurian wives were loved and cherished by

 | DOI:10.1163/9789004380233_002

their husbands as equals. This flies in the face of popular assumptions that love in classical societies was necessarily a matter of gender inequality, where men married only in order to have domestic and sexual servants.

The first section also contains an excursion into gender and love relations in classical Greek thought via the tale of Eros and Psyche in the chapter "Love, Alterity and Gender Relations: Re-thinking the Myth of Eros and Psyche," by Wernmei Yong Ade. Central to the myth of Eros and Psyche, narrated in Apuleius' novel *The Golden Ass*, are the interrelated themes of love and knowledge. Through an analysis of Jungian psychologist and philosopher Erich Neumann's reading of the myth, this chapter argues that, despite objections to the gendered Jungian archetype pervading Neumann's analysis, the tale of Eros and Psyche can indeed contribute something of value towards thinking of love as a means of living ethically, especially where gender relations are concerned. Ade argues that Neumann's insights bear out the conditions necessary in thinking of love as a discourse of alterity, conditions outlined in the philosophical writings of Luce Irigaray. Indeed, the only way to recuperate love as a positive experience for men and women is by understanding it as an experience in which both partners move away from the totalizing domain of sameness, towards otherness and alterity.

The second section of the book, "Inconsistencies in Heterosexual Cultures Today," challenges normative assumptions regarding gender and sexuality. The idea of inconsistencies resonates throughout the three chapters by Dikmen Yakalı-Çamoğlu, Veenu Kakkar and Aanchal Kapur, and Tuija Saresma. All three writers, in different ways, unpack the fault lines in gender norms as they are experienced and represented in heteronormative society. A focus on these fault lines reveals that what we consider to be a given heterosexual culture is not a seamless or unmodulated whole, but a conglomerate of contradictions between perspectives and expectations of different gender subjectivities and positions. Yakalı-Camoğlu's wide-ranging research, described in her chapter on "Characters from a Different Story: Media, Narratives of Love and Construction of Gender Identities in Children's World," deals with the way Disney princes and princesses are received by young girls and boys (aged between 4 and 8), to explore the inconsistency that lies between the heterosexual matrix of patriarchal society and the overt incompatibility of play norms among boys and girls. Yakalı-Camoğlu carefully navigates through an analysis of both the way women and men are portrayed in the Disney narratives – princesses are largely decorative and princes do little other than enact their devotion to their princesses – and the reception of these images by young children, to examine how these representations of femininity, masculinity and love affect gender construction among little girls and boys. This has an impact on relationships between the opposite sexes, leading to a segregated social life along gender lines. The study suggests a startling outcome: incompatible narrative identity constructions of boys and girls contradict the standard objective of cultural discourse, which is to secure reproduction.

Veenu Kakkar and Aanchal Kapur's chapter, "Control and Exclusion of Female Bodies in India: Responding to Ground Realities," addresses a darker side of the failure of men and women to relate to one another due to strict adherence to normative gender expectations. Taking readers through their work with the Breakthrough NGO in India, Kakkar and Kapur shed light on the serious problem of daughter aversion, which constitutes part of a vicious cycle of discrimination and exclusion for women and girls in India. Thankfully, efforts at challenging and changing these oppressive mind-sets across India are being made at the grassroots and policy levels – targeting families, communities, the medical fraternity, governance structures and the media. One state of India where focussed attention is being given to preventing and ending gender-biased sex selection is Haryana, where Breakthrough initiated activism against the Gender-Biased Sex Selection (GBSS) programme in 2012. Violence against women is similarly examined in the next chapter, Tuija Saresma's "The Concept of Love in Masculinist Blogs: A Strategic Ideal," but this time on the internet, where love, often considered as a positive emotion and (ideally) an ethical relationship between people, is used to promote regressive ideologies such as misogyny and antifeminism. As similarly argued in the last two chapters, the advocates of traditional gender order – masculinists or male rights activists (MRAs) – use normative images of heterosexual love, often intertwined with the idealized heterosexual nuclear family, to achieve this end. Saresma demonstrates that the fluidity of the concept of love enables various strategic uses of the ideal of love, often in the service of a repressive, heteronormative ideology in an attempt to re-position women and men within the traditional, rigid gender order.

The third section of the book deals with "Aspects of Love and Gender for Transgender People." The two chapters in this section agree that transgender identities transgress what Sylvia Tidey calls "the straight line" of heteronormative expectation. Tidey's chapter explores gender identities among Indonesian waria (transgender women) and their relatives. Here, despite overtly subverting the dominant gender regime through their gender identity, the waria reveal conformity to the "straight line" by intending to return to the heterosexual fold after a few years of transgender existence. This, Tidey concludes, is testimony to the power to control and police sexual identity through what heterosexual biopower calls "the normal" and the way it is enforced through family and kinship networks. Andrea Mathews' chapter, "What Would Jesus Do? Transgender and

Transsexual Narratives of the Relationships between Religion and Education," similarly explores the ways in which faith schools in the UK, while overtly espousing Gospel values of love and tolerance of diversity, do not enact these by making transgender pupils feel accepted in their school environments. While the schools are (by and large) accepting towards homosexual pupils, the same respect and tolerance are not extended towards transgender learners.

The final section of the book deals with "Fluid Gender, Fluid Love in Postmodernity" and contains three chapters. The first is Kelly Gardiner's chapter on "Fictions of Love: Writing about 17th-Century Ideas of Gender and Love." Gardiner explores the figure of Julie d'Aubigny, known as La Maupin, a seventeenth-century French cross-dressing swordswoman and opera star who was known for her sexual liaisons with both women and men. La Maupin's relentless historical and biographical interrogation of gender norms in an era "before Freud, before queer" casts into question the rigid boundaries between gender positions that may have been assumed to hold in that century. Gardiner's chapter, like many others, highlights the historical malleability and porosity of polarized gender identities, showing up their inherent contingency and susceptibility to being invaded by the other side of the polar opposition. Deirdre C. Byrne's chapter on "Conditions of (Im)Possibility: True Love in Haruki Murakami's *1Q84* and Suzanne Collins's *Hunger Games* Trilogy" explores the concept of "true love" in two postmodern narratives, Haruki Murakami's *1Q84* and Suzanne Collins's *Hunger Games* trilogy. Through an examination of the way the novels' central protagonists do, and do not, conform to idealized gender norms, Byrne concludes that these two texts espouse a pessimistic view of love and gender performativity, despite a degree of gender rebellion. While the texts espouse some gender fluidity, the authors' choice to set them within works of speculative fiction points to scepticism that this can find expression outside the imaginative space of speculative fiction's capacity to disrupt "the real." Finally, Angela Tumini's chapter on "An Unconventional Ménage à Trois: The Fluidity of Love and Desire in Anne Fontaine's *Nathalie*" explores the ultimate fluidity of gender in a film by contemporary film-maker Anne Fontaine, where a woman hires a prostitute to find out whether her husband is unfaithful. As the two women's relationship unfolds in increasing intimacy, they jettison one of the bastions of heteronormative relations, namely women's supposed dependency on men. Once this is out of the way, they create an entirely new kind of non-romantic, but no less loving intimacy with each other. Tumini shows how this relation between two women includes elements of romance, but ultimately reflects more on their individual and collaborative identities as women, both in and through love, and resonates with the ethical dimensions of their identities as described by Neumann and Ade.

The fluidity of the book's title is not, in any simplistic sense, a deconstruction of established verities and binary polarities where love and gender are concerned. The chapters collected here demonstrate that these supposed polarities are coextensive, porous, nuanced and created in response to historical and social contingencies. From Ancient Etruria to postmodern technologically-enhanced social media, the broad categories of love, gender, sexuality and identity are revealed through rigorous scholarly investigation not to be as rigid as they might appear. Echoing Anna Ferguson and Anna G. Jónasdóttir (2014, 1–8), the chapters in this book testify to the continued relevance of love as a field of knowledge, capable of giving new insight into gender relations, power and domination in order to move towards liberation.

Reference

Ferguson, Anna and Anna G. Jónasdóttir. 2014. "Introduction." In *Love: A Question for Feminism in the Twenty-First Century*, edited by Anna Ferguson and Anna G. Jónasdóttir, 1–8. Routledge, New York and London.

PART 1

Historical Insights into Norms for Gender and Love

CHAPTER 1

Attitudes to Deviation from Gender Norms in Israelite and Early Jewish Religion

Marianne Schleicher

Introduction

Hostile responses to Western financial, military, and cultural dominion as well as refugees' wishes to benefit from Western wealth, while expressing reluctance to embrace Western normativity, beg reflections on the extent to which a culture can tolerate difference, normative deviance, and attempts at subversion. In this chapter, I shall juxtapose the Levinasian approach of American philosopher Judith Butler to how tolerance becomes possible with my alternative evaluation based on insights from Israelite and early Jewish religion and explained with reference to Michel Foucault, the earlier Butler and cultural evolutionary theory.

By including historical accounts of tolerance toward deviation from gender norms central to Israelite and early Jewish religion, I shall exemplify how Jewish religious texts reveal a dynamic relationship between the promotion of certain norms and the inclusion of deviant others. The historical material on gender reveals at least how one culture has strived to protect itself against inside and outside threats, how it has sometimes recognised a potential in deviation, and how it sometimes has become tolerant toward it, even including deviant elements in its midst. By learning from history, in this case the history of the Israelite-Jewish religion, I argue for a more realistic strategy to bring about tolerance than that of the later Butler.

Two Approaches to Tolerance

Once an individual or society is wounded, retribution is only one response among many. In a collection of articles entitled *Precarious Life: The Powers of Mourning and Violence* from 2004, Judith Butler reflects on the adequacy of US reactions to the violent attacks on 11 September 2001, given US dependency on the global political community. The dependency on hostile others was exposed that morning when US boundaries were breached and its First World privilege of sovereignty and control was temporarily lost. The attacks revealed

© KONINKLIJKE BRILL NV, LEIDEN, 2019 | DOI:10.1163/9789004380233_003 a national vulnerability that was, however, disavowed along with an all-too-short process of grief, to be replaced by the president's declaration of a war against terror – retaliation by state violence. Butler is calling for an arrest to the circularity of violence through a prolonged process of grief that allows for a reflection on the precariousness of life and a critical assessment of the mechanisms in our national as well as global cultures that distribute vulnerability and "mournability" unevenly (2004, XI–XXI).

Referring to her early critique of how discursive violence renders deviant expressions of gender unintelligible,[1] Butler asks with respect to the casualties of 11 September and the US-led war on terror,

> Who counts as human? Whose lives count as lives? And, finally, What *makes for a grievable life*? .... Loss and vulnerability seem to follow from our being socially constituted bodies, attached to others, at risk of losing those attachments, exposed to others, at risk of violence by virtue of exposure. (2004, 20, original emphasis)

Butler considers the occlusion of the grief of others a part of the discursive distribution of intelligibility, a process of wishful thinking away of unwanted subjects. Even though it is an illusory dream of sovereignty, it involves the discursive violence of non-recognition, which supplements acts of military retribution and promulgates the circularity of violence.

As an alternative to the all-too-short process of grief and retaliation, Butler had hoped for contemplation on national grief over what was lost and on how subjects, as well as nation states, are constituted by their web of relations, by their dependency on others (2004, 21–22). Politically, mourning could have been transformative in that the interdependency of US citizens and Arabs, who were hostile to the US, reveals both parties as vulnerably exposed to each other despite overt differences. Counting the perpetrators as humans – despite the attacks, which Butler in no way justifies – would also have implied an inquiry into the reasons for their attacks, which could have inspired different strategies of self-defence against "an exploitation of that primary tie, that primary way in which we are, as bodies, outside ourselves and for one another" (2004, 27). Butler admits to the near-unfeasibility of such a political strategy, implying the responsibility of a state to protect its own citizens (2004, 140). Nevertheless, she grants her alternative strategy viability based on two deductions. First, she turns to a psychological model of how trust in others derives from a primary

1 Cf. Butler (1990, 144 and 2001, 621–636). Butler points to the similarity herself (2004, 32–33).

reliance of an infant upon others, which images how our survival hinges and has always hinged on our ability to trust those upon whom we depend, despite our differences (Butler 2004, 45–46). Second, she turns to Emmanuel Levinas' illustration of how admitting to the face of the other renders the other intelligible and admits to his or her vulnerability in a way that, if it cannot halt violence, at least reduces it (2004, 138–139).

Despite the beauty of Butler's Levinasian ideal of attributing vulnerability to hostile others, I need to distance myself from it because I find its lack of realism counterproductive to achieving a shared goal of reduced violence and tolerance of otherness. Her ideal runs counter to basic human defence mechanisms that aim at securing individual and cultural survival.[2] Such substantial changes in behavioural patterns across the globe do not come about as a result of ethics-based encouragements to be empathetic toward those we fear. Most people would reply, "Why should we?" Instead, I consider it a much more realistic strategy to invest in increased knowledge about history and its positive memories of how deviance and otherness occasionally become cultural assets, even contributing to individual and cultural survival.

As I shall try to show in my analysis, foundational texts from different historical periods reveal an increasing knowledge of complex identities, which is most likely related to the need of cultures to register knowledge about the dynamic and nomadic, constantly changing, diverse, and composite identities[3] of its members in order to govern them and thus secure cultural survival. Here, I am inspired by French historian Michel Foucault's understanding of power as a multiple and mobile field of force relations, always unstable, a complex strategic situation in an always local society. On the one hand, local culture demarcates and protects itself by means of strong boundaries including unambiguous structures, categories, norms, and laws. On the other hand, culture relies on the presence of counter-discourses that may serve as "a point of resistance and a starting point for an opposing strategy [that] provide for relatively obscure areas of tolerance" (Foucault 1978, 101). To some extent, cultural dynamics imply that culture actually opens itself to include otherness. In the first volume of *The History of Sexuality*, Foucault reflects on how Western culture regulated sexuality by gathering knowledge about the different ways in which sexuality was being performed (Foucault 1978, 11). Foucault also reveals how

2 George Shulman also addresses this problem (2011, 227–235).

3 My understanding of complex identities derives from Deleuze and Guattari's *A Thousand Plateaus – Capitalism and Schizophrenia* (1987); Haraway's "A Manifesto for Cyborgs: Science, Technology, and Socialist Feminism in the 1980s" (1990, 190–233); and Braidotti's *Nomadic Subjects – Embodiment and Sexual Difference in Contemporary Feminist Theory* (2011).

the cultural "will to knowledge" implied an unpremeditated effect of recognition and signification of what was previously unintelligible. Accordingly, the mere act of signification brought identities from unintelligibility to signification, sometimes even to inclusion (Foucault 1978, 92–102). In *Gender Trouble*, Judith Butler also reflects on the premises for the inclusion of alterities. Butler points to how people of complex gender identities, on the one hand, are struck by discursive violence in an attempt at regulation because their genders do not conform to cultural categories and norms (Butler 1990, 144). On the other hand, Butler also describes how rule-generating practices also "enable the assertion of alternative domains of cultural intelligibility" (Butler 1990, 198). Butler's theory of performativity implies that subversive agency requires that individuals work for cultural changes from within their culture by participating in the rule-regulating practices such as religious rituals and other repetitive acts as a testimony to their loyalty toward culture (Butler 1990, 201).

As the analysis of Israelite and early Jewish texts will show, cultural boundaries are negotiable and can be changed from within. Yet, culture demarcates and protects itself whenever it feels threatened by means of strong boundaries, including unambiguous structures, categories, norms and laws. Violence toward local deviants or foreigners decreases only when culture recognises the loyalty of these others to the overall objective of culture to secure its survival. In line with this, I want to include a hypothesis from cultural evolutionary theory that conceives of cultural evolution as driven by increased specialisation, due to the invention of tools and solutions to adapt to the surrounding world and the subsequent need to economise on labour. I choose to apply this hypothesis to the question of tolerance by considering tolerance as a side-effect of cultural specialisation. The invention of tools and other solutions sometimes comes about due to deliberate efforts; at other times it comes about by chance, by failure or refusal to conform to normative performances (cf. Donald 2007, 216–218). Accordingly, one must expect that culture has an interest in not condemning unexpected outcomes or performances – at least until it has evaluated their potential for present or future problem-solving.

Five Gender Norms in Israelite Texts

At the overall level, the Hebrew Bible presents itself as concerned with survival and sees it as depending on God's promise to Israel of land and numerical greatness: "I will make you fertile and numerous, making of you a community of peoples; and I will assign this land to your offspring to come for an everlasting possession" (Gen 48:4).[4] Neglect of the scriptural commandments will endanger this promise, as God threatens:

> You shall be left a scant few, after having been as numerous as the stars in the skies, because you did not heed the command of the Lord your God. And as the Lord once delighted in making you prosperous and many, so will the Lord now delight in causing you to perish and in wiping you out; you shall be torn from the land that you are about to enter and possess. (Deut 28:62–63)

The Hebrew Bible, with its more than 3000-year-old content, edited between 400 BCE and 200 CE, wants to avoid such a catastrophe. Accordingly, it regulates expressions of gender by means of what I have counted as five norms that are constitutive of an intelligible gender identity (Schleicher 2011, 422–435).

The first norm promotes a bipolar conception of gender that rests on a categorisation of human beings into subgroups of males and females. The divine logic behind the gender binary relates to the complementarity of male and female with regard to their reproductive potential, as it is evident from the very first chapter of Genesis where it says: "male and female He created them. God blessed them and God said to them, 'Be fertile and increase …'" (Gen 1:27–28).

Deviation from the gender binary attracts little attention in the Hebrew Bible. There is no mention of androgyny or intersexual identity, despite the fact that about one in a thousand births reveals a child with deviating genital characteristics (ISNA.ORG 2014). These humans have no names in the Hebrew Bible.[5] They are characterised by their absence and invisibility. As such, they are what Butler calls unintelligible and, as such, extremely vulnerable to the pressure to conform to the gender binary on disadvantaged premises. Should they fail to conform but still insist on their deviant presence, it might be interpreted as an attempt at subverting the gender binary as a norm. Sanctions exist against attempts at subversion. This is seen in a prohibition against women's and men's crossdressing, which is spelled out as an offence against God: "A woman must not put on man's apparel, nor shall a man wear woman's clothing; for whoever does these things is abhorrent to the LORD your God" (Deut 22:5). In similar cases of performances described as abhorrent in the eyes of God,

4 Biblical quotations are taken from The Jewish Publication Society TaNaKh Translation of 1985.

5 The Mishnah (ca. 200 CE) was the first Hebrew text to signify people with deviating genital characteristics. The Tosefta (ca. 300 CE) invests in this new knowledge by partially distributing intelligibility and vulnerability to these people, cf. tBikkurim 2:3–7. For more, see Schleicher (2011).

passages describe how God would withhold blessings from the land, or require an expatriation of the entire people from the promised land (e.g. Lev 18:28–29). To avoid a national catastrophe like this, pressure was put on members of the town community to execute deviating individuals (Lev 18:26–30). In other words, cultural violence on more levels is detectable and contributes to dissuade Israelites from challenging the gender binary as a norm.

The second norm rests on a basic hierarchy between males and females, where men are portrayed as superior to women. Within marriage, God orders man to rule over woman (Gen 3:16). Within the extended family, the patriarch rules over his wives, children and slaves. Extended families are headed by men who would then be the family representatives in public contexts, e.g. in the assembly of the town elders or in contexts of God's presence, so they would be characterised by public agency. In both cases, women are expected to succumb to the decisions and representations of their husbands/patriarchs. At Mount Sinai, when the commandments are given to Israel, God only addresses the eldest among the males when the covenant between God and the people of Israel is agreed upon (Ex 19:15), thereby granting men, patriarchs in particular, a more privileged access to holiness, which also becomes evident in the priestly regulations of the Israelite cult. Religiously, God's sanctioning of male superiority reflects a postulated, divine trust in men being better suited, as religious agents and family representatives, to guide the behaviour of the entire people of Israel to maintain God's blessings.

Accounts of deviation from the gender hierarchy, nevertheless, exist. On the one hand, the Book of Exodus makes it clear that women are not to subvert the gender hierarchy by usurping male authority in matters involving God. Miriam and Aaron, siblings of Moses, try to argue that they are just as important as Moses is. As an expression of divine disapproval of this claim, God strikes Miriam, but not Aaron, with snow-white scales and pushes her into a vulnerable situation where she is dependent upon both of her brothers to have God heal her (Num 12:1–15). On the other hand, God deviates from his praxis of sanctioning the authority of men in religious matters in his direct address of a few women beyond Miriam who, despite God's rebuking her, bears the title of prophetess one who leads other women in dance and song (Ex 15:20–21). Other prophetesses include Deborah, who is a prophetess and a judge, i.e., a leader of the people (Judg 4:4); Huldah is also both prophetess and judge (2 Reg 22:14–22/2 Chron 34:22–28); and Noadiah is a prophetess (Neh 6:12–14). Finally, the prophet Isaiah refers to his wife as the prophetess (Is 8:3). These five women reflect the presence of female religious agents who hold public offices and remind us that some cases of deviation from the gender hierarchy are tolerated, while others are not. Miriam's riot is condemned because she does not pay enough attention to the ontological differences between God's revelation to Moses and to ordinary prophets (Num 12:6–8). Noadiah is associated with prophets who accepted bribes. Neither Miriam nor Noadiah seems to be married. The other three prophetesses are married and conform in all other respects. They are also described as acting wisely on insights derived from God, contributing to the overall objectives of securing land and reproduction, which may explain why their otherness, in the form of their deviation from the hierarchical gender norm by holding public office, is tolerated.

The third gender norm promotes restricted heterosexuality, connoting the gender binary and its potential for reproduction (Gen 1:27–28). Yet, the Torah does not allow all heterosexual constellations and expressions of love. Lev 18:6–20 prohibits intimate relations with one's own parents, children, siblings, half-siblings, and one's extended family. The passage also forbids intimate relations with two women at a time if they are related to one another, and with a neighbour's wife, just as sexual practices associated in one way or the other with foreign cultures are prohibited. The norm of restricted heterosexuality reveals that only heterosexual unions that do not cause inbreeding, internal strife in the smaller cultural units of family and clan, and do not threaten the outer boundaries of the culture will be tolerated.[6] Maintenance of God's blessings depends on sexual performances in accordance with the norm of restricted heterosexuality.

God defines deviation from the laws defining restricted heterosexuality as capital crimes. God prescribes the extinction of sexual deviators – be they Israelites or strangers, primarily because the laws are presented as ways to keep the land of Israel holy (Lev 18:29). The sexual laws are explained as ethnic markers in that God justifies the expatriation of the Canaanites from the land that God is now to give to the Israelites because of the sexual practices of the Canaanites that God now defines as sexual deviations (Lev 20:22–23). Divinely sanctioned violence is to strike sexual deviators because their sexual performances do not pledge allegiance to the covenant and its entailed promises of reproduction and land. The execution that follows from a man's intercourse with another man is self-earned: "their bloodguilt is upon them" (Lev 20:13); and as such, their deaths are not to be mourned. Sons who sleep with the concubines of their fathers are not to be mourned either (Gen 9:21–22; 35:22; 49:4). Violence will strike a young woman who has sex while under her father's authority. If she has, "the girl shall be brought out to the entrance of her father's house, and the men of the town shall stone her to death" (Deut 22:21). Finally, the

6 On categorisation of the laws of Lev 18, see Mohrmann (2004, 57–79).

narrative parts of the Hebrew Bible do not mourn the death of men who refuse to produce an heir to their deceased brother, if the latter dies childless. In Genesis 38, Onan does not want to father a child to be considered the offspring of his brother, so he only engages in interrupted intercourse with Tamar, upon which God takes Onan's life (Gen 38:9–10). Judah, now afraid that Tamar will also cause the death of his young and only remaining son, Shelah, sends Tamar away by saying: "Stay as a widow in your father's house until my son Shelah grows up" (Gen 38:11). Yet, once Shelah grows up, Judah does nothing to arrange for the levirate marriage (see below), to which Tamar is entitled. Consequently, Tamar takes matters into her own hands. She dresses up like a harlot, seduces Judah and has extramarital sex with him, and forces him to marry her. She conceives and gives birth to twin boys, thus securing Er's heir. While occluding Onan's loss of life because of his waste of semen and failure to secure his brother's reproduction, the narrative celebrates Tamar's deviancy and ignores the capital crime of having extramarital sex (Gen 38:24), because her sexual deviancy served the greater purpose of securing land and reproduction.

Other examples of positive deviations from restricted heterosexuality occur in the narrative material and include Jacob, who marries two sisters, contrary to the commandment in Lev 18:18. This is not Jacob's original wish, but once Laban has deceived Jacob into marrying the elder before the younger, Jacob performs his marital duty of having sex with both of them (Gen 29:21–30). As a consequence and as warned against in Lev 18:18, rivalry occurs between the sisters (Gen 30:1). However, the function of, not only these two marriages, but also the subsequent marriages with their Hebrew maidservants, Zilpah and Bilhah, that result in the total births of twelve sons and one daughter, points to God's fulfilment of his promise of securing the numerical greatness of the people of Israel (Gen 36:8–27; 49).

The fourth gender norm promotes marriage as the frame for performances of restricted heterosexuality (Deut 7:12–16). Today, marriage in the Western world connotes the romantic ideal of mutual love between two people. However, in the Hebrew Bible, the word for "love"; i.e. "ahavah" (and its cognates) appears 252 times in the context of a relationship between a man and a woman. In the narrative texts, it occurs as a verb, always in the third person masculine singular, except in one case.[7] In view of that, a man who declares his love to a woman never hears a woman replying, "I love you, too!" Scholars explain this lack of mutuality with reference to the hierarchical, covenantal character

7 Cf. 1 Sam 18:20, where Michal, daughter of King Saul, is described as loving David, who was a shepherd at that time.

of marriage. The biblical narratives describe love as a feeling held by a man toward a woman, where love typically occurs after the man has had sex with her – an act that initiates marriage. The word "love" is also used to designate covenants between political allies and the religious covenant between God and Israel. In these political or religious instances, the hierarchically superior agent loves his subject and expects loyalty in return (Van Wolde 2008, 1–24; Ackerman 2002, 437–458). When dealing with marriage as a gender norm in Israelite culture, it is important to understand the different connotations of marriage. This does not rule out mutual affection between a man and a woman, but it clarifies the contractual character of marriage.

A few commandments in the Hebrew Bible contribute to well-functioning marriages. Deuteronomy recognises the vulnerability of newlywed couples by prescribing that "When a man has taken a bride, he shall not go out with the army or be assigned to it for any purpose; he shall be exempt one year for the sake of his household, to give happiness to the woman he has married" (Deut 24:5). Happiness within marriage secures bonding and a stable family unit and thus establishes a secure frame for reproduction as one of the ultimate goals of Israelite culture (Deut 28:54–56). While most lay marriages were monogamous, polygynous marriage was allowed; i.e. a man was allowed to marry more wives, while the woman was required to remain monogamous. Polygynous marriages, beyond obvious advantages for the husband, reflect recognition of the vulnerability of spinsters, widows, and divorcees by offering them an opportunity to re-/marry, which was considered attractive, in that marriage in Israelite culture was the primary way for women to obtain a respected social position, secondary as she might be, and to obtain protection against hostile others. Restrictions were attached to polygynous marriages in that the husband had to be wealthy enough to provide for all of his wives. It says: "If he marries another, he must not withhold from this one her food, her clothing, or her conjugal rights" (Ex 21:10). If he did, the woman was entitled to a divorce. A man was entitled to a divorce with reference to his dislike of her alone (Deut 24:1–4).

Most marriages in the Biblical narratives are between a male and a female Israelite, where the female is often a relative from the groom's paternal lineage. This relates to the prohibition against foreign sexual practices with the purpose of restricting the divine blessings to benefit Israelites only. In line with this, several passages in the Hebrew Bible forbid marriage between an Israelite and a foreigner (Ex 34:16; Deut 7:2–4), while Leviticus considers endogamic marriage a restriction to be applied to Israelite priests alone (Lev 21:14–15). The Hebrew Bible sanctions different kinds of discursive violence toward Israelite men who marry foreigners, fearing that such mixed marriages will lead to apostasy and thus a loss of divine blessings affecting the entire people. Esau's marriage to three Canaanite women justifies his loss of the primogeniture (Gen 26:34–35; 27:46–28:9); divine punishment indirectly strikes King Solomon for marrying 1000 foreign women (1 Kgs 11:1–12); and both Ezra (Ezra 9:1–2; 10:1–3; 10:19) and Nehemiah (Neh 13:23–30) ordered those Israelites who had married foreign women while Israel was under Babylonian rule, to send away their foreign wives. Whatever feelings an Israelite man would have for his foreign wife, they were not considered mournable. Contrary to this, the Book of Ruth portrays how an Israelite's marriage to Ruth, a Moabite, reminds a local community of its ancient laws of inheritance and levirate marriage (see below). In the case of Ruth, marriage to a foreigner became a deviation to be celebrated thanks to her performance from within cultural, yet forgotten, practices.

Once married, women are expected to be monogamous and to engage in sex only with their husband (Deut 7:12–16). Both the man and the woman who engage in adulterous sex are to be executed in order to "sweep away evil from Israel" (Deut 22:22). If a woman is suspected of adultery, she has to drink the so-called spell-inducing water of bitterness. If she is innocent, nothing will happen to her. However, if she is guilty of adultery, God will orchestrate her punishment; i.e., "her belly shall distend and her thigh shall sag; and the woman shall become a curse among her people" (Num 5:27). The bodily permutations may indicate some kind of induced infertility, while the curse probably indicated her subsequent social state of being an outcast.

The fifth gender norm promotes inheritance as an asset available to male children, above all to firstborn sons who are to receive the primogeniture; i.e., a double portion compared to the portion of his brothers. In polygynous marriages, the primogeniture is normally passed on to the husband's firstborn son, not to the firstborn son of the husband's first wife (Deut 21:15–17). This patrilineal norm of inheritance implies that land and property are passed on from father to sons, which explains patrilocality as a side-effect of this gender norm: a woman is expected to leave the locality of her parents to follow her husband to his land. The patrilocal effect of the patrilineal norm of inheritance gives men an advantage over women in that married life supplements a preformed network, whereas women will have to protect themselves against social vulnerability in- and outside of marriage by establishing new alliances.

Laws of inheritance serve the purpose of keeping land and property within the patrilineal tribe and territory, and usually the eldest son with his primogeniture will have this as his prime responsibility when considering where to live and whom to marry. Some of the narratives in the Hebrew Bible, however, sanction deviation from this norm. Esau is elder than Jacob, but with reference to Esau's marriages to three Canaanite women (Gen 27; 28:6–9), the Book of Genesis legitimises deviation from the praxis of privileging the eldest son.

Similarly, Ishmael is older than Isaac, but Ishmael's mother is a foreigner, an Egyptian, and not a patrilineal relative to Abraham as Sarah is, which is why God supports Sarah's wish to have Hagar and Ishmael sent away (Gen 21:8–12).

Deviation from the norm of favouring sons, especially the first-born son, in matters of inheritance is tolerated by necessity in cases where a man has fathered only daughters. The legal parts of the Hebrew Bible address such cases and state that only daughters can inherit from their deceased fathers (Num 27:8) as long as they succumb to endogamic restrictions on whom they could marry. The Book of Numbers states that 'Every daughter among the Israelite tribes who inherits a share must marry someone from a clan of her father's tribe, in order that every Israelite may keep his ancestral share' (Num 36:8). Similarly, a childless widow can inherit from her dead husband. However, the law in Deuteronomy of levirate marriage encourages her remarriage by prescribing that the childless widow "shall not be married to a stranger, outside the family [of the husband]" (Deut 25:5). Instead, the brother of the deceased husband shall marry the widow. In both cases, women's productivity and other assets such as their inheritance had to remain within the patrilineal territory and tribe. The legal sanctioning of female heirs, however, does not increase her intelligibility, because this norm primarily favours the male children to whom these women hopefully will give birth.

In the remaining part of my analysis, I shall turn to deviations from these norms in early Judaism to address the transition from Israelite religion to early Jewish religion with respect to complex gender identities. What logic explains why some literature tolerates deviation from the five gender norms, sympathetically admitting the vulnerability and the humaneness of deviators, while other early Jewish texts attempt regulation of deviators by means of cultural violence, sending deviators off to cultural regions of unintelligibility?

Development of Biblical Gender Norms in Early Jewish Literature

Early Judaism signifies Jewish religion from around the 4th century BCE until the 3nd century CE, during which the people of Israel were first under Hellenistic, then Roman rule. The hegemony of foreign empires inspired new ways of thinking just as it provoked defence of what was now referred to, not as Israelite religion, but as Jewish religion due to the official name of the region: Judea. Similarly, Israelites were now referred to as Jews.[8] Early Judaism is a period

8 Cf. Josephus 11.5.7 and 173; Cohen (2006, 8).

characterised by religious diversity in that the cultic monopoly of the priests was challenged through the rise of sects and denominational movements, all claiming their unique version of Judaism as the normative one. Phenomenologically, Israelite religion, with its archaic focus on divine blessings in the form of fertility, health, and military success, was transformed into a salvific religion, typical of the axial age, that promised transcendent rewards, including participation in the world-to-come, to those who trained their souls and bodies through worship, ascetic practices, and ethically governed behaviour.[9] It is my argument that Judaism's transformation into an axial religion had great significance for its potential to exert tolerance toward deviation from the five biblical gender norms addressed in this chapter on deviation in early Jewish literature.

Sanctions are still directed at men and women who challenge the first biblical gender norm, i.e., the gender binary, by dressing like the opposite gender (4Q159, frg. 2–4; Philo: *On the Virtues* 18). It also seems that Jews were expected to demarcate their gender through the choice of colour for the clothes they wore. Archaeological material from Masada and the Cave of Letters specify that men tend to wear white or off-white clothing, whereas women wear coloured clothing (Magness 2002, 104). A slight change in norms concerning the gender binary is detectable in the works of Philo at a time when the soul is considered dominant in men, while women are associated with the body because they are associated with this-worldly concerns in everyday life.[10] Philo advocates something that I designate "spiritual transgender performances" (*On Flight and Finding* 50–51; *On Abraham* 99–102). He considers it an ideal that women cultivate their souls for them to become more masculine, i.e. ontologically closer to God, who is associated with ultimate masculinity.[11] Even more surprising, Philo encourages men to become feminine on the allegorical level by engaging in what Daniel Boyarin has called men's "couvade"; i.e., male imitation of women's capacity to bear, nurture, and rear children as a way to cultivate and exercise virtues that granted them access to spiritual unification with God as male (cf. Harrison 1994, 50–52; 55; Boyarin 1994, 3–36). Spiritual transgender performances were also promoted on the festival of Sukkot. At first, the Jewish sect-members, known as the Therapeutae, form an all-male and an all-female chorus, but then proceed to co-ed singing (*On the Contemplative Life*, 83–84).

9 Cf. Robert Bellah's periodization of cultural evolution (1964, 358–374 and 2005, 69–89).

10 Quotations from the work of Philo stem from C.D. Yonge's translation.

11 While this ontological distinction between women and men definitely contributed to establishing a hierarchy between genders that challenges modern liberal ideals of gender equality, it nevertheless signifies a historic increase in tolerance of women's religious performativity in that their association with this-worldly matters is conceived as amendable.

The co-ed singing represents an almost ecstatic culmination of the festival. Some scholars see the joining of male and female voices as an imitation of the longed-for spiritual reunification of male and female according to the constituency of the first human, described in Gen 1:26–27,[12] thus revoking the lifting of the gender binary as a foretaste of what awaits humans in the world-to-come. Such deviant performances are tolerated basically with reference to the dualistic worldview of early Judaism, given its overall – especially sectarian – objective to ensure the refinement or even salvation of the soul.

A slight subversion of the second biblical norm posing a hierarchy between man and woman is detectable in the Book of Tobit (ca. 200 BCE). To some extent, Tobit and his wife, Hannah, are portrayed as supplementing and respecting each other. Tobit appreciates the good and abundant Shavuot dinner that Hannah most likely prepared for him (Tob 2:1). Tobit acknowledges his great-grandmother for introducing him to the dietary laws (Tob 2:8). The transmission of the Torah usually rests on the father, but Tobit mentions how he grew up as an orphan, depending on his great-grandmother to transmit such religious information on Jewish tradition. Once Tobit becomes blind, Hannah takes on women's work to earn money for the household by producing handicrafts, where weaving is specified. Tobit and Hannah also quarrel, which is interesting because only equals quarrel. The greater part of Hannah's contributions to the family is performed inside the home. While the private sphere had much less status in Israelite religion, where religion was mainly performed in the public sphere, the diasporic/exilic context, pseudepigraphically portrayed in the Book of Tobit, adds religious status to performances within the home, because the home became the main stronghold for safeguarding the religious involvement of family members in diasporas and exile, where public worship was beyond reach. This may explain the increased tolerance and approval of Hannah's agency.

Deviation from the hierarchy between men and women is also seen in the Book of Judith (ca. 100 BCE), where Judith performs heroic acts in the public sphere. While the Jewish men, including the eldest of the Judaic town of Bethulia, test God, lose faith in God, and are more or less prepared to surrender to the Assyrians, Judith acts courageously by beheading the Assyrian general, Holofernes, within his own camp (Jud 13:1–10), securing not only the survival of the Jewish people, but Judea's victory over the Assyrians. Tolerance and approval of Judith's agency is explained with reference to her religiosity, piety,

12 See Meeks (1973, 165–208, especially 179) and Boyarin (1993, 39).

beauty, and especially her ascetic performances during her three and a half years of widowhood (Jud 8:3–6).

Deviation from the biblical hierarchy between men and women is also tolerated in the mother martyr-accounts portraying women as active religionists of Judaism. According to the various books of the Maccabees, women protested in the streets to demonstrate their anguish in the face of the desecrated temple in 167–164 BCE (2 Macc 3:19; 4 Macc 4:9). While the historical accuracy of these accounts is debated, the books entertain the thought of women suffering slavery or death for their insistence on Jewish ways of living under Hellenistic rule, introducing into the history of religion the concept of martyrdom (2 Macc 5:13; 5:24; 7). The contributions of these women to uphold Jewish practices also included their religious agency as circumcisers of their baby boys (1 Macc 1:60; 2 Macc 6:10; 4 Macc 4:25; cf. Haber 2006).

The Dead Sea Scrolls reveal small conceptual changes with respect to women's active religious roles within their descriptions of an ideal ascetic community. The Damascus Document (4QD) mentions the presence of women, female servants, widows, young girls, and mothers (cf. 4QD vi 16; xi 12; xii 10; CD xiv 15). As Eileen Schuller asks: "The more difficult question is whether women could advance beyond this initial stage to full membership" (Schuller 1994: 121).[13] One scroll testifies to women receiving daily training on the content of the Torah (1QSa 1:4–5:7). We also know that children, both boys and girls, are to receive education from the age of 10 to 20 (1QSa 1:6–15; 4QD 14:16–17; 4Q266, 9, iii:4–7). While the exact purpose of the document 4Q502 is disputed, it indicates that women as well as men are given honorific titles, which means that women, too, have some communal functions and a certain status within the community hierarchy (cf. Baumgarten 1983, 125–135; Schuller 1994, 118; Crawford 2003, 177–191, especially 178–180). In the ritual described in the document, presumably celebrating the community elders, women are given the task of reciting a text. Female members are also referred to as "companions of men" or "daughters of truth, intelligence, and knowledge" (4Q502, frg. 2:3), as "elders" in the sense of being not necessarily old, but part of a leadership group (4Q502, frg. 19:2), and as "sisters", indicating recognition of their status as members of the community (4Q502, frg. 96:1). Furthermore, young men about to be married are encouraged to respect and honour their wives and recognise how they are complemented by their wives (4Q416: 2, ii 21; iii, 21). Tolerance of women

13 Eileen Schuller was among the first to emphasise the consequences for our knowledge of gender and religion in antiquity if women's active presence in the community as described in the scrolls could be documented (1994, 115–131; 121; 130).

seemingly depends upon their contributions through ascetic performances to preparing the community for the world-to-come.

Finally, I want to mention the religious performances of the female Therapeutae. In some of his other works, Philo distinguishes between men and women by rendering women positive only when they accept passivity (*The Special Laws* I, 201; *Allegorical Interpretation* II, 38). Female activity outside the home was positive, according to Philo, only when a woman had to go to the temple (*The Special Laws* III, 171). This statement sheds light on Philo's lack of scorn at the presence and activity of the female Therapeutae in the common holy place of the sect on Sabbaths and on Sukkot (*On the Contemplative Life* 32; 68). As mentioned above, men as well as women were active in singing hymns to God. Philo also explains how men and women sat separately on Sabbaths to preserve the modesty of the women, yet these women had "the same feelings of admiration as the men, and hav[e] adopted the same sect with equal deliberation and decision" (*On the Contemplative Life*, 32; 68). Women's religious agency becomes apparent from this quote, where religious belonging stems from the ascetic women's own active and deliberate decision to belong to the group and from their access to public religious performance. Furthermore, women had access to climbing the ladder of religious authority, once they had proven their honour and excellence, in that the community would confer leadership upon such women (*On the Contemplative Life*, 87). Within the context of asceticism, Philo thus promulgates the relationship between men and women as one of relative equality, encouraging both men and women to doff their sense-controlled behaviour as men and women to enable contemplation on the spiritual aspects of life.

Deviation from restricted heterosexuality is not tolerated. In the Book of Tobit, sex with foreigners is discursively condemned. Set in the Assyrian and Median diasporas, Sarah witnesses how the demon Asmodeus killed her seven foreign suitors on their wedding nights, just before they were about to have intercourse with her. The narrative never ascribes mournability to the death of the foreign suitors, nor to the feelings of loss among their families. Their disappearance ensures Sarah's sexual integrity and future contributions to the people of Israel through a marriage arrangement with her patrilineal relative, Tobias, who conforms to restricted sexuality when he pledges that "not because of lust am I taking this kinswoman of mine, but with sincerity" (Tob 8:7).[14]

14 Quotations from the *Apocrypha* are taken from New English Translation of the *Septuagint*, viewed on 22 October 2015, http://ccat.sas.upenn.edu/nets/edition/.

The unrestricted sexual desire of foreigners is directly addressed in the Book of Judith and stands in direct contrast to the ascetic, abstinent life of Judith. The Assyrian general, Holofernes, is overcome by his sexual desire for the beautiful Judith to such an extent that he cannot control his drinking. He becomes too drunk to carry out his intention of having sex with her and falls asleep, which enables Judith to cut his throat (Jud 12:10–12). While it is of advantage to the Jews that uncontrolled sexuality characterises the enemy, it is still a cause for condemnation in the guise of ridicule. Surely, killing Holofernes was Judith's main objective, but his uncontrolled sexuality and the potential threat of a foreigner who could have succeeded in having sex with the pious Judith not only excuses the narrative violence directed at him, it even causes celebrations in the entire country (Jud 16:20) – a clear case of mournability not granted to a foreign enemy.

Compared to sexual regulations in the Hebrew Bible, the Dead Sea Scrolls reflect intensified regulation. Matrimonial sex is acceptable as long as it is licit, which now precludes intercourse with a pregnant wife and other non-procreative sexual activities. Men and women obtain purification from semen (or menstrual bleeding) not with one immersion, but with two, just as clothes need to be washed not once, but twice on the first and third day. For three days they are not allowed to access the community (11QT 45:7–12). The *Temple Scroll* promulgates this intensification of the purity rules with reference to the overall sectarian objective of gaining access to the world-to-come, characterised by God's presence, which explains the focus on ritual purity.[15]

Distinguishing between Jews in general (*On the Cherubim,* 43) and Jewish ascetics, Philo approved of ascetics being sexually abstinent. Philo describes with admiration how the male Therapeutae had left their families behind, i.e., their access to legitimate sex, and had, instead, inverted the structures of forbidden sexuality by seeking erotic union with God. The erotic union was expressed through metaphors, such as the metaphor of God's spiritual impregnation of ascetic men and women and their subsequent spiritual childbearing, applying the imagery of God sowing "the seed of happiness in good and virgin soil" (*On the Cherubim,* 49). The female members were referred to as "virgins". "Virginity" was considered a prerequisite in order to be impregnated by divine wisdom. Ascetic performances turned these female sect members, no matter their age, into such "virgins" (*On the Contemplative Life*, 68).

The fourth norm on marriage was exacerbated in some sects by forbidding certain marital unions that used to be licit in Israelite religion (Lev 18:13). The

15 For more on this intensification of the purity rules, see Japhet (1993, 75–76; 79).

Dead Sea Scrolls as well as the Book of Jubilees (ca. 160–150 BCE) forbid marriages between uncles and nieces (Jub 2:19–22; CD, iv 12–v 11; 4Q251, 17; 11QT 66:15–16; 11Q270 5:7–11).[16] In its rewriting of Genesis, the Book of Jubilees even tries to erase all traces of marriages between uncles and nieces in this founding narrative, indicating its opposition to such marriages. The Damascus Document (4QD) also prohibits the act of "taking two wives in their lifetime" (4QD 3:11), based on the monogamous relationship of Adam and Eve in Gen 1–3.

When it comes to tolerance of otherness, I consider the respectful portrayal of Hannah's contributions to family life in the Book of Tobit a novelty relative to its historical context.[17] In spite of many descriptions of gender-conforming actions and emphasis on the importance of patrilineal marriage, it is important to notice how Tobit's wife has a name; i.e., Hannah (Tob 1:20) and how it is within reach of the author's imagination to conceive of her as a substitute breadwinner for the family, when Tobit becomes blind, which I consider a matter of normative expansion. The Book of Tobit is also unique because it constitutes the first source to document the scripting of marriage contracts. Sarah's father, Raguel, called his wife, Edna, "and told her to bring a scroll, and he wrote out a contract, a scroll of marriage, that he gave [Sarah] to [Tobias] as wife according to the decree of the law of Moyses" (Tob 7:13). The next morning after the consummation of the marriage, Raguel hands over half of his property to Tobias as a dowry, and furthermore, as an inheritance the father promises the groom the other half, including the responsibility for Edna once he dies (Tob 8:21).[18] The marriage celebration ends once the bride is transferred to the groom's patrilocal area, house, and family (Tob 11:17). In the description of this transferral, the Book of Tobit recognises, but refuses Raguel's attempt to persuade the newlywed couple to choose the locality of the bride (Tob 10:8). This part signifies the vulnerability, grief and worries of families – not to mention the brides – for sending their daughters/sisters far away to sometimes remote places with hardly any network in the immediate surroundings.

---

16 Schuller (1994, 119); Bernstein (2004); *Dead Sea Discoveries* 11.2 (2004): (191–211) 201; 202n25.

17 Amy-Jill Levine (1992, 42–51, 64) considers the portrayal of Hannah's sharp tongue a negative one and also points to the approving portrayal of a passive and mute Sarah. My reading of the Book of Tobit as slightly subversive of the hierarchy within the gender binary is much more in line with Schuller (2012, 377); Machiela and Perring (2014, 124); Hieke (2005, 103–120, especially 105). For a nuanced discussion, see Bow and Nickelsburg (1991, 127–143).

18 This promise indicates the custom also witnessed in Judith 8:7 that widows were allowed to live in the house and administer the property of their late husbands until their own death.

The Book of Judith also emphasises marriage to a patrilineal relative as a norm to be pursued. Judith was married to Manasseh, a patrilineal relative (Jud 8:1–2). After Manasseh's death, Judith's love for her husband is so strong that remarriage is not an option. Instead of remarriage, she becomes the head of the household, with the freedom to express her gratitude over her maid's loyal companionship by setting the maid free (Jud 16:23), thus lifting social hierarchical barriers to allow for the increased agency of another woman. Also, it is worth noticing how Judith emphasises how she has been capable of protecting herself and guarding her own chastity during her public performance (Jud 13:16). Her ascetic way of life promulgates a new way of living as a widow after marriage. In this way, the portrayal of Judith as a widow deviates from the biblical expectation of widows to return to their parental house, to their husband's family, or to poverty, perceived in all biblical contexts as nothing else but an extra mouth to feed.[19]

According to most Dead Sea Scrolls, marriage was a legal and liturgical theme, presumably reflecting the presence of men, women, and children in the sect (CD 7:6–7). Not carnal love, but having children was the only purpose of marriage. Accordingly, "they put their wives to the test for a three-year period and only marry them after they have by three periods of purification given proof of fecundity" (Josephus: *The Jewish War* ii 161), cf. Schuller (1994, 120). Once reproduction had been secured, husband and wife ought to unite in their pursuit of spiritual goals. Contrary to this line of procedure, Philo considers procreation within marriage a fitting thing to strive for once male and female have become purified through ascetic exercise (*Questions and Answers on Genesis* II, 49).

Matters of inheritance dominate in the Book of Tobit because both Sarah and Tobias are only children. In this respect, Num 36:6–9 on Zelophehad's daughters – heirs to their father because he had no sons – functions as an important intertext.[20] Its relevance becomes obvious once the words of Sarah are recalled: "I am my father's only begotten, and he has no other child to be his heir" (Tob 3:15). Sarah shares the unique situation of the daughters of

19 For more on the living conditions of widows, see Galpaz-Feller (2008, 231–253). For more on the distinction between on the one hand women whose husbands have died but who are still or will be included in an extended family; and on the other hand women who are infertile/post-menopausal as well as homeless in the sense that they are not included in a patriarchal family unit, see Leeb (2001, 61–67). Leeb argues for her distinction by pointing to the fact that the biblical texts only refer to someone from the latter group as "widow" and that they are characterised by their incapacity to contribute with their fertility and labour to the extended household of a patriarch.

20 See Soll (1998, 166–175, especially 171).

Zelophehad, which is why the Book of Tobit does not merely promote endogamic marriage,[21] but must focus on patrilineal marriage. However, Sarah was initially convinced that her father had no "near kinsman or other relative that I should keep myself as a wife for him" (Tob 3:15). This explains the hope and exaltation once Tob 6:11–14; 6:16; and 7:6–9 point to the patrilineal relation between Tobias and Sarah. In addition, it should be emphasised that the marriage agreement between Sarah and Tobias is a double celebration of God's role in uniting two only children: "blessed are you because you had mercy on two only children" (Tob 8:17). Tobit's and Raphael's instruction to Tobias to find a wife among his own people, even his own tribe and kin, emphasises that the property of males, especially only male children, were to be kept within the immediate collective, too. In other words, ethnic concerns to keep property in family hands set up restrictions, not only for only daughters, but also for only sons, especially in diasporic contexts. Hereditary concerns with its implications for patrilineal marriage even become a disciplinary force in this book's conceptions of love. The narrative states that it is news on the patrilineal connection that arouses Tobias' protagonistic love for Sarah (Tob 6:18).

With respect to inheritance, the Book of Judith is unique in its deviating portrayal of how Judith after her husband's death, becomes the head of the household. In Jud 8:4; 16:21, the house and property are referred to as hers, whereas in Jud 16:23 they belong to her husband. The property that he used to possess is passed on to Judith and includes gold and silver, servants and maids, and cattle and fields. With no children, she receives his property. Her ability to guard it is specified in "she still had all of these things in her possession" (Jud 8:7). Once Holofernes is decapitated and the inhabitants of Bethulia have conquered his camp, they decide to give Judith the tent of Holofernes, all of "his silver, the beds, the vessels and all the other equipment" (Jud 15:11). In other words, throughout her life she increases her fortune and becomes a very rich and powerful woman. If Judith and Manasseh had had any adult male

21 It seems to me that many scholars confuse the terms "endogamy" and "patriliny" in their readings of the Book of Tobit, such as Bow and Nickelsburg (1991, 133). Within Jewish studies, endogamy refers to marriage with a fellow countryman or -woman, whereas patriliny refers to marriage with a descendant from one's father's bloodline. While anthropologists use the term "endogamy" to signify kinship marriage, scholars of Judaism use the term more broadly to be able to address marriage norms after the reforms of Josiah, cf. Deut 7:3–4, and Ezra, cf. Ezra 10:2, where Israelite men are forbidden to marry foreign wives. Soll's discussion of kinship relations in the Book of Tobit specifically has no references to these reforms and thus fails to see a basic distinction in Judaism between endogamy, positioned as an ideal for the ethnic group in general, and patriliny in specific cases of only daughters inheriting (1998, 172–173n12).

children, the eldest would most likely have become the head of the household. As childless, Judith is the administrator of the land and the property. However, she is still not the heir. Prior to her death, she needs to distribute her vast possessions to all Manasseh's relatives. The innovative part lies in the fact that she also passes on possessions to the closest of her own blood-relatives, making them recipients of an inheritance from a woman (Jud 16:24).

Within more sectarian communities, like the one described in the Dead Sea Scrolls, neither men nor women are to inherit due to the shared property in the community. In addition, a word like inheritance takes on a metaphorical meaning, pointing forward to otherworldly blessings, equally accessible to both men and women (Murphy 2001, 173).

Conclusion

According to this analysis, Israelite culture can be seen as resting on the intertwining of a hierarchical bipolarity of gender, restricted heterosexuality, patrilocality and patrilineal laws of inheritance through the institution of marriage. On the premise of commitment to what I have counted as five norms concerning gender, Israelite culture protects its members against internal and external threats to secure the overall survival of the culture. Deviation from the five norms is tolerated if deviation contributes to preventing loss of land and the weakening of cultural boundaries. In the transition from Israelite to early Judaism, the history of Jewish religion exhibits recognition and to some extent a growing tolerance and accommodation of complex gender identities, basically because early Jewish religion turns to an axial emphasis on the importance of the soul and ascetic practices that seek to refine it in accordance with dualistic ideals. What this history does not reveal is any sign of culture pushing aside its categories, norms, and boundaries in situations where culture sees its overall objectives of either survival or salvation being threatened. While I do treasure Butler's endeavours to reduce violence through an even distribution of intelligibility, vulnerability, and mournability to deviant others, I do not see any evidence in the course of Jewish history for an unmotivated, discursive admittance to the face of deviant others, especially those who seem to pose a threat. Instead, and based on insights from the gender history of Israelite-Jewish religion, I see hope for tolerance and respect for variant identities in information on how cultural violence is reduced whenever it invests in the gathering of knowledge about complex identities and how they have contributed to the success and survival of the culture. If deviant others participate, as the early Butler stresses, in the repetitive acts and rituals of a particular culture, participation itself signals loyalty to the culture, which becomes the key to expanding, maybe even subverting, its very norms. Following Foucault, my estimate is that such gathering of knowledge will ultimately lead to recognition, possibly also to accommodation of complex identities, in all those cases where culture can realise that complexity does not pose a threat.

References

Ackerman, Susan. 2002. "The Personal Is Political: Covenantal and Affectionate Love in the Hebrew Bible". *Vetus Testamentum*, 52 (4): 437–458.

Baumgarten, Joseph M. 1983. "4Q502, Marriage or Golden Age Ritual?" *Journal of Jewish Studies* 34 (2): 125–135.

Bellah, Robert. 1964. "Religious Evolution". *American Sociological Review* 29 (3): 358–374.

Bellah, Robert. 2005. "What is Axial about the Axial Age". *Archives Européennes de Sociologie* 46 (1): 69–89.

Bernstein, Moshe J. 2004. "Women and Children in Legal and Liturgical Texts from Qumran". *Dead Sea Discoveries* 11 (2): 191–211.

Bow, Beverly and George W.E. Nickelsburg. 1991. "Patriarchy with a Twist: Men and Women in Tobit". In *'Women Like This': New Perspectives on Jewish Women in the Greco-Roman World, Early Judaism and Its Literature*, Vol. 1, edited by Amy-Jill Levine, 127–143. Atlanta: Scholars Press.

Boyarin, Daniel. 1993. *Carnal Israel: Reading Sex in Talmudic Culture*. Berkeley: University of California Press.

Boyarin, Daniel. 1994. "Jewish Masochism: Couvade, Castration, and Rabbis in Pain". *American Imago* 51 (1): 3–36.

Braidotti, Rosi. 2011. *Nomadic Subjects – Embodiment and Sexual Difference in Contemporary Feminist Theory*. New York: Columbia University Press.

Butler, Judith. 1990. *Gender Trouble: Feminism and the Subversion of Identity* (1999 edition). New York: Routledge.

Butler, Judith. 2001. "Doing Justice to Someone: Sex Reassignment and Allegories of Transsexuality". *GLQ: A Journal of Gay and Lesbian Studies* 7 (4): 621–636.

Butler, Judith. 2004. *Precarious Life: The Powers of Mourning and Violence*. London: Verso.

Cohen, Shaye J. D. 2006. *From the Maccabees to the Mishnah* (2nd edition). Louisville: Westminister John Know Press.

Crawford, Sidnie White. 2003. "Mothers, Sisters, and Elders: Titles for Women in Second Temple Jewish and Early Christian Communities". In *The Dead Sea Scrolls as Background to Postbiblical Judaism and Early Christianity*, edited by James R. Davila, 177–191. Leiden: Brill.

Deleuze, Gilles and Félix Guattari. 1987. *A Thousand Plateaus – Capitalism and Schizophrenia*. London: Continuum, 1987.

Donald, Merlin. 2007. "Evolutionary Origins of the Social Brain". In *Social Brain Matters: Stances on the Neurobiology of Social Cognition*, edited by Oscar Vilarroya and Francesc Forn i Argimon, 215–222. New York: Rodopi.

Foucault, Michel. 1978. *The History of Sexuality – Volume 1: An Introduction*. New York: Pantheon Books.

Galpaz-Feller, Pnina. 2008. "The Widow in the Bible and in Ancient Egypt". *Zeitschrift für die Alttestamentliche Wissenschaft* 120 (2): 231–253.

Haber, Susan. 2006. "Living and Dying for the Law: The Mother-martyrs of 2 Maccabees". *Women in Judaism: A Multidisciplinary Journal* 4 (1): https://wjudaism.library.utoronto.ca/index.php/wjudaism/article/viewFile/247/320

Haraway, Donna J. 1990. "A Manifesto for Cyborgs: Science, Technology, and Socialist Feminism in the 1980s". In *Feminism/Postmodernism (Thinking Gender)*, edited by Linda Nicholson, 190–233. New York: Routledge.

Harrison, Nonna Verna. 1994. "The Feminine Man in Late Antique Ascetic Piety". *Union Seminary Quarterly Review* 48: 49–71.

Hieke, Thomas. 2005. "Endogamy in the Book of Tobit, Genesis, and Ezra-Nehemiah". In *Book of Tobit: Text, Tradition, Theology*, edited by Géza G. Xeravits and Jósef Zsengeller, 103–120. Leiden: Brill.

Japhet, Sara. 1993. "The Prohibition of the Habitation of Women: The Temple Scroll's Attitude Toward Sexual Impurity and Its Biblical Precedents". *Journal of the Ancient Near Eastern Society* 22: 69–87.

Leeb, Carolyn S. 2001. "The Widow in the Hebrew Bible: Homeless and Postmenopausal". *Proceedings Eastern Great Lakes and Midwest Biblical Society* 21: 61–67.

Levine, Amy-Jill. 1992. "Tobit. Teaching Jews How to Live in the Diaspora". *Bible Review* 8 (4): 42–51.

Machiela, Daniel A. and Andrew B. Perring. 2014. "Tobit and the Genesis Apocryphon: Toward a Family Portrait". *Journal of Biblical Literature* 133 (1): 111–132.

Magness, Jodi. 2002. "Women at Qumran?" In *What Athens Has to Do with Jerusalem: Essays on Classical, Jewish, and Early Christian Art and Archaeology in Honor of Gideon Foerster*, edited by Leonard V. Rutgers. Leuven: Peeters.

Meeks, Wayne A. 1973. "The Image of the Androgyne: Some Uses of a Symbol in Earliest Christianity". *Journal of the History of Religions* 13: 165–208.

Mohrmann, Doug C. 2004. "Making Sense of Sex: A Study of Leviticus 18". *Journal for the Study of the Old Testament* 29 (1): 57–79.

Murphy, Cathrine M. 2001. *Wealth in the Dead Sea Scrolls and in the Qumran*. Leiden: Brill.

Schleicher, Marianne. 2011. "Constructions of Sex and Gender: Attending to Androgynes and *Tumtumim* through Jewish Scriptural Use". *Literature and Theology* 25 (4): 422–435.

Schuller, Eileen. 2012. "Tobit". In *Women's Bible Commentary: Revised and Updated*, edited by Carol A. Newsom, Sharon H. Ringe, and Jacqueline E. Lapsley, 376–382. Louisville: John Knox.

Schuller, Eileen. 1994. "Women in the Dead Sea Scrolls". In *Methods of Investigation of the Dead Sea Scrolls and the Khirbet Qumran Site: Present Realities and Future Prospects*, edited by Michael O. Wise, Norman Golb, John J. Collins, and Dennis G. Pardee, 115–131. New York: The New York Academy of Sciences.

Shulman, George. 2011. "On Vulnerability as Judith Butler's Language of Politics: From 'Excitable Speech' to 'Precarious Life' ". *Women's Studies Quarterly* 39 (1/2): 227–235.

Soll, Will. 1998. "The Family as Scriptural and Social Construct in Tobit". In *The Function of Scripture in Early Jewish and Christian Tradition*, edited by Craig A. Evans and James A. Sanders, 166–175. Sheffield: Sheffield Academic Press.

Wolde, Ellen van. 2008. "Sentiments as Culturally Constructed Emotions: Anger and Love in the Hebrew Bible". *Biblical Interpretation* 16: 1–24.

CHAPTER 2

The Art of Etruscan Love

Bridget Sandhoff

What can one say about love? It is a difficult term to define because it affects humans in such diverse ways and creates radically different experiences and perspectives. Also complicating the situation are the various expressions of love: spiritual, altruistic, amorous, platonic, and erotic. Generally love is a positive emotion associated with the romantic coupling of men and women or other pairings. The intensity of this feeling and the longing to bond with another human being has made love one of the most common topics found in literature and the visual arts, even in antiquity.

Ancient Greek and Roman literature did not avoid the topic of love, and it demonstrates the same diversity that we see today. One of the most catholic of topics is the relationship between husbands and wives. Modern Western beliefs assume couples marry for love, and that their affection for each other will carry on into the afterlife. However, love was not necessarily the motivating factor for men and women to marry in classical antiquity. Romantic love in marriage implies a level of reciprocity between husband and wife in which they are equals who share a common desire for one another (Goldhill, 2004, 48–50; Flacelière, 1962, 187–188). To achieve this level of intimacy in a Greek or Roman marriage was possible but difficult to achieve, if we trust the extant literature and artwork. Prevailing gender norms dictated marital behaviours. Wives/mothers had to follow strict codes of conduct (i.e., interaction with men who were non-relatives), while husbands/fathers were free to do as they pleased (i.e., extramarital affairs).

This is not to say that marriages in the ancient Mediterranean lacked affection: far from it. Writings and artwork survive that show more tender portraits of marital relations. Greek marriage hymns and personal correspondence of Romans discuss longing for a loved one. Artists illustrate married couples on Roman funerary monuments and brides and grooms on Greek vases. In spite of these examples, the extant writings often discuss the less ideal aspects of marriage. Betrayal, infidelity, jealousy, and bastard children become the fodder for ancient writers, and conjugal bliss was treated as a childish fantasy. Art follows the same path. Sexual desire rarely accompanies happy marriages, but adulterous affairs do, especially in mythology: Ares and Aphrodite or Zeus and his multiple conquests. Erotic Greek vase paintings and Pompeian wall frescoes seldom

 | DOI:10.1163/9789004380233_004

depict husbands and wives (real or mythical) but prostitutes and paramours. When wedded couples appear, they appear sombre and devoid of any emotion. Thus, the Greek and Roman point of view on marital love paints a muddled and ambiguous picture.

One ancient culture, however, that showed more explicit affection between husbands and wives was the Etruscans. Their approach to conjugal relations appears more transparent. This early Italic society was noted for its unusual attitudes about women and marriage. While Etruscan literature does not survive, their art does, and it provides the foremost evidence for our understanding of Etruscan marital love. Though it is important not to read the artwork too literally, the sheer volume of the imagery depicting loving couples, especially on engraved bronze mirrors, tomb paintings, and sarcophagi, should not be overlooked. I believe that these affectionate images, whether projections of an ideal or reflections of reality, were valued and probably shaped Etruscan attitudes, behaviours, and ideology. These works promoted the significant role that family life played within their society, which was only possible through the successful bonding of husbands and wives. Subsequently, their happy union would produce children who ensured the family name would live on but also guaranteed the continuation of Etruria.

Perceptions of Marital Love in Ancient Greece and Rome

A *Greece*

Greek literature provides a wealth of insight on love among wedded couples. However, it should be noted that to reconstruct a human emotion and all its psychological workings from the past is nearly impossible. Though numerous writings survive that provide a glimpse into the mind of an ancient Greek or Roman, these works are not without their flaws; the evidence provides a very limited perspective, primarily male and aristocratic. Translation issues also compound the problem. Nonetheless, one can develop a general picture about the relations between husbands and wives, which is complex and often contradictory. Overall, Greek literature provides a sceptical view about romantic love among couples, but some beautiful examples of marital affection can be found too. For example, longing for a spouse is exemplified in the mythical couples of Hector and Andromache and Odysseus and Penelope. Their stories play out in Homer's epic tales, *Iliad* and the *Odyssey* (both eighth century B.C.), which illuminate their perfect marriages and devotion to their partners.

Marriage hymns, *epithalamia*, were composed frequently in antiquity. They were sung at weddings, usually declaring the appeal of the wedding/married life

(Johnson and Ryan 2005, 61). The female poet Sappho (late seventh-early sixth centuries B.C.), famous for her erotic odes about women, also wrote sentimental yet playfully sensual *epithalamia*. One of the surviving stanzas states: 'Joyous bridegroom, your marriage has reached fruition for which you prayed … Your body is graceful, gentle your eyes … And love pours over your beautiful feature … Aphrodite bestowed great honour upon you' (Sappho *Fragments* 112, in Johnson and Ryan 2005, 68–70). One of the earliest complete hymns comes from Theocritus, a third century B.C. pastoral poet. His *epithalamium* honours the marriage between Helen and Menelaus, wishing them a happy life together and blessed with children (Theocritus, *Idyll* 18, in Johnson and Ryan 2005, 71–73).

In addition to the literature, funerary inscriptions display more romantic declarations of spousal harmony and suggest that love carried throughout life and into death. Many mention the pain and suffering in losing one's beloved: 'In this tomb lies Chaerestrate. Her husband loved her as long as she lived. When she died he grieved for her' (Epitaph for Chaerestrate, *EG* 44.2-3 (from Piraeus, fourth century B.C.), in Johnson and Ryan 2005, 83). They also typically recall the exemplary life of the deceased who conformed to and promoted proper behaviours, such as Aspasia: 'Of a worthy wife this is the tomb … of Aspasia, who is dead; in response to her noble disposition Euopides set up this monument for her; she was his consort' (Epitaph for Aspasia, *CEG* 167.G (from Chios, c. 400 B.C.), in Lefkowitz and Fant 1992, 16). Another memorial for a woman named Dionysia praises the devotion she showed to her husband:

> It was not clothes, it was not gold that this woman admired during her lifetime; it was her husband and the good sense that she showed in her behaviour. But in return for the youth you shared with him, Dionysia, your tomb is adorned by your husband, Antiphilus. (Epitaph for Dionysia, *IG* II2.11162.G (from Athens, fourth century B.C.), in Lefkowitz and Fant 1992, 16)

These loving examples, however, did not necessarily mirror reality. Marriage among elites was viewed in practical terms. It was regarded as a business contract instead of a love match in which the children of aristocratic families were sacrificed in order to strengthen each individual group. Therefore, marriage was used as a tool to secure political alliances, procure economic security, strengthen the *polis*, and bear legitimate children (Johnson and Ryan 2005, 1–3). With this in mind, love was of little concern. Moreover, wives had to follow rules of decorum within the marriage, especially in terms of sex. Husbands were not bound to the same regulations. Married men were granted sexual freedom not accorded to their spouses. While Greek society demanded marital fidelity of women, it was only expected that men would do the same, but it was *not* obligatory. If they wanted, husbands could frequent prostitutes, especially *hetairai* (courtesans who catered to an aristocratic clientele) or even engage in sexual relations with the slaves in their own households. In addition, men, especially in Athens and Sparta, could develop *pederastic* relationships with young male citizens. Apollodorus, a fourth century B.C. Athenian citizen, gave a speech at a trial against a supposed prostitute. His words speak about the situation perfectly: 'We have the *hetairai* for delectation, slaves to see to our daily sexual needs, and wives to bear legitimate offspring and to be faithful protectors of the household' (Preserved in Demosthenes 59.119, in Skinner 2014, 119). In this respect, a conjugal disparity is created in which men reign and women obey.

Many Greek authors share the same admonishment of marriage, and believed that it ultimately led to the destruction of men. Early writers, including Hesiod (late eighth-early seventh centuries B.C.) and Semonides (seventh century B.C.), make inflammatory remarks concerning marriage and wives. They believed all women were evil and were created to torture men. Hesiod's *Theogony* reinforces these attitudes. This well-known poem discusses the creation of the world with the gods at the helm. It also relays the punishment of mankind because Prometheus gives humans the power of fire. Zeus' punitive act is to create women who become irresistible to men; thus, they desire women and wish to possess and contain them (i.e., in marriage) (Hesiod, *Theogony* 585–594, 602–612, in Johnson and Ryan 2005, 62).

The poet Semonides of Amorgos writes in the same mode as Hesiod. His infamous poem outlines the various types of wives, comparing them to animals. He believes wives are inherently flawed and because of this fact, they are inferior to men. The following excerpt highlights his invective:

> At the beginning, the god made the mind of woman different. One kind he fashioned out of a bristled sow, throughout whose household is a pile of filth; she, messy with muck, rolling about on the floor, unwashed, in dirty clothes, squats in shit, growing fat. (Semonides, *Poem* 7, in Johnson and Ryan 2005, 63–68)[1]

Indeed, this sentiment pervades the literature more frequently than professions of love between husbands and wives. Desire, lust, and longing fall under the most dangerous aspect of love, *eros*, or in other words, mindless sexual desire. It is a powerful force that, if left unchecked, could lead to dire situations that endanger the home (*oikos*) or city (*polis*). The first lessons Greek children learned were not to succumb to excess, whether it was with food or material

1 A few of the other animals include a dog, weasel, horse, and ape.

goods. Giving into one's desires constituted a lack of self-control, an essential human quality that distinguished man from animal. Therefore, amorous feelings for one's life partner could potential destroy a family home, the foundation of Greek society. Duty and obligation in marriage were fostered, not love (Goldhill 2004, 50–52; Johnson and Ryan 2005, 1–3).

When Greek authors talk about conjugal bliss, it is usually an ideal construct for couples to emulate. Even Odysseus and Penelope, the paragons of fidelity, show no burning passion. In its place, we see a love that is proper and one that follows the rules of society. Moreover, characters from Greek mythology usually illustrate the foibles of love: Helen and Menelaus, Medea and Jason, Apollo and Daphne, and Eros and Psyche (see Wern Mei Yong's chapter in this volume reassessing the myth of Psyche and Eros) (Goldhill 2004, 51–52; Flacelière 1962, 187–231). In fact, desire for one's wife or husband is the source of ridicule in the literature and is often the topic for comedies. An example of this mockery can be found in Aristophanes's play *Lysistrata* (late fourth century B.C.).[2] The elite wives try to end the Peloponnesian War by refusing to sleep with their husbands. Mysteriously, all other outlets (e.g., prostitutes) for their sexual gratification have disappeared. As a result, the men go crazy with desire for their wives. It should come as no surprise that Greek love poetry is rarely addressed to a wife or husband but to some other paramour (Bing and Cohen 1991, 3, note 6). It all amounts to codes of proper conduct for respectable citizens. Any public display of affection would be criticized. Such tenderness was left to the confines of the private realm including personal letters or love poetry.

In Greek art nuptial imagery regularly decorated Attic Greek vases, especially the wedding procession which transferred the bride to the groom's home (e.g., the marriage of Peleus and Thetis). The processions usually show a line-up of characters displaying no emotion. By the mid-fifth century B.C., "feminine" topics became more common, including domestic scenes and bathing/dressing the bride. The movement of the bride to her new home also continued to be depicted. Aphrodite's son Eros was often incorporated into the imagery to indicate desire, but these vases typically show the groom pulling his (reluctant?) bride along by the wrist in an urgent manner. No hugging, kissing or any other intimacy is present. So, why this change in subject? The answer probably stems from a change in Athenian law, which ensured the legitimacy of its residents. It denied citizenship to anyone not born from legal Athenian

2 See Jeffrey Henderson's Loeb Classical Library translation: *Aristophanes*, Vol. 3 (2000, 254–441).

citizens (Skinner 2014, 129–131).[3] Therefore, marriage became critical in securing a stable *oikos* and *polis* in Athens.

The only monumental expressions of conjugal bliss were reserved for funerary monuments (e.g., gravestone inscriptions or portraits). The married pairs show little affection and appear stiff and formal. One example can be seen on a Greek tombstone depicting a man and woman immortalized in a large marble relief (approx. 5'10") from Rhamnous, 330–300 B.C (Robertson 1989, 138, fig. 189; Dillon 2010, 76, fig. 32).[4] Hieron and Lysippe stand together, and although a father and daughter has been suggested, the two probably represent a married couple since fathers are usually paired with sons, not daughters (Figure 2.1).

The mature bearded male rests in a three-quarters view and in a soft contrapposto stance; his left leg crossed over the other. His upper torso is bare, but his lower body is swathed in drapery. He looks intently at his partner, who rests in a subtle contrapposto position to his left. She stands frontally with her physique enveloped in clothing; it clings to her body, revealing the outline of her form. Her youthful face is in profile as she looks directly at her older companion. Both are missing arms, but most likely they were holding hands because other grave monuments show similar pairs engaged in the same action, perhaps welcoming the deceased into the afterlife.[5] Their gazes indicate their connection, but Hieron and Lysippe do not push the boundaries of impropriety; they show the legitimate amount of affection. Comparable scenes of emotion are expressed among families on funerary monuments not necessarily matrimonial pairs (e.g., mother and daughter, father and son, and small family groups).[6]

B *Rome*

Understanding attitudes about conjugal love in ancient Rome poses the same problems as it does in Greece. A wealth of information survives in the literature and art, but it often presents a skewed perspective: male, elite, and incongruous. The Romans prided themselves as being practical, rational people. Everything had a purpose, even their art which borrowed heavily from Greek sources. Roman society, just like Greece, also valued self-control and moderation, but a surprising amount of emotion can be found in their literature, even writings about husbands and wives.

3 See in particular, fig. 3.18, which shows a *loutrophoros* (ceremonial wedding vase) with a bridal procession. The groom grabs his modestly dressed betrothed by the hand and leads her to his home.

4 National Archaeological Museum, Athens, inv. no. 833.

5 See Boardman (1995, 223, fig. 123) for a comparable example.

6 For examples of Greek couples, see Blundell (1999, fig. 24) and Boardman (2001, 95, fig. 129).

FIGURE 2.1 Marble relief of Hieron and Lysippe from the grave monument of Hierokles, Rhamnous, 330–300 B.C. National Archaeological Museum, Athens. KOSTAS XENIKAKIS (PHOTOGRAPHER).

The diverse oeuvre of Catullus, first century B.C. poet, is mostly distinguished by his bawdy works,[7] but he also composed romantic poetry, including a wedding hymn for a real Roman couple. The *epithalamium* for Junia Aurunculeia and Manlius Torquatus paints a happy portrait of the wedding and marriage. The hymn invokes gods/goddesses, eases anxieties, and offers well wishes to the couple, especially for male children (Catullus, *Poems* 61, in Shelton 1988, 40–43; Johnson and

7 For examples, see Bing and Cohen (1991, 197–215), especially nos. 6, 32, 37, 41, and 42, which are particularly vulgar.

Ryan 2005, 73–78). Two female poets named Sulpicia (first century B.C. and first century A.D.) provide a rarefied articulation of a woman's experience. The earlier Sulpicia speaks of love in a more sensual manner, but the latter poet shows more restraint discussing her chaste desire for her husband.[8]

A more insightful understanding can be drawn from personal letters, which are less guarded in their sentiment, including those by Cicero (Dixon 1992, 84–85) and Pliny the Younger. Pliny's (late first-early second centuries A.D.) letters to his third wife Calpurnia still survive and illustrate his contentment with his young love. In one letter he explains the tender commitment that she shows to Pliny: '… and she loves me, surely an indication of her virtue. She has even, because of her affection for me, taken an interest in literature …' (*Letters* 4.19, 2–4, in Shelton 1988, 45–46). A more poignant letter exhibits his passion for her while they are separated by her convalescence in the country:

> It is incredible how much I miss you, because I love you and then because we are not used to being separated. And so I lie awake most of the night haunted by your image; and during the day, during those hours I used to spend with you, my feet lead me, they really do, to your room; and then I turn and leave, sick at heart and sad, like a lover locked out on a deserted doorstep. The only time I escape these torments is when I am in the Forum, wearing myself out pleading cases for my friends. Judge for yourself what my life is like when I find relaxation in work and relief in problems and anxiety … (Pliny the Younger, *Letters* 7.5, in Shelton 1988, 46; Johnson and Ryan 2005, 87)

Similar sentiments of pining can be found on funerary stelai and sarcophagi. The inscriptions, as in Greece, exalt the deceased, but also demonstrate the bond between husbands and wives. Both men and women honour their deceased spouses in affectionate ways. One tombstone has Paternus eulogizing his wife:

> … To Urbana my sweetest, chastest, and rarest wife. Surely no one more distinguished ever existed. She deserved honour also for this reason, that she lived every day of her life with me with the greatest kindness and the greatest simplicity, both in her conjugal love and the industry typical of her character. I added this so that those who read may understand how much we loved one another … (Epitaph for Urbana, *CIL* VI.29580/ILS 8450 (from Rome, third century A.D.), in Lefkowitz and Fant 1992, 20)

8 Their writings are preserved in the works of Tibullus (3.14L, 3.15, 17, 18, 13.L) and Martial, *Epigrams* 10.35, respectively (Lefkowitz and Fant 1992, 8 and 169).

Conversely, women occasionally erected funerary monuments for their husbands who passed away. Furia Spes laments her dead spouse Sempronius Firmus, imploring the spirits of the dead to treat her husband favourably. She also declares her desire to be with her husband in the next realm soon:

> ... When we were still boy and girl, we were bound by mutual love as soon as we met. I lived with him for too brief a time. We were separated by a cruel hand when we should have continued in happiness. I therefore beg, most sacred Manes, that you look after the loved one I have entrusted to you and that you be well disposed and very kind to him during the hours of the night, so that I may see him, and so that he, too, may wish to persuade fate to allow me to come to him, softly and soon. (Epitaph commissioned by Furia Spes, *CIL* 6.18817/*ILS* 8006, in Shelton 1988, 48)

While the Romans appear more demonstrative than the Greeks, ancient Rome closely mirrored Greek ideas of elite marital relationships. The purpose of marriage was essentially the same: it linked aristocratic families together, secured hegemonic rule, bolstered fortunes, and procured political partnerships. Marriage was done out of a sense of duty to the family and the state, not out of affection for another person. As in Greece, elite Roman children had little say in who they married; match-making was left to the elders in the family. The primary resolve of the union was bearing and raising legitimate male heirs. In these males were the aspirations of the family, largely to cement higher social standing and prestige.[9]

Unlike Greek women, Roman matrons had more freedom within their marriages. They could inherit property and had more public visibility, but despite this independence, wives were not equals with their husbands in marriage. The *paterfamilias*, the head of the household, had final say and authority over its members. Females also had to follow regimented codes of decorum or suffer bringing shame upon the family. (Sadly, a similar situation faces women in modern India, as Veenu Kakkar and Aanchal Kapur explain in their chapter in this volume.) Men, too, were regulated by similar rules but were rarely held accountable with the same rigour. The concept of *concordia* or harmony was aspired to in marriage but hardly realized. Solidarity within the household equated to stability of the state, which was especially true for the imperial family as it signified their effectiveness to rule (Dixon in Rawson 1996, 107–108).[10] In this regard, marriage was a civic duty, not a personal choice.

9 For more on Roman marriage, see D'Ambra (2007, 46–91) and Rawson (1996).

10 *Concordia* was a concept that emperors utilized consistently to cement their rule, both literally and visually.

Thus, the mostly male Roman authors were hardly sentimental about marriage. While Ovid (first century B.C.) wrote impassioned letters to his wife (Dixon 1992, 85–87), he gained notoriety instead because of his infamous love manual that taught men and women how to find a lover. The same contradiction is found in the first century B.C. writings of Stoic philosopher, Seneca (the Younger). He also expresses love for his wife Paulina but also shares decidedly moralizing opinions about unscrupulous women and marital relations: '… to sleep with one's wife like a lover is as disgusting as adultery' (Seneca, *de Matrimonio* (frag. 13), in Dixon 1992, 87; Goldhill 2004, 50).

Moreover, Latin satirists Horace, Martial and Juvenal (first century B.C.-second century A.D.) examine the inherent evils of marriage and wives (Dixon 1992, 84). Marriage was often considered a necessary nuisance. This belief is highlighted in the speech of a late second century B.C. censor, now preserved in the writings of Aulus Gellius (second century A.D. grammarian). Q. Caecilius Metellus Numidicus made a famous speech about the inconvenience of marriage that is nonetheless an obligation for a Roman male citizen:

> If we could manage without a wife, Romans, we would all avoid that nuisance; but since nature has laid it down that we cannot live peacefully with them but not at all without them, we must consider the long-term benefit rather than immediate satisfaction. (Quoted by Aulus Gellius, *Noctes Atticae* 1.6.2, in Dixon 1992, 84; D'Ambra 2007, 46)

It was generally believed that satisfaction, especially sexual, was sought outside the marital bond (Dixon 1992, 86; Bing and Cohen 1991, 12–13; Wyke 2002).

Adultery was apparently such a significant problem in the late Republic/early Imperial period that the emperor Augustus instituted laws to deter straying husbands and wives. He was also appealing to the more conservative sect of Roman society who longed for the good old days of the virtuous Republic. These measures did not stop most husbands though from fraternizing with prostitutes and slaves within their homes or even the mistress of the house taking a lover or two (Bing and Cohen 1991, 16; Shelton 1988, 54–55, 58).[11]

Furthermore, the founding myths of Rome are based on acts of sexual violence against women: the rape of the Sabine women and the rape of Lucretia.

---

11 See Dixon (1992, 71–83) for Augustus' Julian laws, but also about his hypocritical behaviour (i.e., Augustus' own extramarital affairs).

In these myths, the women resigned to their fate and became the model of appropriate behaviour for Roman matrons – obedient and faithful. Suzanne Dixon sees the literary and visual evidence riddled with problems when trying to extrapolate on marital love. For example, authors borrowed from Greek models. Epitaphs run rampant with clichés and formulaic constructions. Widowhood was common, as well as easy divorces and extramarital affairs. No moral or religious restrictions dissuaded Romans from divorcing; in simplistic terms, marriage was a contract (Treggiari in Rawson 1996, 31–46).

Dixon also believes that the inscriptions and artwork express an ideal rather than reality (1992, 86–90). The Romans, a very image-conscious people, tried to promote this stereotype of the virtuous couple. Nuptial imagery in Roman art survives in large numbers, but it is typically superseded by family portraits or busts of significant family members/ancestors. Depictions of weddings are not frequent but when they are found, they usually show the preparation of the bride (e.g., bathing, adorning, and dressing) or the couple holding their right hands, symbolizing their union (*dextrarum iunctio*).[12] These hand-holding scenes are the only display of real intimacy between the pair, and again they exhibit a sober and reserved attitude.

Imperial portraiture, as expected, is plentiful but emphasizes legacy over conjugal bliss. And since children were the primary goal of any marriage, they are often promoted especially imperial ones. A highly unusual artwork is the Severan family portrait, ca. 200 A.D., from Faiyum, Egypt (Figure 2.2) (Kleiner 2007, 233, fig. 16-4).[13] This is unique because it is the only surviving painted imperial family portrait. The round wooden panel (approx. 14″ in diameter) depicts the emperor Septimius Severus with flecks of grey in his hair, his wife Julia Domna sporting her jewellery, and their two sons, Caracalla and Geta (Geta was later erased from the piece because of a *damnatio memoriae* issued by his elder brother). They all pose frontally, like busts, with the children placed in front of their parents. The handsome crew is dressed in their finest garments, and mom and dad wear crowns to indicate their status. Naturally, Severus is slightly larger than the other three since he is the emperor. The havoc that beset Rome prior to Severus' ascendancy certainly inspired him to promote the theme of *concordia* throughout his entire reign: within his family (*two* sons to rule after his death) and the state.

12 For examples, see plates 1, 2, 4–6 in Dixon (1992, 166–170) and figures 18–19 in Stewart (2003, 105–106).

13 Antikensammlung, Staatliche Museen Preussischer Kulturbesitz, Berlin, inv. no. 31329.

FIGURE 2.2 Severan Family Portrait (Septimius Severus, Julia Domna, Caracalla and Geta), Faiyum, 200 A.D. Antikensammlung, Staatliche Museen zu Berlin-Preussischer Kulturbesitz.

The most frequent representations of husbands and wives are found, however, on funerary monuments commissioned by former slaves, especially in the first century B.C. These freedmen, once they had enough money, would have portraits of themselves carved and then placed into the façades of their tombs. Typically, the rectangular stone slab is carved in shallow relief with busts of the husband and wife, along with an inscription; surviving children are often included. The figures are posed frontally, staring directly at the audience. They generally lack any affection towards each other and appear only as if to document their existence. The inscriptions could be more effusive but usually are formulaic in nature.

A fine example resides in the Museum of Fine Arts in Boston. The tomb relief of Publius Gessius and family was found near Viterbo (late first century B.C.), and portrays Publius in the centre flanked by his wife and son (Figure. 2.3) (Kleiner 2007, 83, fig. 6-9).[14] All three stare out at passers-by with rather dour expressions on their faces; no emotional connection is

14 Museum of Fine Arts, Boston, inv. no. 37.100. Kleiner, however, believes that his wife could actually be his daughter.

FIGURE 2.3 Marble relief of Publius Gessius and family, near Viterbo, late first century B.C. Museum of Fine Arts, Boston.

depicted between the husband and wife or the parents with the child. Their faces are rendered realistically, particularly in terms of their age which was the style at the time. A large age difference between the couple shows typical Roman marital practice: older men marrying younger women. Other than their shoulders, no touching or gestures indicate a burning passion, but they reflect the ideal relationship: stoic and unaffected. Family was important in all levels of society, and these newly freed people wanted to declare their new status, not necessarily proclaim their love. Freedmen art, in order to remove the stigma of slavery, tried to emulate imperial models, hence their reserved, decorous mood.[15]

The Exceptional Etruscan View on Marital Love

The absence of Etruscan literature is a major setback in our understanding of Etruria, let alone their view on marital relations.[16] Though usually biased and one-sided, ancient Greek and Roman writings at least provide first-hand insight into their own cultures as well others like Etruria. Foreign writers provide commentaries about the Etruscans, which can provide some answers; however, more often, these authors intended to scandalize and shock their conservative readers with the outrageous, barbaric

15 For more affectionate couples, see the marble sarcophagi of the late Roman period (second-third centuries A.D.) in Wrede (1990, 15–46). The sarcophagus types, however, mimic Etruscan examples.

16 Mostly inscriptions survive which do not provide much insight. They simply furnish the names of characters or real people. The lengthier inscriptions usually outline business contracts.

behaviours of Etruria. The general belief is that the Etruscans were luxurious barbarians, and that they, particularly the women, enjoyed partying. Etruria was a place where aristocratic wives behaved outside normal gendered decorum.

Theopompus, a fourth century B.C. Greek historian, wrote one of the longest but most scathing reviews of Etruscan society. Scholars often dismiss his comments as pure invective. A further problem is that his comments are preserved second-hand in the work of Athenaeus of Naucratis (early third century A.D.). *The Deipnosophists* (The Learned Banquet) features of group of educated men discussing various topics over several days, including a chat about the Etruscans. Despite these issues, it is fascinating to see that Theopompus was mostly concerned with martial relationships in Etruria, especially the role of Etruscan wives:

> ... further, they dine, not with their own husbands, but with any men who happen to be present, and they pledge with wine any whom they wish. They are also terribly bibulous and very good looking. The Etruscans rear all the babies that are born, not knowing who the father is in any single case ... (Athenaeus, *Deipnosophistae* 12.517D-18B, in Gulick (trans.) 1969, 329, 331)

Athenaeus also mentions Aristotle, who confirms Theopompus' beliefs: 'And Aristotle, in his *Customs of the Tyrrhenians,* said "The Tyrrhenians (i.e., Etruscans) dine in company with their women, lying back under the same robe"' (Athenaeus, *Deipnosophistae* 1.23G, in Gulick (trans.) 1969, 103). In the same way, Theopompus notices how different women acted and were treated within Etruria, which seems to be corroborated with the surviving evidence. Yet, Etruria was a patriarchal society, and women understood their duties to the family. What was considered unacceptable in Greece and Rome (e.g., having a loving relationship) was normal and encouraged in Etruscan society.

Instead of written texts, the material and visual culture provide our best evidence on how the Etruscans viewed conjugal love. Again, similar issues come to the fore – not an authentic, but an idealized, elite view. Whether truthful or romanticized, Etruscan art does show what they deemed important. Just like Greece and Rome, no extant public monuments were dedicated to couples, but they were ostensibly confined to the funerary realm. Based on a brief analysis of engraved bronze mirrors, tomb paintings, and sarcophagi, the Etruscans were more candid in their representations of husbands and wives. Couples dancing, eating together on banquet couches and showing affection permeate these works. Rather than concealing their feelings, the Etruscans were more apt to declare their love and on a grander scale.

A *Engraved Bronze Mirrors*

Engraved bronze mirrors comprise the largest body of artwork to survive in Etruria.[17] The numbers are staggering when compared to other Etruscan art forms as well as the number of mirrors in Greece and Rome. The ubiquity of the objects suggests its almost banal status but also their pivotal role in Etruscan society. Though men certainly used them, engraved bronze mirrors were primarily feminine objects and probably given as wedding gifts or to mark other significant life events. The 3000–4000 extant examples imply that most aristocratic women in Etruria owned at least one mirror, perhaps more. And at the end of a woman's life, the mirror followed her to the grave (where most are often found), and ostensibly, to the next realm. They could also be given to the next generation as heirlooms (De Puma 2013).

Etruscan mirrors are noteworthy because of the engravings on the reverse sides. The enormous variety of subjects provides a veritable encyclopaedia of information about Etruscan culture. One of the most common topics is love or variations on this theme: affectionate couples, wedding adornment, and birth. The topics shaped and reinforced Etruscan ideology on the importance of family, which hinged on a successful partnership between husbands and wives. The engravings, no doubt, had a strong impact on the owners, who used their mirrors every day. A wife's personal appearance was not regarded as frivolous but created a potent public image of the individual family as well as desire within her spouse. It helped crystallize the love bond between the married pair.

Turan (Aphrodite/Venus) shows up frequently on mirrors because of her connection to beauty. She often helps out in adornment scenes, but it is her love affairs that often take centre stage, particularly with her young love, Atunis (Adonis). Interestingly, Turan is rarely depicted with her husband Sethlans (Hephaestus/Vulcan), but rather with her youthful lover. The preference for Atunis over Turan's husband probably stems from the lack of mutual affection between them. The intensity of Turan and Atunis' passion was more meaningful, and one that Etruscan couples may have aspired to themselves. One beautifully engraved mirror, dating to the fourth century

17 In the nineteenth century, Eduard Gerhard was the first to catalogue all known mirrors (five volumes of *Etruskische Spiegel*). It is an invaluable resource, but today, most scholars also use the modern *Corpus Speculorum Etruscorum* (CSE). The series was started in the late twentieth century to re-document all known mirrors in a more thorough and scientific manner.

B.C., depicts Turan and Atunis locked in an adoring embrace in the centre of a circular frame (Van der Meer 1995, 187, fig. 89; Gerhard 1867, pl. 322).[18] An oversized swan named Tusna, a symbol of Aphrodite, and Zipna, a Lasa, flank the couple. Outside this frame six more Lasas fly around the edge of the mirror, and a chubby little satyr kneels, flanked by two feline creatures, on an overturned amphora in the exergue.

Zipna and the rest of her winged entourage belong to a large collective group of supernatural beings called Lasas. Most scholars liken them to Greek nymphs because of their multiplicity and helpful nature. Though they are difficult to define and identify sometimes, Lasas tend to be young, pretty, winged females (either semi-nude or clothed) and typically serve as beauty attendants (Rallo 1974). This role seems to be illustrated on this mirror. The outer Lasas, a mix of beautiful winged women and men, hold items to aid the lovers: lyre, alabastron and perfume dipper, small leafy branches, and long ribbons. Zipna, the main Lasa, rests against the circular frame. Her glorious wings rise up next to her head. She is fabulously dressed, coiffed, and bejewelled (just like her mistress) and she holds a long, thin alabastron and perfume dipper in her hands. She looks at the couple and seems to be anointing them with a pleasant scent. This coincides with another Lasa duty: to protect lovers. All of the Lasas seem to facilitate their love affair by creating the right ambience. The human-sized Tusna looks happily at the couple too.

Despite the bevy of characters, Turan and Atunis are the primary focus. The alluring goddess of love wears a long chiton and mantle, posh hairstyle, jewellery, and fancy shoes. She faces her paramour with arms wrapped around his adolescent body and looks down into his eyes. The youthful Atunis replies, looking up at his mature lover with his left hand touching the back of her head, possibly to move her closer to kiss. He sports a necklace of bullae (good luck charms) and opens his garment to expose his upper torso. Curiously, his revealing action mimics the gesture used by brides (i.e., *anakalypsis* or "unveiling"). Their embrace, gaze, and erotic atmosphere all speak of the fondness they share for one another. This type of intimacy is lacking in comparable Greek and Roman examples.[19] Their desire is clear, and Turan and Atunis may have served as a model for the mirror owner to imitate.

A similar mirror probably depicts the couple again but in a more erotic manner. The so-called Northampton mirror, ca. 300 B.C., shows Turan and Atunis in

18 Hermitage Museum, St. Petersburg, inv. no. V.505.

19 We do see, however, similar gestures of affection – embracing, kissing, touching – on Greek vases but in pederastic scenes between young men (*eromenoi*) and older gentlemen (*erastai*) or symposia scenes with *hetairai* and male guests.

the central frame unaware of the seated female and standing Menrva (Athena/ Minerva) on either side of them (Izzet 2005, 2, fig. 1; Van der Meer 1995, 21, fig. 6; Gerhard, Klügmann and Körte 1897, pl. 191).[20] A rich foliate border surrounds the group of four, and a snaky, winged male rests in the exergue below their feet. Most scholars discuss this mirror in terms of the dedicatory inscription on Menrva's shield that she rests her hand upon[21] or try to explain the curious combination of characters (Izzet 2005, 9–11).[22] However, the intensity of their relationship is most provocative and begs for greater examination.

Just like the prior work, Turan and Atunis embrace in a sensual manner. They both stand frontally in mirror contrapposto stances *pressing* their bodies into each other; even their faces touch with eyes locked on one another, suggestive of their desire. Atunis' right arm hugs her neck and shoulder while the left arm rests at his side. Turan gestures with her right hand as if making a point. The other arm (not shown) probably rests on his back. The pair seem detached from reality and engulfed in a haze of love. What heightens the eroticism is Atunis' conspicuous nudity. In contrast with Turan's elegant dress, hair, and jewellery (just like her female companions), Atunis lacks any clothing, footwear or embellishment. Nothing stands between his well-muscled form and his lovely lady. The only hint of nudity that Turan displays is the outline of her breasts beneath her garment. Her breasts, his nakedness, and the pressing of their bodies together illustrate the passion in their relationship. The popularity of the couple (Van der Meer 1995, 185)[23] indicates their appeal and more than likely inspired the owner to achieve to a similar connection with her husband.

Another equally engaged couple can be found on a Vulcian mirror, ca. 400–350 B.C. (Van der Meer 1995, 184, fig. 87; Sassatelli 1981, 196, fig. 41a).[24] The labelled figures do not appear to be mythical but could possibly represent a real, nude Etruscan couple.[25] The uncluttered mirror shows Cruisie (male) and Talitha (female) nude, standing in the centre and facing each other. He holds an alabastron while she carries a cista. A simple horizontal line serves as the

20 Private collection, Northampton, United Kingdom.

21 The inscription states that it was commissioned by Tite Cale, who seems to have given the mirror as a sacred gift to his mother or possibly a mother deity. See Izzet (2005) and Van der Meer (1995, 20–22) for more discussion.

22 Izzet suggests the seated figure could represent Uni (Hera/Juno), based on the belief that the engraving could be a conflation of the Judgment of Paris with Turan and Atunis.

23 Van der Meer has counted 22 epigraphic mirrors that identify and show Turan and Atunis together.

24 Museo Civico, Bologna, inv. no. 1071.

25 Van der Meer (1995, 184) attempts to interpret their names: Talitha = *talida* = marriageable girl and Cruisie = *Croesus* (wealthy Lydian king). He believes the engraving could represent an episode from King Croesus' life; however, I am not convinced by the argument, since it does not correspond with any known event in his life.

ground, and underneath this line an ivy plant grows with vines sprouting berries and leaves that encircles the outer edge of the mirror.

Nudity of both the man and woman together is quite shocking but may be explained by their physiques and the paraphernalia they hold. Both stand in three-quarter views which show off their rather athletic forms. His upper torso is well defined with articulation in his pectorals, biceps and abdominals. Talitha's body also shows muscle development with her flat stomach and lean legs. The alabastron and cista in their hands are typical objects used for beautification, but they are also employed by athletes. Whether they represent athletes or not is beside the point; their affection is poignant. They both gaze lovingly at each other. Cruisie holds up a flower to his partner, and Talitha responds with a caress to his cheek. This tender moment plainly demonstrates their fondness for each other and stresses the importance of the relationship. Their similarly short hair and analogous, nude bodies evoke a visual harmony that exemplifies the unity of the couple.

B *Tomb Paintings*

The Etruscans had a strong belief in life after death, and much of their art centres on funerary practices and the tomb. Based on their material culture and visual record, the Etruscans thought that life carried on in a different realm of existence after death, so they equipped their deceased loved ones with the necessary tools in order to live. The funerary rituals, preparation of the bodies (i.e., inhumation or cremation) and burial/tomb types varied among Etruscan territories but all had one goal in mind – to take care of the dead.

In Tarquinia the residents tended to paint their underground tombs with frescoes. A common subject was the funerary banquet in honour of the deceased. These banquets show a jovial atmosphere with eating, drinking, conversing, music, and dancing. More importantly, married couples feature prominently at these festivities and are shown enjoying the parties together.[26] One such example can be found in the Tomb of Hunting and Fishing, Tarquinia, 520 B.C. (Steingräber 2006, 86–87). The two-chambered tomb is brilliantly painted (in reds, oranges, blues and greens) with activities mentioned in the title: dancing and hunting in the first room and fishing and a banquet in the back chamber. In the pediment area of the backroom, an elegant husband and wife lounge together on a mattress blissfully unaware of the attending slaves (or children?) (Figure. 2.4).

---

26 Examples include the Tomb of the Lionesses, Tomb of the Bigas, Tomb of the Leopards and Tomb of the Triclinium; all the tombs date to the late sixth-early fifth centuries B.C. See Steingräber's seminal work on the Etruscan wall painting (2006, 94, 103, 130, 136–139).

Much like the Turan/Atunis mirrors, the focus is on the husband and wife, who are fully engaged with each other. The elegantly-styled woman decked out in jewellery and fine clothing lies on her stomach and hands her mate a garland. She also touches her husband's bare chest and looks directly into his eyes. The bearded spouse responds to his wife's affection: he faces her and returns her gaze. His right arm reaches out to rest his hand on her shoulder, and he places his leg on her back. His other arm helps prop up his upper body as he holds a phiale in his hand. The tender, intimate scene speaks of the keenness that they share for each other and again paints a potent image of love in Etruria.

A much later tomb shows the same topic with similar verve but emphasizes family lineage and pride. The Tomb of the Shields (Tarquinia, 350–300 B.C.)

FIGURE 2.4 Painting of a husband and wife banqueting, Tomb of Hunting and Fishing, Tarquinia, 520 B.C.

was the final resting place for the Velcha family, whose portraits still remain along with the genealogical inscriptions (Figure. 2.5) (Steingräber 2006, 188; 204; 221–224; Haynes 2000, 310–311, figs. 249–250). Painted shields on the walls give the burial its name; it was common practice to decorate Etruscan homes with shields, suggesting a military/warfare connection. The much larger tomb has several small rooms, but in the antechamber, members of the Velcha family repose at banquet. A bearded Larth Velcha, founder of the tomb, lies recumbent on a well-cushioned decorative couch or *kline*. He wears a laurel wreath in his short, dark hair and a garment surrounding his lower body that exposes his upper chest. At the foot of the *kline* sits his wife, Velia Seitithi, fashionably dressed, bejewelled, and coiffed. A table laden with food sits before them. Though more reserved than the prior couple, Velia and Larth convey their feelings through gentle glances and the exchange of an egg, a symbol of rebirth common in funerary scenes. She also gently rests her hand on her partner's shoulder.

FIGURE 2.5 Portraits of Larth Velcha and Velia Seitithi, Tomb of the Shields, Tarquinia, 350–300 B.C.

Comparable affection is also represented in the earlier generation. Larth's parents – Velthur Velcha and Ravnthu Aprthnai – are also depicted in a similar fashion in the same tomb (Figure 2.6). Velthur lies on the couch like a banqueter, and Ravnthu rests at the end of the *kline*. Musicians provide song, and food awaits them on the table. Ravnthu wears similar garments as her daughter-in-law, but they are not as flashy. Just like his son, Velthur is wreathed and bare-chested but holds a phiale in his hand. The other hand lies on Ravnthu's shoulder, and he looks intently at her. His spouse reacts with a hand on his shoulder too and touches his forearm. The depiction of the two is clearly the purpose of the painting: it is meant to preserve their memory and glorify this aristocratic family. However, the way they are commemorated is significant. Their affection was imperative and necessary for the relationship to thrive, but more importantly, it suggests that their love will carry on, even after death.

FIGURE 2.6 Portraits of Velthur Velcha and Ravnthu Aprthnai, Tomb of the Shields, Tarquinia, 350–300 B.C.

FIGURE 2.7 Couple sarcophagus, Cerveteri, 530–520 B.C. Louvre, Paris.
HERVÉ LEWANDOWSKI (PHOTOGRAPHER). © 2015, COURTESY OF RMN-GRAND PALAIS/ART RESOURCE, NY.

C *Sarcophagi*

Sarcophagi are another avenue of expressing Etruscan ideology on marital love. Just like the tomb paintings these works with depictions of husbands and wives were meant to commemorate the couple as well as to ensure their bond would last in the next life. The most iconic works of Etruscan art are the couple sarcophagi from Cerveteri, ca. 530 B.C. (Haynes 2000, 214, fig. 176a (Paris); Brendel 1995, 230–231, figs. 158–160 (Rome)). These life-size pieces, now in Paris and Rome, depict a husband and wife on a banquet *kline* (Figure 2.7).[27]

The similarities between the two works indicate that they were mass produced but for a wealthy clientele. They show a husband and wife reclining on a thick mattress, which is supported by a wooden frame. They prop themselves up on their left elbows and face the viewer as their legs stretch out on the couch. The men rest behind their wives, placing their right arms on their partners' shoulders. Presented like the previous male banqueters, they are bearded and bare-chested with their lower bodies covered. The elegant wives wear the latest fashions: chiton, mantle, tall, pointed boots, jewellery (now missing), and conical hat. Their rope-like hair lies on their chests and backs. The women hold up their hands as

27 The illustrated example comes from Paris: Louvre, Paris, inv. no. Cp 5194.

if they held something, perhaps an egg like Velia from the Tomb of the Shields. Despite the quirky stylizations prevalent at the time, the couples exude a vivacity that enhances the intimacy between them. The monumentality and their bond are palpable and testify to their congenial relationships.

Later sarcophagi and ash urns continue to portray husbands and wives together on the lids as well as on the receptacle itself.[28] Probably the most unique depictions of marital love and perhaps in all of antiquity can be found on a pair of stone sarcophagi from Vulci, late fourth century B.C. (Haynes 2000, 288, fig. 232a and 290, fig. 233).[29] Instead of being propped up on a couch, the lids present the couples lying in bed together. The later sarcophagus shows Arnth Tetnies and Ramtha Visnai, an older couple, embracing each other under a single blanket (Figure 2.8). Both lie angled towards each other with their arms wrapped around their partner's body. Ramtha sports a light-weight chiton, earrings, and bracelet, but her husband is nude. Their lower bodies are concealed, but the fabric reveals the outline of their heavier physiques; their feet peek out from underneath the blanket. Their mature faces and fuller frames indicate middle age, and it illustrates an interesting choice in not representing themselves as young lovers. This very rare depiction probably infers that the two share the marital bed, and that their love and its physical expression will carry on into the next realm.

As elite members of their community Ramtha and Arnth wanted to safeguard not only their relationship but also their station. On the long side of the sarcophagus the couple is represented coming together in the centre, followed by servants who hold items indicating their position: symbols of a magistrate and Ramtha's beauty items (Haynes 2000, 289, fig. 232b). The pair stands facing each other as Arnth, bare-chested, grabs hold of her hand and wrist; his posh wife wraps her arm around his neck. The carved ends show the duo again, one on each side, driving or sitting in a conveyance that is probably symbolic of their journey into the afterlife (Haynes 2000, 289, figs. 232c-d). Indeed the sarcophagus was meant to demonstrate their power but also their affection for each other. This lid is the epitome of wedded bliss; however, its companion sarcophagus trumps even Ramtha and Arnth's love.

The earlier sarcophagus shows a more youthful, idealized couple on the lid but in a more erotic manner. The two represent Larth Tetnies and Thanchvil Tarnai, the son and daughter-in-law of Ramtha and Arnth (Figure 2.9). They also share the marital bed together. The two embrace each other, like Ramtha and Arnth, but rest on their sides facing and looking directly into

28 For a few later examples, see Haynes (2000, 366, fig. 288 and 368, fig. 290).

29 Museum of Fine Art, Boston, inv. nos. 1976.799 (Arnth and Ramtha) and 86.145. See also Rowland (2008).

FIGURE 2.8
Sarcophagus lid depicting Arnth Tetnies and Ramtha Visnai, Vulci, 300–280 B.C. Museum of Fine Arts, Boston.

FIGURE 2.9 Sarcophagus lid depicting Larth Tetnies and Thanchvil Tarnai, Vulci, 350–300 B.C. Museum of Fine Arts, Boston.

each other's eyes. Larth's well-muscled arm reaches over and rests his hand on Thanchvil's shoulder. Her arm lies underneath her lover's with her hand placed on his ribcage. She also cradles her other hand around his neck. The two are clearly young with no imperfections present on their youthful faces and slender bodies, which are covered with a beautifully carved sheet. This blanket serves as their clothing because both Larth and Thanchvil are nude underneath, making the meaning obvious: these two are engaged in a carnal embrace that was meant to illustrate their strong living bond but a bond that would not break after death. Moreover, their sexual act symbolically illustrates rebirth in the afterlife (Bonfante 1996, 285–286; Bonfante 2000, 158–159). To represent such explicit passion between a husband and wife and on such a large scale is unparalleled in the ancient Mediterranean, even for the Etruscans, but it is not unusual for Etruria when considering the significance of the wedded couple as well as the importance placed on their love.

Conclusions

So what can we say about marital love in the ancient Mediterranean? Certainly there are no black and white answers. When it comes to human emotions, nothing is guaranteed because it varies greatly from person to person. The only thing that can be said with certainty is that the representation of marital love is variable. In ancient Greece and Rome an ambiguous picture of conjugal relations can be drawn from the literary and visual evidence. Both positive and negative perceptions abound, but one thing is definite: marriage was a necessary component of a functioning society. Whether the partners cared for each other or not was left up to the individuals in the relationships. An ideal image of a loving couple was promoted but typically not realized. Visual representations of this paradigm show a subdued love but nothing too effusive. The lack of Etruscan writings makes it difficult to determine the perception of love between husbands and wives in Etruria. More than likely, they too shared similar conflicting views like their neighbours. Marriage could be a political tool and not about love. However, it is my belief that the Etruscans placed greater value on the relationships between husbands and wives. Whether or not aristocratic couples truly loved each other is impossible to determine, but it was a philosophy that they promoted in their artwork.

But why worry about individual relationships? Why promote this ideal? The Etruscans presented marital love and affection so vividly because of the importance placed on family and its creation. The wedded couple was the cornerstone of Etruscan life (Nielsen 2009, 171–181). Without family a community and ultimately Etruria would cease to exist. The husband and wife worked together to establish a home and name for themselves, but more importantly to bear and raise children. Children were of vital importance because they signified the continuation of the family name and established a degree of immortality. On a greater level it cemented the strength of Etruria, which would live on another day.

Survival underscores much of the Etruscan philosophy on beauty, love, marriage, and family. This is not an unusual idea considering death was a regular part of life, but the Etruscans seem to have been particularly sensitive to endings and the passage of time. One of the major predictions about Etruria (stated in their sacred ritual books) was that it had a limited life expectancy, approximately 1000 years.[30] If this knowledge was pervasive, it would be reasonable to assume that the Etruscans were constantly battling the passage of time. The only way to combat this prediction was to privilege the family where life originates. Moreover, the fourth century B.C. marked the slow decline of Etruscan power, and their eventual conquest by the Romans. It is no coincidence that many marital images date to this period or later. No doubt the threat of Rome loomed large and seemed to reinforce the prophecy. Families retaliated by continuing to procreate but also by building large ancestral tombs and creating images of family members. These monuments secured their memory, which established a measure of immortality that would hopefully last.

The role of women also played a key factor. Wives were not considered a nuisance but a critical member of the family unit. They brought their own prestige and wealth to the family; they owned property, retained their own family names and were probably educated. Rather than being thought of as property or a liability, an elite Etruscan woman shared in the responsibility of creating a family with her husband which he could not do on his own. I am convinced the Etruscans understood that without a solid marital bond, their society could not function. Husbands and wives were thought of as relative equals who worked in tandem for the greater good. And in order to solidify the relationship bond, love, desire, and affection were probably fostered and reflected in Etruscan visual culture. The Etruscans wanted and needed love that would last forever, and indeed, it seems as if it has.

References

Athenaeus. 1969. *The Deipnosophists.* Translated by Charles B. Gulick. Cambridge, MA: Harvard University Press.

Bing, Peter, and Rip Cohen. 1991. *Games of Venus: An Anthology of Greek and Roman Erotic Verse from Sappho to Ovid.* New York: Routledge.

Blundell, Sue. 1999. *Women in Ancient Greece.* Cambridge, MA: Harvard University Press.

30 These beliefs were preserved in Censorinus, a third century A.D. Roman author: 14.6; 17.5–6. He states that each Etruscan person as well as each Etruscan city had a predetermined time span. Ultimately Etruria would survive for only ten centuries (Maras 2013, 480–482).

Boardman, John. 1995. *Greek Sculpture: The Late Classical Period*. London: Thames & Hudson.

Boardman, John. 2001. *The History of Greek Vases*. London: Thames & Hudson.

Bonfante, Larissa. 2000. "Classical Nudity in Italy and Greece". In *Ancient Italy and Its Mediterranean Setting: Studies in Honour of Ellen Macnamara*, edited by David Ridgway, Francesca Serra Ridgway, M. Pearce, Edward Herring, Ruth Whitehouse, and J. Wilkins, 271–293. London: Accordia Research Institute.

Bonfante, Larissa. 1996. "Etruscan Sexuality and Funerary Art". In *Sexuality in Ancient Art*, edited by Natalie B. Kampen, 155–169. Cambridge: Cambridge University Press.

Brendel, Otto. 1995. *Etruscan Art*. New Haven: Yale University Press.

Bücheler, Franz, and Alexander Riese, eds. 1895–97. *Carmina Latina Epigraphica* (*CLE*). Leipzig: B.G. Teubner.

Henzen, G., I. B. de Rossi, E. Bormann, C. Huelsen, and M. Bang, eds. *Corpus Inscriptionum Latinarum VI* (*CIL*). 1876–. Berlin: Georg Reimer.

D'Ambra, Eve. 2007. *Roman Women*. Cambridge: Cambridge University Press.

De Puma, Richard D. 2013. "Mirrors in Art and Society." In *The Etruscan World*, edited by Jean MacIntosh Turfa, 1041–1067. London: Routledge.

Dessau, Hermann, ed. 1892–1916. *Inscriptiones Latinae Selectae* (*ILS*). Berlin: Weidmann.

Dillon, Shelia. 2010. *The Female Portrait Statue in the Greek World*. Cambridge: Cambridge University Press.

Dixon, Suzanne. 1992. *The Roman Family*. Baltimore: The Johns Hopkins University Press.

Dixon, Suzanne. 1996. "The Sentimental Ideal of the Roman Family". In *Marriage, Divorce, and Children in Ancient Rome*, edited by Beryl Rawson, 99–113. Oxford: Clarendon Press.

Flacelière, Robert. 1962. *Love in Ancient Greece*. Translated by James Cleugh. New York: Crown Publishers, Inc.

Gerhard, Eduard. 1867. *Etrusckische Spiegel IV*. Berlin: Gedruckt und Verlag bei Georg Reimer.

Gerhard, Eduard, Adolf Klügmann and Gustav Körte. 1897. *Etrusckische Spiegel V*. Berlin: Gedruckt und Verlag bei Georg Reimer.

Goldhill, Simon. 2004. *Love, Sex & Tragedy: How the Ancient World Shapes Our Lives*. Chicago: The University of Chicago Press.

Hansen, Peter A., ed. 1983–. *Carmina Epigraphica Graeca* (*CEG*). Berlin: Walter de Gruyter.

Haynes, Sybille. 2000. *Etruscan Civilization: A Cultural History*. Los Angeles: The J. Paul Getty Museum.

Henderson, Jeffrey, ed. 2000. *Aristophanes, Vol. 3*. Cambridge, MA: Harvard University Press.

Kirchner, Johannes, ed. *Inscriptiones Graecae II.2* (*IG*). 1913–1940. Berlin: Georg Reimer.

Izzet, Vedia. 2005. "The Mirror of Theopompus: Etruscan Identity and Greek Myth". *School Papers of the British School at Rome* 73: 1–22.

Johnson, Marguerite and Terry Ryan. 2005. *Sexuality in Greek and Roman Society and Literature*. London: Routledge.

Kaibel, Georg, ed. 1878. *Epigrammata Graeca.* (*EG*). Berlin: Georg Reimer.

Kleiner, Fred S. 2007. *A History of Roman Art*. Belmont, CA: Thomson Wadsworth.

Lefkowitz, Mary R. and Maureen B. Fant. 1992. *Women's Life in Greece & Rome: A Source Book in Translation*. Baltimore: The Johns Hopkins University Press.

Maras, Daniele F. 2013. "Numbers and Reckoning: A Whole Civilization Founded Upon Divisions". In *The Etruscan World*, edited by Jean MacIntosh Turfa, 478–491. London: Routledge.

Nielsen, Marjatta. 2009. "One More Etruscan Couple at the Museum of Fine Arts, Boston". In *New Perspectives on Etruria and Early Rome*, edited by Sinclair Bell and Helen Nagy, 171–181. Madison, WI: University of Wisconsin Press.

Rallo, Antonia. 1974. *Lasa: iconografia e esegesi*. Florence: Sansoni.

Rawson, Beryl, ed. 1996. *Marriage, Divorce, and Children in Ancient Rome*. Oxford: Clarendon Press.

Robertson, Martin. 1989. *A Shorter History of Greek Art*. Cambridge: Cambridge University Press.

Rowland, Ingrid. 2008. "Marriage and Mortality in the Tetnies Sarcophagi". *Etruscan Studies* 11: 151–164.

Sassatelli, Giuseppe. 1981. *Corpus Speculorum Etruscorum: Italia 1: Bologna 1*. Rome: L'ERMA di Bretschneider.

Shelton, Jo-Ann. 1988. *As the Romans Did: A Source Book in Roman Social History*. New York: Oxford University Press.

Skinner, Marilyn B. 2014. *Sexuality in Greek and Roman Culture*. Hoboken, NJ: John Wiley & Sons, Inc.

Steingräber, Stephan. 2006. *Abundance of Life: Etruscan Wall Painting*. Translated by Russell Stockman. Los Angeles: The J. Paul Getty Museum.

Stewart, Peter. 2003. *Statues in Roman Society: Representation and Response*. Oxford: Oxford University Press.

Treggiari, Susan. 1996. "Divorce Roman Style: How Easy and How Frequent Was It?" In *Marriage, Divorce, and Children in Ancient Rome*, edited by Beryl Rawson, 31–46. Oxford: Clarendon Press.

Van der Meer, Bouke L. 1995. *Interpretatio Etrusca: Greek Myths on Etruscan Mirrors*. Amsterdam: J.C. Gieben.

Wrede, Hennig. 1990. "Der Sarkophagdeckel eines Mädchens in Malibu und die frühen Klinensarkophage Roms, Athens und Kleinasiens". In *Roman Funerary Monuments in the J. Paul Getty Museum, Vol. 1*, edited by Marion True and Guntrum Koch, 15–46. Malibu: The J. Paul Getty Museum.

Wyke, Maria. 2002. *The Roman Mistress: Ancient and Modern Representations*. Oxford: Oxford University Press.

CHAPTER 3

Love, Alterity and Gender Relations: Re-Thinking the Myth of Eros and Psyche

Wernmei Yong Ade

Luce Irigaray's work on love constantly circles back to the belief in love, described as a "clearing for the advent of a dialogue or conversation between the two parts of humanity in the respect of their otherness to one another" (2002, XII). This ethical encounter between two as two, staged as a dialogue in difference, lies in opposition to the widely accepted idea of love as a union or fusion of opposites; philosophically, this popular conception of love as fusion is informed by a Hegelian dialectical overcoming of two, to arrive at absolute synthesis. For Irigaray, absolute synthesis amounts to a narcissistic, solipsistic love, being the love of one, or of the Same, almost always that of the male figure in heterosexual love. Her philosophy of love is grounded in a belief in love as an encounter with alterity, the truly other; a situation in which two maintain their positions of difference, where neither subjects the other, and where both remain subjects in love. Partly indebted to the thought of Emmanuel Levinas, the encounter with alterity also grounds Irigaray's conceptualisation of a philosophy in the feminine, one that attempts to re-vision love. In this philosophy of the feminine, "the values of intersubjectivity, of dialogue in difference, of attention to present life, in its concrete and sensible aspects, will be recognised and raised to the level of a wisdom" (2002, VII). This chapter evaluates a crucial aspect of the amorous relation central to Irigaray's re-vision of love: touch, that is, love in its concrete and sensible aspects. My examination of touch as opening up the possibility of an ethical loving relation will be limited to Irigaray's engagement with the work of Levinas, particularly the latter's conception of the feminine and the caress as outlined in "Phenomenology of Eros" in *Totality and Infinity*. Ultimately, I am interested what is being contested in Irigaray's re-vision of love *qua* Levinas: the body of the woman in love.

The revaluation of the sensible and concrete aspects of love towards an appreciation of alterity has significant implications for the way women and men love. As observed by Eileen Clements in her conference paper entitled "The (Im)possibility of Love: Women and the Problem of the Feminine", the hierarchical order that exists between dualistic terms such as mind/body, reason/passion, transcendence/immanence, masculine/feminine, terms which

© KONINKLIJKE BRILL NV, LEIDEN, 2019 | DOI:10.1163/9789004380233_005

ground Plato's theory of ideal love and therefore wisdom in love, has resulted in a "devaluation of the feminine in western thought, [and] combined with the oppression of women in the material world, has produced a society lacking in love, with women who cannot love – particularly themselves – as embodied representations of the feminine" (2014, n.p.). Clements thus concludes that only a revaluation of the embodied feminine can lead to ethical relations between men and women, and identifies this as the impetus that drives Irigaray's re-vision of love. Indeed, a critique of love can hardly ignore the patriarchal conventions of love that have come to delimit the way men and women love. As observed by Adrienne Rich:

> The choice still seemed to be between "love" – womanly, maternal love, altruistic love – a love defined and ruled by the weight of an entire culture; and egotism – a force directed by men into creation, achievement, ambition, often at the expense of others, but justifiably so. For weren't they men, and wasn't that their destiny as womanly, selfless love was ours? We know now that the alternatives are false ones – that the word "love" is itself in need of re-vision. (1979, 46–47)

Rich thus urges the need for a new narrative of love, one in which the act of re-visioning, comprising the "act of looking back, of seeing with fresh eyes, of entering an old text from a new critical direction," would serve as "an act of survival" for women, who face the "challenge and promise of a whole new psychic geography to be explored" (1979, 35). "Re-vision" is Rich's prescription for the female writer's active relationship with her literary past, one that would serve the project of decolonisation of language and basic habits of thought. Forty years after the publication of Rich's essay, love still remains in desperate need of re-vision, as evidenced in Tuija Saresma's study of the way love continues to be used as a repressive tool to lock women and men within conventional gender roles. In her conference paper, "Love as a Repressive Concept in Masculinist Blogs", Saresma evaluates the ways in which *Angry Harry*, a self-professed masculinist blog, exploits love as a "justification for the restoration of the traditional, patriarchal gender order within which the white heterosexual Western male dominates, subordinating people of any other gender, sexuality or ethnic background" (2014, n.p.). It is precisely the old narratives of love, such as those outlined by Rich, which enable the continued oppression of women, and thus need to be re-visioned. This article represents a small contribution towards that process, for which Erich Neumann's critique of the tale of Eros and Psyche serves as a useful starting point. Indeed, Rich's reference to "a whole new *psychic* geography to be explored" gestures towards a revaluation of the role that

Psyche as female lover and seeker of wisdom, can play towards the possibility of an ethical loving relation.

As a philosophy in the feminine, Irigaray's re-vision of love is invested in both Platonic views of the love of wisdom and the wisdom of love. The problem with love, going as far back as Plato, as Clements demonstrates, is its heavy reliance on binaristic thought. In "Sorcerer Love", reprinted in *An Ethics of Sexual Difference*, Irigaray contrasts the nature of Diotima's dialectic with the Hegelian dialectic, in order to demonstrate the presence of an intermediary term in love in the former's conceptualisation of ideal love. In the Hegelian dialectic, one begins with two opposites, which finally achieve synthesis after a process of passing into one another. Diotima, on the other hand, establishes, from the outset, an intermediary. This intermediary is love, and it is what permits progression, being both the path as well as that which leads the way. In Plato's text, this path is figured by Diotima in terms of an ascent towards ideal love, a figuration that is fraught with problems, exposed by Irigaray later in her essay. During their dialogue, Diotima leads Socrates through the same process of cross-examination as Socrates will later lead Agathon, a process that culminates in the mistaken conclusion drawn by Socrates that love must be ugly and bad. Diotima's response to this is to posit an intermediate stance, outside of dualism: "Do you think that anything which isn't beautiful must necessarily be ugly?" (Plato 1999, 37). Socrates responds to Diotima's question in the affirmative. Correcting Socrates, Diotima draws his attention to the existence of an intermediary state between wisdom and ignorance, the ugly and the beautiful.

Diotima proceeds to tell the story of the origins of Eros, child of Poverty and Resource. At the birthday of Aphrodite, Resource gets drunk and Poverty "formed a plan of relieving her lack of resources by having a child by Resource" (Plato 1999, 39). There is thus always, within us, some of the other that we desire; that while we may lack it, we certainly do possess some knowledge of it, and this is why the lover falls in between "wisdom and ignorance" (Plato 1999, 40). Eros himself lies between mortal and immortal, being both of the in-between and a go-between: as a demi-god, he interprets and carries messages from humans to gods and from gods to humans. This halfway position also prepares the ground for the idea of the philosopher's quest and the philosophic *eros* as the halfway position, which can be viewed not as a permanent state, but as a stage in the progression towards something more advanced and better (Hunter 2004, 84). As the dialogue between Diotima and Socrates demonstrates, Socrates' mistake was to assume that if Eros is not in possession of beauty, then he must be ugly, a form of reasoning which begins with two opposites: beauty and ugliness. Diotima corrects Socrates, and says that a person who lacks beauty already has some knowledge of beauty, since it is only then that he can know what he lacks. Unlike Socrates, Diotima posits an intermediary state between beauty and ugliness, wisdom and ignorance. This state of being in-between is, firstly, what motivates the lover-philosopher to love, and to seek wisdom. This in-between state also constitutes the path the lover-philosopher will take, one s/he never abandons, and is key to Irigaray's re-vision of love, where "each one attends to remaining oneself," and takes the form of a "return to oneself, in oneself, becoming oneself which does not stay in suspension in immutable truths or essence but which provides a faithfulness to oneself in becoming" (2002, XIV).

Self-realisation as it is understood here is not self-congratulatory, narcissistic or solipsistic, which amounts to an "objectal factuality of an '*étant*' – being" (Irigaray 2002, XIII). Appropriating Heidegger in *The Way of Love*, Irigaray contrasts *étant* with *être* – to be – to refer to the conscious act of assuming the fact of one's existence in the present, specifically the fact of always existing, in every instance, in relation with an other. Moving along this path in relation with an other, one thus resists falling back into immutable truths or fixed essences, that is, into *étant*. This is exemplified in the path of love, where the self is always in relation with an other; and where the self returns to itself even as it moves towards the other, thus ensuring the preservation of difference, alterity and an ethical loving relation. What constitutes existing is the path towards self-realisation, a journey taken, in the instance of *Eros and Psyche*, by the female lover, to be distinguished from the beloved woman, who, in loving, "tends toward her own fulfilment, already unfolds herself to gather in more" (Irigaray 2001, 126). Psyche is perhaps, other than Diotima, the first female lover-philosopher in the feminine. Diotima also alerts Socrates to the notion of possession in love: one's happiness lies in the possession of something good, forever: "Love is the desire to have the good forever" (Plato 1999, 43), and so "the object of love is not beauty ... [but] reproduction and birth in beauty," because "reproduction is the closest mortals can come to being permanently alive and immortal. If what we agreed earlier is right, that the object of love is to have the good *always*, it follows that we must desire immortality (permanence) along with the good" (Plato 1999, 44). There is thus a change in emphasis from possessing the beautiful to gazing on the beautiful, which is the difference between the desire to possess and true love. True love constitutes a vision of unfailing beauty – no longer a mere desire to possess, but "the creative relationship of 'begetting'" (Osborne 1994, 102).

It is also at this point that Irigaray sees Diotima's argument begin to unravel. Irigaray identifies a central contradiction in Diotima's argument, where Diotima oscillates between positing love as intermediary, and love as a result of a cause, specifically the desire to have the beautiful and the good forever.

Diotima had first of all claimed that love is an intermediary, and that love is the process of generation and regeneration itself. Diotima comes to the conclusion that love is the condition necessary for procreation, as well as being procreation itself. It is both the condition and the way. Having said this, Diotima goes on, however, to seek a cause for love in the animal world (properly understood as the physical, mortal world), which is procreation. Diotima ends by saying that love is the love for the beautiful forever, which drives us to reproduce. It is on this count that she contradicts herself. Where she starts by saying that love has no object, that love is a process and a becoming, she undermines herself by attributing a cause to love, which is the desire to have the beautiful forever. In mortal love, the child comes to represent having the beautiful forever, and as the product of love, the child becomes a symbol of immortality. Love has therefore now lost its intermediary status that Diotima posited to start with. Love is now motivated by something else, which is to have the child in which we immortalise ourselves, love forever, and in which we have the good and the beautiful forever. This leads Irigaray to a further objection to Diotima's argument. Because the desire for immortality takes place on two levels (the body and the soul), these are placed in a hierarchical relationship. Immortality of the soul, or the mind (artistic reproduction), is privileged over that of the body (physical reproduction). Furthermore, this hierarchy is gendered: love between men (which will lead to superior spiritual reproduction by default) is privileged over love between men and women (which will lead to inferior physical reproduction). As Clements observes, "Plato conceives of love as being attained by the intellectual purification of Eros – intimate, passionate, sexual love – from carnal into ideal form. Plato argues that Eros is initially felt for a person, but with contemplation it can become […] an appreciation for beauty itself in an ideal sense" (2014, n.p.). In the ascent from bodily to ideal love, women's reproductive abilities, and women's bodies, are placed low on the ladder towards love. According to Plato then, women, being fecund only in body and not in mind, are less deserving of love than men are. Clements concludes that it is this very hierarchisation of gender relations that leads women to devalue their bodies, hindering any possibility of self-love, and by extension loving relations between self and other (2014, n.p.). This is why Irigaray insists that a re-vision of love, one in which women can love as equals, must concern the concrete and sensible aspects of love. To neglect to re-vision love perpetuates the debasement of the body, and of the feminine. As noted by Kate Ince, for Irigaray, it is the "reduction of fecundity to productivity [that] marks the failure of love, including for the child, whose role is reduced to that of mediator in its parents' relation" (1996, 122–140, especially 129). It is also for this reason that Irigaray rejects Levinas's abstraction of the Eternal Feminine, and in his conceptualisation of the not-yet in the figure of the child.

Irigaray's chapter "The Fecundity of the Caress: A Reading of Levinas, *Totality and Infinity*, 'Phenomenology of Eros'" (2001) is one of two responses crafted by Irigaray to Levinas's conceptualisation of sexuality and femininity in *Totality and Infinity*, the other being "Questions to Emmanuel Levinas" (1991). While most agree that Irigaray regards Levinas's approach to the Other in his conception of alterity as central to developing her own formulation of the loving relation, Irigaray nonetheless finds fault with the apparent neutrality of Levinas's ethics, which recognises only the male subject. Irigaray is certainly not the first to take issue with an ethical theory that is apparently gender-neutral, where the masculine perspective masquerades as the neutral. As explained by Ince, "one central issue which gets left out when ethics ignores gender is of course, embodiment: an ethics which is universalizable [...] has to function independently of any particular corporeality" (1996, 3). This chimes with the urgency expressed by Clement over the need to revalue feminine embodiment, which brings us to the issue Irigaray takes with Levinas's conception of the feminine. The rejoinder to Levinas that opens "Questions to Emmanuel Levinas" gives us a fairly good idea of the feminine in Levinas as Irigaray understands it, and which she challenges:

> Is there otherness outside of sexual difference? The feminine, as it is characterized by Levinas, is not other than himself. Defined by "modesty," "a mode of being which consists in shunning the light" (see *Time and the Other*), the feminine appears as the underside or reverse side of man's aspirations toward the light, as its negative. The feminine is apprehended not in relation to itself, but from the point of man, and through a purely erotic strategy, a strategy moreover which is dictated by masculine pleasure (*jouissance*), even if man does not recognize to what limited degree his own erotic intentions and gestures are ethical. (1991, 109)

Irigaray accuses Levinas of reducing the feminine to abstraction. Ince sums it up succinctly by saying that "Levinas's erotics are not bodily enough for Irigaray" (1996, 131). Carl Cedeberg argues, however, that even though Levinas associates the male perspective with the loving subject's perspective, Irigaray is mistaken to claim that Levinas universalises the male perspective. Defending Levinas, Cedeberg points out that for Levinas, neutrality "distorts the representation of human existence in general, which [Levinas] understands always from intrinsically non-neutral interhuman relations" (2012, 211). Ince likewise argues that Irigaray's accusation that the feminine other in Levinas is merely a function of a love premised on the idea of the Same, is misplaced. Ince posits that the feminine and the feminine face are in fact forms of alterity in the work of Levinas, and proceeds to demonstrate how the concepts of the feminine as articulated by Levinas have more to contribute to Irigaray's ethics than she seems to think, thus exposing the very same prejudices in Irigaray's work as the latter finds fault with in Levinas's work.

While Ince and Cedeberg offer us very convincing arguments about Irigaray's misunderstanding of Levinas' erotics and therefore ethics, I would like, however, to point out that there is something relevant in Irigaray's accusations that there is not enough of the concrete body in Levinas's erotics and ethics, particularly where the female is concerned. This is apparent in the fact that Levinas never names Psyche in his chapter "Phenomenology of Eros". The lover, being the God of Love, is named (Eros), while Psyche is not. She is referred to as the Beloved, in abstract feminine terms:

> The Beloved, at once graspable but intact in her nudity, beyond object and face and thus beyond the existent, abides in virginity. The feminine essentially violable and inviolable, the "Eternal Feminine," is the virgin or an incessant recommencement of virginity, the untouchable in the very contact of voluptuosity, future in the present. Not as a freedom struggling with its conqueror, refusing its reification and its objectification, but a fragility at the limit of non-being wherein is lodged not only what is extinguished and is *no longer*, but what is not yet. (Levinas 1991, 258)

This supports Irigaray's objections: that where the male lover is given concrete existence, given over to the full gamut of human experiences of being "hungry, happy, sexually aroused, in pain, etc," (Cedeberg 2012, 211), the female in love is given over to abstraction, functioning as the underside of man. As the Eternal Feminine, Levinas's conception of the feminine falls back into *étant*, into immutable truths and fixed essences. Linked to Levinas's failure to recognise the female lover (as opposed to the Beloved) in the loving relation, is also his notion of the promise of a not-yet, invested in the figure of the child. As outlined above in her reading of Plato's *Symposium*, Irigaray objects to the child as the end product, as that which motivates love, since this reduces love to a mere means to an end. She says in "Fecundity of the Caress", that "when the lovers, male or female, substitute for, occupy, or possess the site of those who conceived them, they founder in the unethical, in profanation. They neither construct nor inhabit their love. Remaining in the no longer or the not yet. [...] Sterile, if it were not for the child." Furthermore, the idea of the child as the embodiment of the not-yet fixes women once more in their reproductive capabilities, such that "while he, the lover, is sent back to the transcendental, she, the beloved, is plunged into the depths" (Irigaray 2001, 121). And so, where both the Platonic and the Levinasian accounts of love fail, the loving encounter between Psyche and Eros appears to bear more hope for an ethical relation. Specifically, it is Eric Neumann's analysis of the account that provides the initial sketches of a possible scenography for philosophy in the feminine.

Despite serious feminist objections to Neumann's invocation of gendered archetypes in his work, there are aspects of Neumann's reading of *Eros and Psyche* that can be usefully appropriated for a feminist re-vision of love staged as an encounter between the two, as two. Due to the limitations of this chapter, I merely identify points in the encounter between the lovers staged by Neumann that correspond to the encounter sketched out by Irigaray, to reveal some surprising similarities between the way both writers conceptualise the process of individuation of the female subject in love. Frances Gray observes that Irigaray's work "has been susceptible to complaints by some feminist scholars that mirror complaints made about Jung" (2008, 133). With this in mind, it perhaps comes as little surprise that Irigaray's and Jung's work on love should share some similarities. Feminist scholars such as Naomi Goldenberg have shown hostility towards archetypes, observing that Jungian psychology has become "a form of patriarchal religion" (1976, 444) and that, while Jung appeared to revere the feminine, his reverence "involved only recognition and support for the feminine principle in men and did not value the actual experiences of women themselves" (Lauter and Rupprecht 1985, 7). There are some who argue, however, that a re-vision, rather than a rejection, of the archetype might serve a feminist critique. Estella Lauter and Carol Rupprecht point out that Neumann himself never assumed the archetype to be eternal, but viewed it as "a formless structure of the psyche itself that is known only through its changing manifestations" (1985, 11). Far from a timeless pattern, the archetype "assumes different forms according to the personal and social history of the person who manifests it" (Lauter and Rupprecht 1985, 11). Most valuable of all, Lauter and Rupprecht recognise that culturally determined gendered qualities are equally available for development by either sex (1985, 5). Gray offers a similar argument for rethinking essence in Irigaray, as a product of one's "causal history" (2008, 141), concerned with "the giving of the cause of something's being what it is" (Gray 2008, 140), rather than as properties or universals. While I appreciate the problems that archetypal theory and essentialism hold for feminist criticism, this analysis finds justification in the possibility of reclaiming the archetype and essence for a feminist critique of love. In fact, Irigaray argues that in order for us to have a theory of alterity, we need a theory of difference, but not one that endorses differences that are eternally fixed, which is precisely the point on which Irigaray questions Levinas's ethics.

But before moving further, let us first consider the narrative in question, "Eros and Psyche" as told by Apuleius, and read by Neumann in his 1956 publication, *Amor and Psyche: The Psychic Development of the Feminine, A Commentary on the Tale by Apuleius*. Very briefly, the tale goes that Psyche, in spite of her beauty, can find no one to marry her. Aphrodite, angered by the fact that her own beauty and power as a Goddess has been usurped by that of a mere human, sends her son Eros to punish Psyche by making sure she falls in love with, and marries, a vile-looking man. Meanwhile, an oracle pronounces that the fate awaiting Psyche is a marriage to death. As her family prepares to send her to her death, Psyche is, instead, transported to a paradise because Eros has fallen in love with her. Eros, however, imposes a condition on their love: he forbids her knowledge of his identity. They thus spend their days loving in darkness. Psyche grows lonely in her paradise, as her companion visits her only in the night, and expresses a desire to see her two sisters. At the behest of her jealous sisters, who manage to convince her that her lover is fact a murderous beast, Psyche vouches to reveal his identity and to kill him. Holding up a lamp to her sleeping lover, she discovers he is in fact the God of Love himself. Overcome with shock and anxiety, she accidentally pricks herself on his arrow: "So all unwitting, yet of her own doing, Psyche fell in love with Love" (Neumann 1956, 26). In her passion, a drop of oil from her lamp spills onto his shoulder, and he wakes. Because of her betrayal, Eros flees from her, and thus begins Psyche's journey to win her lover back.

Acts of seeing and touching are central to the tale of Eros and Psyche. Neumann's reading of the tale centres on the light-bringing as the point of Psyche's death and rebirth: the death of her dependence, ignorance and passivity, and rebirth into womanly initiative, and most significantly, into agency and subjecthood. For Neumann, the two-fold wounding of Psyche and Eros first gives rise to love, and "creates the possibility of an encounter, which is a prerequisite for love between two individuals" (1956, 86). Neumann's reading thus bears out the conditions necessary in thinking of love as an ethical relation: "Psyche's act leads, then, to all the pain of individuation, in which a personality experiences itself in relation to a partner as something other, that is, as not only connected with the partner" (1956, 85). More significantly, the moment of light-bringing is also the moment of a face-to-face encounter, where the lovers had previously not seen each other, and therefore marks the beginning of an ethical relation. The initial conditions in which Eros and Psyche love bear out the tension between touch and sight outlined in Irigaray's philosophy of the feminine, specifically in relation to Psyche having to love in darkness, literally and figuratively. Irigaray describes touch as naïve ("this naïve or native sense of touch, in which the subject does not yet exist" (2001, 119)) and contrasts it with an eros whose origins lie in a subject that sees. The latter is a subject already "fixed," one that "already knows its objects and controls its relations with the world and others" (Irigaray 2001, 119). In contrast, touch, or sensual pleasure, can:

> ... reopen and reverse this conception and construction of the world. It can return to the evanescence of the subject and the object. [...] *Eros* can arrive at that innocence which has never taken place with the other as other. (Irigaray 2001, 120)

Elsewhere, Jean-Luc Marion has also argued that to see the other, to subject the other to my gaze, is to immediately disqualify subjects from participating in the loving encounter, since "everything that I perceive and comprehend, I experience first and finally in my consciousness, and not outside of it" (2002, 74). To love, "the other must remain invisible so as to offer himself to a possible love, because if, by chance, I saw him, he would be ipso facto already disqualified as other" (Marion 2002, 80). In contrast to the touching of bodies, the act of gazing upon the beloved "reduces her to less than nothing if this gaze is seduced by an image, if her nudity, not perceived as endlessly pulsating, becomes the site of a disguise rather than of astonishment at something that moves, unceasingly and inwardly" (Marion 2002, 125). Sensual pleasure, however, initiates a return to an encounter before *seeing* and thus *knowing* of one's gendered status. More importantly, touch is a caress that "without going through me, gives me back the borders of my body" (Marion 2002, 121).

Psyche's initial situation is one of paradise, certainly, one in which, for her at least, sight is subject to touch. She loves Eros in touch, not sight. But this loving in darkness is no genuine paradise; Eros can in fact see her. His falling in love with her is based on sight, seduced by her beauty, her image. This inequity undermines the innocence of the loving touch, for he dictates the conditions of their love. This is not love between equals, because one sees and the other is denied sight. This paradise disguises what for Neumann is an ideological situation: the powerful male subjects the woman to his desires, yet refuses her knowledge of him, even as he gains full access to her. From them to love as equals, Psyche needs to be given equal access to her lover, for "though she yielded to him in the darkness, she had not loved him [...] It is in the light of knowledge, her knowledge of Eros, that she begins to love" (Neumann 1956, 81). In his analysis of the psychic development of the feminine, as revealed in Psyche's story, Neumann is interested primarily in the transformation Psyche goes through at the moment of revelation. She moves from being passive to a woman who acts: "Psyche emerges from the darkness and enters upon her destiny as a woman in love" (Neumann 1956, 81). Her act of defiance also ushers in the age of human love, by which Neumann means an age where love is determined by human action, rather than being subject to the power of the Gods. After all, Aphrodite's punishment for Psyche was precisely that Eros should make Psyche fall in love with a beast. Psyche, however, by her own action, falls in love with Eros, and from this time forth, does everything she can to win him back. Her new action-driven self is not limited to pursuing her lover; she also enacts a cruel revenge upon her sisters that leads to their deaths. Neumann thus identifies the moment of love as the moment she sees his face, in the light of her knowledge of Eros. More importantly, her act of bringing to light her lover's face marks the beginning of an ethical relation. But the sight of his face, which begins the ethical relation, appears incompatible with philosophy in the feminine, since, as Irigaray and Marion note, in love, neither must be visible to the other. However, Neumann goes on to adduce that the moment Psyche sees, and loves, is also the moment she has to suffer loss and individuation. She must experience Eros' absence, and to continue to love him in his absence:

> … she deprives Eros of his divine power over her. Psyche and Eros now confront one another as equals. But confrontation implies separateness. […] By her courageous readiness to embark on her independent development, to sacrifice him in order to know him, Psyche drives Eros and herself out of the paradise of uroboric consciousness. (Neumann 1956, 83)

Her separation and individuation thus constitutes a gesture of return to oneself, in oneself, becoming oneself. This brings us to the question of the nature of Psyche's separation and individuation. When the two sisters tell Psyche that her husband is a monster, she is conflicted: "In the same body," the tale reads, "she hated the beast and loved the husband" (Neumann 1956, 72). According to Neumann, Psyche's revelation brings with it a new psychic situation, in which opposite terms enter into conflict with one another: beast and husband. This is congruent with the phase of separation, manifest here as a polar relation of opposites. The trials she undergoes to win Eros back become a means of bridging these opposites, towards what Neumann refers to as "the highest manifestation of the archetype of relatedness: a divine Eros joined with a divine Psyche" (1956, 110). As such, "Psyche's course from labour to labour becomes a *way*" (Neumann 1956, 98) and "through her love for him, Psyche develops not only toward him, but toward herself" (Neumann 1956, 110). Paradoxically, while Psyche moves towards Eros, she moves, at the same time, towards herself, and hence remains separate from him. This paradox underlines the process of individuation which, for Neumann, is necessary in love as an encounter between two, or as Irigaray argues, a philosophy in the feminine. What happens to Psyche adheres to the notion of love as a path or a way. She is led precisely by her love for Eros, who is Love himself, and the trials Aphrodite sends her are the path of love, towards Love. In my understanding of Neumann, Psyche is the lover-philosopher in search of wisdom. Her conflict of hating the beast but loving the husband places her in-between the states of love and hate, in the presence of beauty and ugliness. Although the light makes visible the terms of opposition, as suggested by Neumann – in shining her light, she now sees that he is a God, not a beast – this is followed by her immediate loss; armed with the knowledge of the beautiful but lacking in it, she goes in pursuit of the beautiful. This is the path she never abandons, just as Plato's lover-philosopher knows beauty but lacks it, and whose pursuit of it constitutes love.

This moment of seeing and loss is accompanied by a somatic instant; she is pricked by his arrow, and he is burned by the oil of her lamp. Interestingly, while touch is involved, it is nevertheless one that is mediated by objects associated with each of them: his arrow that pricks her, and her oil that burns him. Significantly, the caress, usurped now by her sight, gives way to mediated touch. And it is in their separation that she is spurred to consider the other, a separation ushered in by the initial face-to-face encounter. Warning Psyche about her sisters, Eros says, "Those false she-wolves are weaving some deep plot of sin against you, whose purpose is this: to persuade you to seek to know my face" (Neumann 1956, 18). Undaunted by his refusal, Psyche begs for him to let them see her: "By your locks that hang all round your brow, sweet as scent of cinnamon, by the soft delicate cheeks so like mine, by your bosom that burns with strange heat, I implore you, by my hopes that at least I may behold your face in the face of our babe …" (Neumann 1956, 19). Eros' refusal to allow Psyche to see his face suggests a refusal of an ethical relation, which is a consequence of one's necessary confrontation with the other. It is only when one has to negotiate between one's existence and another that the ethical relation arises. Accepting that she will never, in her lifetime, see the face of her lover, Psyche hopes instead that she may see his face in the face of their child. The child then comes to embody "the evanescence of the caress [that] opens on a future," which is distinct from "an approach to the other's skin here and now" (Irigaray 2001, 122). As end product, the child in whose face the female lover beholds the face of her male lover, thus signifies attention not to present life, or *être*, but to love as future investment and future pleasure. It is perhaps fitting then that the child will not be the way of love for Psyche: she is abandoned by her lover, forced into separation and a process of individuation, culminating in a sleep as deep as death, "no better than a sleeping corpse" (Neumann 1956, 50). At this point, Eros wakes her up, and they come face to face, for the second time, significantly after Psyche's journey is complete.

After Psyche's sisters convince her a second time to expose the murderous beast who is her lover, the tale describes Psyche's state of mind thus: "Impatience, indecision, daring and terror, diffidence and anger, all strove within her, and, worst of all, in the same body she hated the beast and loved the husband" (Neumann 1956, 25). To whom does this body refer? Psyche? Eros? Both? The conflict expressed here comes at a time prior to her seeing his face, and so, prior to separation and individuation. The ambiguity here is unsurprising, since she has yet to realise her self. I previously pointed out that Levinas never names Psyche, but as it turns out, neither does Irigaray. While Irigaray does at least acknowledge the female lover, a step closer to the ethical relation from Levinas's conceptualisation of the Eternal Feminine or the Beloved Woman, her failure to name Psyche is inimical to her attempts to revalue the concrete and sensible aspects of love as a first step towards her philosophy in the feminine. It stands to reason that concrete bodily experience belongs to a particular lived and living body. Arguably, it would seem that even Irigaray's erotics are not bodily – understood as particular and bounded – enough, a point of contention feminist critics of Irigaray's work will be familiar with. For this reason, I see Neumann's evaluation of the loving encounter between Psyche and Eros, one that preserves the identity of Psyche the female lover, as indeed having something of value to contribute to thinking of love as a means of living ethically, especially where gender relations are concerned.

References

Cedeberg, Carl. 2012. "Accusing the Erotic subject in Levinas". In *Phenomenology of Eros*, edited by Jonna Bornemark and Marcia Sá Cavalcante Schuback. USA: Soderton University.

Clements, Eileen. 2014. "The (Im)possibility of Love: Women and the Problem of the Feminine". Unpublished paper presented at the Gender and Love 4th Global Conference, Mansfield College Oxford, 24–26 September.

Goldenberg, Naomi. 1976. "A Feminist Critique of Jung". *Signs* 2 (2) (Winter): 443–449.

Gray, Frances. 2008. *Jung, Irigaray, Individuation*. London and New York: Routledge, 2008.

Hunter, Richard. 2004. *Plato's Symposium*. Oxford: Oxford University Press.

Ince, Kate. 1996. "Questions to Luce Irigaray". *Hypatia* 11 (1): 122–140.

Irigaray, Luce. 2002. *The Way of Love*. Translated by Heidi Bostic and Stephen Pluhácek. Continuum: London and New York.

Irigaray, Luce. 2001. "The Fecundity of the Caress: A Reading of Levinas, *Totality and Infinity*, 'Phenomenology of Eros'". In *Feminist Interpretations of Emmanuel Levinas*, edited by Tina Chanter, 119–144. Pennsylvania: The Pennsylvania State University Press.

Irigaray, Luce. 1985. "Sorcerer Love": An Ethics of Sexual Difference. Translated by Gillian C. Gill. New York: Cornell University Press.

Irigaray, Luce. 1991. "Questions to Emmanuel Levinas: On the Divinity of Love". Translated by Margaret Whitford. In *Re-reading Levinas*, edited by Robert Bernasconi & Simon Critchley. Bloomington & Indianapolis: Indiana University Press, p. 109–118.

Lauter, Estella and Rupprecht, Carol Schreier. 1985. *Feminist Archetypal Theory*. Knoxville: The University of Tennessee Press.

Levinas, Emmanuel. 1991. "Phenomenology of Eros". In *Totality and Infinity*, translated by Alphonso Lingis. Kluwer Academic Publishers: Dordrecht, Boston, London.

Marion, Jean-Luc. 2002. *Prolegomena to Charity*. Translated by Stephen E. Lewis. New York: Fordham University Press.

Neumann, Erich. 1956. *Amor and Psyche: The Psychic Development of the Feminine*. Translated by Ralph Manheim. New York: Princeton University Press.

Osborne, Catherine. 1994. *Eros Unveiled*. Oxford: Clarendon Press.

Plato. 1999. *The Symposium*. Translated by Christopher Gill. London: Penguin Books.

Rich, Adrienne. 1979. "When We Dead Awaken: Writing as Re-vision". In *On Lies, Secrets, and Silence*. New York: W.W. Norton & Company.

Saresma, Tuija. 2014. "Love as a Repressive Concept in Masculinist Blogs". Unpublished paper presented at the Gender and Love 4th Global Conference, Mansfield College Oxford, 24–26 September.

PART 2

Inconsistencies in Heterosexual Cultures Today

CHAPTER 4

Characters from a Different Story: Media, Narratives of Love and Construction of Gender Identities in Children's Worlds

Dikmen Yakalı-Çamoğlu

Introduction[1]

The representations of femininity and masculinity in popular culture present us with two distinct sets of stereotypical character traits. The first set belongs to women's cultural forms, which attribute certain themes and traits to femininity and masculinity; and the second set is for men's cultural forms, which present totally distinct sets of traits for masculinity and femininity. The existence of these distinct stereotypical representations seems to construct an infrastructure of emotion and communication for girls and boys as they grow up. Although patriarchal discourse, in order to prevail, seeks to secure reproduction through heterosexuality, and does so through the narratives of romantic love, popular culture seems to compromise this aim. This chapter seeks to explore how and in what ways popular culture segregates the two sexes from childhood onwards, through positioning them in two different sets of narratives and giving them narrative identities with two sets of expectations.

As a beginning, I identified stories for girls such as *Cinderella*, *Snow White*, *Beauty and the Beast*, *Sleeping Beauty* and Disney's version of *The Little Mermaid*; and, for boys, stories of Marvel characters (such as *Hulk*, *Spider-man*, *Action-man* and *X-Men*) and *Ben 10*. The tales of these characters are also significant intertextual stories to which children are exposed in the form of fairy tales, books, television shows, plays, computer games and feature animations and films. Thus, with every different form they take, the characters and the stories become more familiar for the children.

As a next step, I examine how the representations of femininity and masculinity affect gender construction among Turkish children through semi-structured interviews conducted with 28 children aged 4–8. The aim of my analysis in this chapter is to explore the inconsistency between the gendered

1 Parts of this study have been published in Dikmen Yakalı-Çamoğlu, 'Heroes and Villains in Gendered Narratives for Children' (2012).

 | DOI:10.1163/9789004380233_006

narratives; the way they inculcate incompatible play norms and foster the segregated social life of boys and girls. This study seeks to understand how children relate their own narrative identities to the characters of such stories and how they place and perceive the opposite sex within this context. I also propose this question for further scrutiny: if there is a discrepancy over the constructions of the opposite sex in the narratives of each gender, then how might they live "together" and construct a common narrative? How can they have a common narrative of heterosexual love?

I therefore aim to answer the following questions: How can the inconsistency between the gendered narratives, incompatible play norms and segregated social life of boys and girls be explained? And what are the societal consequences of this inconsistency? The results challenge existing scholarship on gender because the incompatible narrative identity constructions of boys and girls contradict the standard objective of cultural discourse: to secure reproduction – and, as such, they also challenge many explanations of cultural discourses.

This chapter links the two sections of this volume. From the discussions on the metanarratives of love in the first section, we arrive at the inconsistencies in the heterosexual discourse across different cultures. While I discuss how the patriarchal discourse uses narratives of love to establish heteronormativity, Tuija Saresma explores how performing gender is in the very core of the blogs that she surveys, and argues that love is used to justify the restoration of the traditional, patriarchal gender order where white heterosexual Western males dominate, subordinating people of all other genders, sexualities, or ethnic backgrounds. However, Veenu Kakkar shows us how the same heteronormative discourse takes on more aggressive forms and is reflected in the actual experiences of women in India.

Methods and Data

The data consist of:

- Narrative analyses of 20 issues of *Princess* (Disney) magazine (published between 2005 and 2014); these are monthly magazines for girls aged between 4 and 8.
- Narrative analyses of 20 issues of boys' magazines: various issues of the superhero magazines *Action Man*, *Spider-Man*, Marvel *Super Macera* (Adventure), Marvel *Kahramanları* (Heroes) and *Ben 10* (published between 2007 and 2014). These magazines are for boys aged 5–10. Although the boys' magazines outnumber those for girls, the former all centre on the same superhero characters.

- Semi-structured interviews conducted with 15 children aged 4–6 (mean age: 4.9; seven girls and eight boys).
- Semi-structured interviews conducted with 13 children aged 7–8 (mean age: 7.4; six girls and seven boys).

Through a textual analysis of the magazines, I identify several recurring themes and concepts. These categories reflect the number of times that they occurred as main themes in the little stories which appear in the magazines. Semi-structured open-ended interviews were conducted to see if the same themes were used in the construction of the narratives of the sample girls and boys. I made use of a "narrative approach", which leads the interviewees to give individual and subjective information in a "story" form. I used themes which were driven by the texts to encourage the interviewees as far as possible to speak about the same topics.

All the interviewees were the children of middle-class university graduates who worked outside of their homes. They all resided in Istanbul. All the children were asked questions about the forms of popular culture which they consumed. Then they were each asked to create a story and a game whose main character was themselves. The next step was to learn about their relationships with the opposite sex. I asked questions about the games they played together and the activities they shared in and outside of the school. Most of the time, I ended up hearing complaints and gossip. Finally, they were shown the magazines *Princess*, *Marvel Heroes* and *Ben 10* and were asked to comment on them and the characters in them.[2]

Theoretical Assumptions

The theoretical background of this study is derived from poststructuralism and assumes that gender is narratively constructed in culture. Narratives are considered as a way of mediating the construction of meaning. The self is narratively constructed by way of thinking about ourselves autobiographically and by way of telling our life stories to others. Through storytelling, we give life a feeling of order and confer meaning on the events. Through emplotment, we can "integrate the past, present and future and thereby constitute stable, coherent identities on both a personal and communal level" (Hinchman and Hinchman 2001, 2). Narratives give life a feeling of order, for events have no

2 The project which yielded the data on which this chapter is based was approved by the Research Ethics Committee of Doğuş University.

meaning in themselves unless we confer it on them with our stories.[3] In short, the self is narratively constructed and communicated (Gergen 2003, 65–77).

People construct identities by locating themselves or being located within a repertoire of prototypical emplotted stories.[4] We are led to act in certain ways on the basis of the estimations, hopes and memories that we copy from a limited repertoire of available social and cultural narratives, which are institutionally mediated (Somers 1994, 614; Ricoeur 1991, 20–33; Holstein and Gubrium 2000, 3). Narrative identity, then, is "coherent but fluid and changeable; historically grounded but 'fictively' reinterpreted; constructed by an individual but constructed in interaction and dialogue with other people" (Ezzy 1998, 247); and it undeniably influences our future actions.

This study assumes that the social repertoire of prototypical emplotted stories is first learnt in childhood and that the media constitute some of the primary sources which convey them. Änggård argues that children's story-books could be considered as repositories of primary genres, on the thematic content of which the style and compositional structure of everyday communication is built (2005, 544). The forms of popular culture, in particular when they present the same themes intertextually, present children with limited options; and the tales in question, their structure and characters become the prototypes for children to base their own narratives on. The representations of masculinities and femininities in comic books or magazines construct and mediate social narratives, and in so doing provide us with definitions of who we are. The prototypical stories mentioned above are constructed within a discourse which, in return, produces subject positions with specific perceptions, understandings and expectations.

Power is an important category of analysis, because it usually appears to be the foundation of narrative identities which are discursively constructed. As will be seen from the data analysis, when individuals choose emplotments from the repertoire, they do so on the basis of "power". This power should be understood in Foucault's conceptualisation of it as "productive"; it is "the name that one attributes to a complex strategical relationship in a particular society".[5] It is exercised upon the dominant as well as the dominated, meaning that it is multidirectional and can manifest itself on the "micro" level, which starts in the ordinary activities of daily life (cf. Foucault 1979). It is never fixed or stable, but always negotiated.

3 See Paul Ricoeur, "Life in Quest of Narrative" (1991, 20–33) and "Narrative Identity" (1991, 188–200).

4 See Margaret R. Somers (1994, 614); Mark Freeman (2001, 287); Hinchman and Hinchman (2001, XXIII).

5 Foucault (1978, 93). Also see Foucault, *Discipline and Punish: The Birth of the Prison* (1979) and Foucault, "Afterword" (1982, 208–226).

In this conceptualisation, the individual is thought of as an effect rather than an essence. Under one of "the prime effects of power", Foucault argues, "certain bodies, certain gestures, certain discourses, certain desires, come to be identified and constituted as individuals" (1980, 98). In line with Foucauldian analysis, we can argue that power relations produce particular types of identity. Foucault does not think of power as simply a site of oppression, and believes that identities are formed in negotiation and play; on this basis, I will argue that masculine and feminine identities are effects of power within a patriarchal discourse, and that we come to be who we are as men and women as we negotiate power with the opposite sex and with the discourse itself as a whole. This process begins in childhood and childhood play, as we shall see in the results of the research.

Heteronormative society needs to regulate identities as feminine and masculine in order to prevail. Patriarchal societies use a number of regulatory discursive practices – themes – in order to make sure that men and women form relationships and reproduce. The narratives of romantic, eternal love, soul mates and marriage are such themes, on which the reproduction of the patriarchal discourse, heteronormative society and culture is founded. Looked at from a distance, girls' and boys' narratives seem to conform to this aim. First, they narrate two stereotypical identities so distinct that they are almost antithetical to each other. Femininity is narrated in and as opposition to masculinity in order to guarantee that both sexes are clearly distinct but complementary. Thus, traditional romantic love is narrated as the attraction of opposites who complement each other in practical matters. As we see in the narratives of princesses, women are seen as the creators of everything domestic, whereas, as seen in the action men narratives, men are the defenders and preservers of everything outside the house.

Nevertheless, I argue that although the discourse makes use of these narratives in order to prevail, when we consider the way that they are presented to children and the discourse of resistance within them, these same narratives seem to threaten the continuity of the heteronormative discourse. In short, as this feminine/masculine dichotomy gets stronger in narratives, so the discourse ironically endangers itself from within.

As individuals negotiate their identities within possible narratives against a patriarchal, heteronormative cultural backdrop, counter-discourses and counter-identification are constructed as a form of resistance within the very same discourse. Various narratives of queer sexuality, which once constituted discourses of resistance, have now become another dominant discourse, situating non-normative sexualities within a narrative of "performativity" as opposed to "normativity". On the one hand, the younger generation is being raised with narratives that are heteronormative in theme, as considered below. On the other, especially in Western and Northern countries, the possibilities of identification with the available subject positions are proliferating after the gay rights movement and the general acceptance of LGBT as "normal" in the dominant discourse. This means, in practice, that young adults have many more possibilities of identification without even having to accept them as core identities. Gender identity has itself become a "play", a performance which one can change as many times as one wishes throughout a lifetime. Today, with the possibility of myriad subject positions and fluid gender identities, and when selves are understood as narrative identities, the younger generation does not feel entrapped by the heterosexual code. It is because of this, I argue, that the heteronormative discourse is jeopardising itself with all these narratives of princesses and action men, making it impossible for the two sexes to find themselves in the same narrative of love.

Results: Analysis of *Princess*

The recurrent categories which can be derived from the stories in this magazine are: "goodness", "self-sacrifice", "body", "beauty", "dressing/clothing", "love", "marriage", "anniversary", "jewels (riches)", "friendship", "dancing", "parties", "romantic acts", "jealousy" and "magic/fairies".

The little stories in these magazines usually take on the character of a fairy tale after the original tale has finished; in other words, they are about the later lives of princesses. They cover the life stages of Cinderella, Aurora and Snow White immediately after marriage to their princes. Bella of *Beauty and the Beast* lives with the Beast in his castle. They are in love and seem to have a perfect relationship, but curiously the Beast has not turned out to be a Prince yet.

Although they live in palaces or castles, we see that the princes go out every morning after breakfast as if they belonged to the middle classes of an industrial city. The princesses stay at home, engaging in activities such as picking flowers, rearranging the house or shopping. In short, princesses and princes conform to the sex roles typical of patriarchal, capitalist societies.

The main theme of the stories within the magazine is "love", which is exercised in monogamy, heterosexual, eternal and self-sacrificing. The aim and meaning of life for the princes and princesses are to make their partners happy. The most clichéd romantic acts are celebrated under the name of "romanticism", making a clear-cut depiction of a perfect relationship and a happy couple. Thus, "love" is associated with "romantic" activities, such as dancing after a candle-lit dinner or rowing on the river in a prettily-decorated boat under a moonlit sky. Anniversaries are the main issue in the lives of the princesses. They are seen as the ultimate signifier for the greatness of their love. In one of the stories Snow White becomes unhappy when she thinks that her Prince has forgotten their wedding anniversary. She is relieved to find that his seeming forgetfulness is a part of his plan for a super-romantic surprise party in the woods (*Prenses* 2007/6, 29–32).

For little girls, the infrastructure of emotion and communication seem to be built around the character of the "prince". The eternal romantic partner presented to girls by this character is docile and ready to cooperate with the princess at all times. The princes are all handsome, in their shining uniforms (except the Beast). They pose in the most elegant way, keeping a constant smile. However, they do not demonstrate any kind of strong personality. The sole purpose of their existence seems to be to make the princesses happy. They do not conform to the traditional role of prince as a "knight" who has proven himself on the battlefield. They never engage in aggression or violence. Their most heroic acts are actually trivial achievements, such as rescuing a small animal or mending a magical jewellery box. Another important function of the prince is to console the princess when she is unhappy about some petty matter, such as an accident concerning the cake which she was baking for him. His happiness, equally, seems to be about "little things": he may adore a decoration arranged by the princess or a cake which she has baked. He is thus a puppet, living only for the princess, always smiling, performing the activities she wishes and using all his powers only to make her happier.

Although the kind of femininity in girls' magazines conforms to the patriarchal norms and roles, this does not make the princess less powerful, submissive or dominant in her own genres. She seems to be waiting for the prince at home, but she still controls him and the house. Since the girls find more agency and more powerful positions in their own narratives, though apparently subject to men in the boys' genre, it is no wonder that they prefer to narrate their own stories with the above themes from the princess tradition. A parallel phenomenon can be seen in the boys' magazines, where the action men have all the agency and power, while the action woman is there only to help and make the action man feel better about himself.

Analysis of Boys' Magazines

Just as the girls have their princesses, the boys have superheroes of their own. The recurring themes in the stories published in the magazines are "fighting", "personal strength", "special power/weakness", "scientific innovations", "technology", "weapons", "danger", "saving the world", "keeping secrets", "villainy" and "transformation". In contrast to the seeming triviality of everyday life in girls' stories, life appears to be highly portentous in boys' magazines.

The key category in boys' magazines is "action". All these characters engage in action and their main accomplishment is either "saving the world" or fighting the "bad" people who try to ruin the order of society. They fight for the system and its preservation. The actions which they undertake are in striking contrast to the ones performed by the princes in *Princess*. They are never trivial, but cardinal to the safety of society, if not the world.

A significant category is "transformation". The action characters have more than one role and identity. In their "real" lives, these heroes are ordinary people (Spider-man is a shy photographer, Hulk and Iron Man are scientists and Ben 10 is a mere schoolboy). However, they have the ability to transform themselves into extraordinary beings with great powers. Transformation is also about having a secret. The heroes have secrets which they are reluctant to share with others. For example, Spider-man tries to hide his real identity even from those who are closest to him. Thus, in the boys' world, nothing is as it seems and the central characters are under the heavy burden of hiding from others important information about themselves. This is why they are not talkative characters.

Many of the heroes make use of technology, which appears as another recurrent category. Technology and scientific innovations seem to be the reason or originator of most of the heroes and their heroism. In direct opposition to the magic and fairies in the girls' stories, there is no spiritual or metaphysical dimension of reality in the boys' worlds. Weird or strange as some may seem, every character or phenomenon has a scientific, empirical explanation, which is presented in a thoroughly credible way.

In all this action, the only engagement with girls, who are largely absent from boys' magazines, occurs when a hero saves a girl's life, coming to the rescue of a damsel in distress; the damsel in question is aligned with the princess character. What I would like to focus on here, though, is the character of the action women. These are female superheroes; they are limited in number and always less powerful than the heroes. However, these women demonstrate more agency in the magazines over the damsel in distress.

These heroines, notwithstanding their special powers, appear in minor roles in the boys' stories. Super heroines are not as elegant as princesses, but, with their tight costumes, are sexy in a pornographic sense. They are good at fighting and are not the sort to be anxious about the beauty of a ball dress or an anniversary. They are more practical women, who seem to have "real" problems and a super career. They do not engage in or seek romantic activities.

Through action women, the boys are presented with a type of woman whose understanding of love and romanticism is totally different from that of the princesses. The question now is: To what extent are children affected in their development by these narratives as they construct their own gender narratives and relationships with the opposite sex?

The Interviews: Romantic Stories of the Girls

The interviewees were asked to create/play a game through which they could express themselves and a story in which the central character was themselves. Most of them named a Princess or a Princess Barbie. The main themes of the girls' games and narratives conform to the general themes in the magazine content and to the understanding of femininity in a patriarchal society.

The game most often played by the girls was named "The Princess". Basically, this game involves acting out the fairy tale. Sometimes, the fairy tale may be edited to fit more than one princess. "The Princess" is a game that can be played like "playing house" but in a regal context, combined with the romantic activities of the Princesses.

For example Demet (8) is Bella and "he [a friend of hers] becomes the Beast and tries to get hold of and kidnap Bella by force. I try to resist him but because he is a strong beast, I am imprisoned in the Castle. Then we spend some 'good' times together. We eat, we read to each other and play games". Although the Beast gets hold of her by force, in the end, he gives in to her feminine charms and he is domesticated through love. The power shifts from the Beast to Bella as a result of "love" and he surrenders all his power and riches to his beloved. She tames the beast through love but, at the same time, accommodates violence and cruelty in the name of love.

Derin (8), in her narrative, focuses on jealousy between the females and "winning" the love of the popular male. In her favourite game, she wants to be Barbie: "There are some popular girls who envy Barbie. She goes somewhere and buys a bracelet with a magic booklet. Whatever she writes in her diary turns out to be real .... That is how she gets to dance with the guy she loves at a dance party". This is also a version of the Barbie feature film, *Barbie Diaries* (2006).

Tuğçe (4) told me the story of a skating princess focusing on dancing, parties and romantic actions. The story took place in a mediaeval setting, where she herself was a skating princess.

Lara (7) also wanted to be the Princess Barbie: "The queen would say 'My child, can I have my pills, please?', and I would run and fetch my mother's pills.

The queen would make me ride a horse and I would wander around the gardens of the palace on my horse and take my sister with me, too". Lara's power as a protagonist is derived from goodness and fulfilling the expectations of her family as a female. Here the focus is on familial love.

Ece (7) also wanted to tell her own story as a princess. She touched nearly all the categories in a single narrative: "There would be a fairy and her twin. There would also be a witch who is bad. I am very beautiful and rich as a princess and I have many friends and a thousand cousins ... and a handsome prince".

In short, the girls focused on the themes of "goodness", "self-sacrifice" and "romantic actions", conforming to the main themes found in the magazines. Love was always a main theme, even if not romantic love.

Action Stories of Boys

The games favoured by the boys are those in which they can engage in some action and "win", e.g., police, soldiers, team games with a ball, Ninja Turtles, Spider-man and Transformers. Like girls, they also acted out the familiar stories, fitting and bending them according to their toys and as they pleased.

In the younger group, three of the boys' favourite characters were Ninja Turtles. Another three loved Spider-Man most and the remaining two liked Pinocchio and Casper. Most of the boys in the older group (5 out of 7) favoured Ben 10. Just over half (4 out of 7) also picked Ben 10 as the central character of their own life stories.

When I asked them to narrate a story with themselves in it, they used characters such as Spider-man or Ninja Turtle and joined in the action. In these self-narratives they fought to save the world, or Turkey. However, when asked why the world or their country was in danger, they could not answer properly. For example, Kerim (8) said, "I don't know", with a gesture implying that my question was completely irrelevant to the story. Later on, he said that the villains came from outer space and that they were really bad. He wanted to transform himself into Four Arms (a hero from *Ben 10*) and defeat them, saving the world. Deniz (8) told a story about a big rocket which was turned towards Turkey and said that he would send it back with a shield so that it would hit the aliens instead. In this story, he was very brave, with the ability to jump very high; he was as tall as his father, with curly hair. He used a laser, string and a rocket launcher to fight the enemy. "Power" in the boys' narratives was not located in "little things" as it was in the girls' stories. Power was always the main theme and was more oppressive.

The "Other"

Neither sex liked the forms of popular culture intended for the other group. The girls said that they did not read the magazines for boys because "they are for boys". Most of the little girls said that they did not want to read the boys' magazines because their characters were "ugly". For example, Pelin (4, f) said: "I would not be any of the heroines in the Marvel magazines. I do not like Spider-Man, either, because he has got only one costume and wears the same outfit every day". It should be noted that the Prince also has only one costume but he is found to be handsome, whereas Action Man is not.

For example, Öykü (8, f) said that she would always prefer the princes in the girls' magazines to the action men because "they are elegant; they are not scary and they do not transform into anything. The boys' characters, on the other hand, are wild, scary and strange". *Ben 10*, as a magazine, looks "all right" but still she does not like the characters who fight. The girls did not like boys' magazines because they contain "war" or "fighting characters".

Selçuk (5, m) said that "boys like things about war". He did not buy the *Princess* magazine because it is for girls. After a pause he added, "Actually, I like it ... But I like Action Man more because it is about war". In the younger group, I observed that their likes and dislikes were more "memorised" than "internalised". However, in the process of internalising, as the boys struggled to establish their place in a gendered world, they could express quite strongly how they feel. Barış (4.5, m) said he wanted to "vomit" when he was read *Cinderella*, because it had a bad ending. When asked what the bad ending was, he said "Cinderella wins and they get married". It was interesting to find that he believed that the Prince was a loser for committing himself to a girl. Tuncay (5, m) was the only boy who declared that he did not like things with "war" in them. But still, his favourite character was Ninja Turtle, a character who fights.

After they were asked questions about the girls in the girls' magazines, the boys were asked to comment on the girls who appeared in the boys' magazines. They were shown pictures of heroines with superpowers. Most of the boys liked the girls "with real superpowers who can fight like men" and preferred them to the princesses. For example, Deniz (8, m) liked "the girl with the power of invisibility; or the one who can control the weather". He said that he would prefer these action girls to the princesses, since they "are more beautiful than the princesses and they are fighters with special powers".

The boys, asked to comment on the princes in the girls' magazines, said that they did not like them and they all said that they would never want to take such roles in a game. For example, Emir (7, m) said that he "would never be the prince as he liked to be wild". Kerim (8, m), who refused at first even to look at the *Princess* magazine, said that he "actually liked the prince in *Snow White* as he is handsome". But he added that he "still would neither like to be him, nor watch these animations"; Murat (7.5, m) said that *Cinderella* was "disgusting" because "it is a girl thing" and her prince was "unbearable". He would not like to be a prince because "they never fight". Tolga (7, m) would not like to be a prince because "he loves Snow White and gives her flowers". Hasan (8, m) was the only interviewee who was prepared to be a prince. However, this was a prince who "would fight the bad people as he was a knight and then he would save Snow White". I asked him if they would get married in the end. He answered with confidence that they would. However, later on he added that it would be better if the princesses could fight.

Another peculiar point was that the boys did not think that the princesses were beautiful. On the contrary, they found them "ugly". For example, Emir (7, m) said that "Bella is disgusting; I want to put her eye out". Later on I gathered that he objected to the feminine manners and girlish worries he associated with the princesses. I found out that the very manners that the girls think "cute" are in fact despised by the boys.

It was quite obvious that the boys did not aspire to the "prince" character of the girls' narratives, since he was not a powerful character; and equally the girls were not the "action" girls of the boys' narratives. In other words, they were the characters of different stories. If there is such a discrepancy over the constructions of the opposite sex in the narratives of each gender, then how might they live together and construct a common narrative of love? This is why I believed that the next step was to investigate whether they could be reconciled and play together in a common narrative.

Is Reconciliation in Play Possible?

The interview data suggests that reconciliation in play, or in a common narrative, seems unlikely. One of the main problems of the girls (in life) is that they cannot play with boys, since the boys who were playing with girls would not agree to take the part of "the Prince" or "the Knight". Sometimes, even if they agreed to take such a part, the girls did not like the results. These princes never did what the Princesses asked, such as getting married, picking flowers for them or dancing at a ball. Our little princes preferred to join in journeys full of action. They fought with swords as "real" knights should do or "spoiled" the game by becoming space princes or cowboys. For example, Selçuk (5, m) said that he would agree to play "princess" with the girls. However, when asked about the part he would take, he answered: "I would be the prince and fight the dinosaurs". This is exactly why two of the girls were on the point of tears as they told me how bad boys were and how they never did what they asked them to do, but "spoiled" everything.

The boys in the younger group said that they did not want to play with girls. The reasons are that the girls wanted to play Barbie all the time or they wanted to play Princess. Barış (4.5, m) said: "I never play with the girls. They want to play with Barbie or be a princess. I could play Robin Hood with them. One of the girls will be the 'beautiful girl' and I would defend her". However, the girls hate to be in such powerless situations. Tuncay (5, m) said that he would play with the girls if they agreed to play boys' games, but not the game of Princess. Doğu asserted that he "would never play Princess because it is a girls' game".

Deniz (8, m) said: "Sometimes the girls ask us to play with them. We say 'no'. There is only one girl that I play with. We have been friends since we were babies. We play hide and seek or tag. She is not like the other girls". Murat, Kerim and Atlas agreed that they can play with the girls when they play hide and seek, tag in the garden or ride their bikes together. However, these were not the favourite games of the girls and it was understood that this hardly ever happened and only when they could not find a playmate of their own sex.

Some of the boys felt that the girls wanted to control the game. Tolga (7, m) said that he "would never play princess with the girls as he would refuse to do such things as giving flowers to girls". However, Emir (7, m) summarised the place of power in the relationship with girls. He said that when they "played with the girls, they tell the girls what to do or what to be. So the girls do not actually join the games but act like maids or helpers. That is why the girls do not like to play with the boys. I never play house or doctor or Princess with them". Obviously, both sexes wanted to control the other, set the games according to the themes of their own segregated genres and were disappointed when they could not do so. This is why they led segregated lives and played and socialised only with their own sex.

Conclusion

The analysis of the data shows that there are two distinct sets of popular social narratives, one for girls and the other for boys. The results also demonstrate that the narratives embedding the existence of "princesses", "princes", "action girls" and "action men" act as infrastructures of emotion and communication in the relationships of children. This affects their relationship, making it impossible for them all to be characters in the same narrative. The children, young as they are, express resentment, disappointment and disillusionment when they talk about their relationships with the opposite sex.

The image of "the prince" in the fairy tales appears to be both the reflection and the constructor of a set of expectations for the little girls. In the most popular narratives for girls, time and time again, we see that the prince (rich, handsome, smart, popular, brave, powerful in every way; and elegant, polite, sensitive, understanding, romantic, generous and protective) surrenders to love; saves the girl; makes her a princess and designates her happiness as the top priority in his life. This blissful, perfect relationship also carries the woman to a higher social status. Love, in a patriarchal society, seems to be the only area where a woman can have a more powerful position than her beloved. Even if the girl seems to save the man (as in *Beauty and the Beast*), her prize is once more to become a princess, with a devoted prince at her feet. Thus, this narrative of a prince who surrenders all his powers at the feet of the beloved woman becomes the foundation for a social narrative of "love" for women. This is the prototype on which all the other stories of love are constructed, either as a basis or an object to react against. Many romantic comedies for adults are constructed on the premise of this prototype: finding a modern prince; discussing whether the prince exists in the real world; finding that "an 'ordinary' guy can be your 'prince' ". However, he still has to display the two characteristics of every prince: first, he should surrender to his partner as a result of his love; and second, making his partner happy (through romantic actions above all) should become his priority. Thus, in their own genres the girls never feel themselves "powerless", oppressed or dominated by men. And, because the men in their genres are easily controlled, they want a "prince" to love/control. This is why they are inclined to like these genres and characters more than the action girls.

As seen above, when girls base their expectations on such images, it becomes almost impossible to have narratives in common with the opposite sex. Girls try to communicate with boys using the signs that are available to them in their own segregated social narratives. The boys, however, attach totally different connotations to the very signs that they receive from the girls, based on their own repertoire. Becoming a "prince" connotes losing one's identity and masculinity; it means becoming a "girl", which is an unacceptable narrative in a patriarchal society. The girls, in contrast, are disappointed as they realise that the boys are not as elegant, polite, sensitive and understanding as the characters portrayed in the narratives and culture presented to girls. This expectation is their emotional infrastructure. They become "unhappy", "disappointed" and "disillusioned", narrating "sad" stories about the opposite sex. As the girls turn into women, this belief in the existence of such characters is reflected and reinforced in popular adult forms with the theme "a search for 'the one' ".

Boys have totally distinct prototypical stories, where they are burdened with heavy responsibilities and take action to save the world. As they do not take on the role of the prince, nor any of the traits assigned to this image, they also become "unhappy" with the girls and their expectations. The girls are either absent from the boys' popular cultural forms or they are physically strong, practical and wholly understanding about the boys' need to be in the thick of action. As the boys realise that the practical "action" girls who are understanding and powerful are not among the girls in their circle, they prefer to retreat to a world from which girls are totally absent.

Although all these representations belong with the hyperreal, these narratives become the social repertoire through which people construct their narrative identity and communicate with the opposite sex. It seems that men and women are not from different planets but, to put it simply, they are not characters from the same story. In other words, if and when the characters from the two stories are totally distinct – when the women of the girls' narratives are totally different from the women of the boys' and when the men of the girls' narratives are totally distinct from the men of the boys' narratives, how on earth can these two sets of characters construct a love story whose main theme is not disappointment?

Now we come back to our first question: Foucault argues that the standard objective of the discourse of patriarchy is to secure reproduction. In other words, society needs its subjects to be heterosexual and engage in sexual relationship in order to prevail. Romantic love seems to be invented to secure this activity. However, as I have argued above, we invent stories that separate the two sexes and segregate them. In a time and culture where gender identities are accepted as fluid and performative, and identities are only temporarily fixed through narratives, presenting a heterosexual love story with the main theme of "disappointment" can only – ironically – jeopardise the aims and objectives of the heteronormative discourse.

The general acceptance of fluid gender identities is what we have worked for, and we still have a long way to go in many societies and cultures. However, we also need to change the gendered narratives that children read and consume. If and when we make girls and boys the characters of the same story, if we can make the next generations forget about the princesses and the action-men, they may have a chance of narrating a common story with the theme of "love".

References

Änggård, Eva. 2005. "Barbie Princesses and Dinosaur Dragons: Narration as a Way of Doing Gender". *Gender and Education* 17 (5) (December): 539–553.

Dreyfus, Hubert L. and Paul Rabinow. 1982. *Michel Foucault: Beyond Structuralism and Hermeneutics*. Brighton: Harvester Press.

Ezzy, Douglas. 1998. "Theorizing Narrative Identity: Symbolic Interactionism and Hermeneutics". *Sociological Quarterly* 39 (2): 239–53.

Foucault, Michel. 1972. *The Archeology of Knowledge*. New York: Harper and Row.

Foucault, Michel. 1973. *The Order of Things: An Archeology of the Human Sciences*. New York: Random House.

Foucault, Michel. 1978. *The History of Sexuality: The Will to Knowledge*. London: Penguin.

Foucault, Michel. 1979. *Discipline and Punish: The Birth of the Prison*. New York: Vintage.

Foucault, Michel. 1980. "Two Lectures". In *Power/Knowledge*, edited by Colin Gordon. Brighton: Harvester.

Foucault, Michel. 1982. "Afterword". In *Michel Foucault: Beyond Structuralism and Hermeneutics*, edited by Hubert L. Dreyfus and Paul Rabinow, 208–226. Brighton: Harvester Press.

Freeman, Mark. 2001. "From Substance to Story: Narrative Identity and the Reconstruction of the Self". In *Narrative and Identity*, edited by Jens Brockmeier and Donal Carbaugh, 283–289. Amsterdam and Philadelphia: Johns Benjamin Publishing Company.

Gergen, Mary. 2003. "Life Stories: Pieces of a Dream". In *Social Construction: A Reader*, edited by Mary Gergen and Kenneth Gergen, 65–77. London: Sage.

Hinchman, Lewis P. and Sandra K. Hinchman. 2001. "Introduction". In *Memory, Identity, Community: The Idea of Narrative in the Human Sciences* by Lewis P. Hinchman and Sandra K. Hinchman, XIII–XXXII. New York: State University of New York.

Holstein, James A. and Jaber F. Gubrium. 2000. *The Self We Live By: Narrative Identity in a Postmodern World*. Oxford: Oxford University Press.

Ricoeur, Paul. 1991. "Life in Quest of Narrative". In *On Paul Ricoeur: Narrative and Interpretation*, edited by David Wood, 20–33. New York: Routledge.

Ricoeur, Paul. 1991. "Narrative Identity". In *On Paul Ricoeur: Narrative and Interpretation* edited by David Wood, 188–200. New York: Routledge.

Somers, Margaret R. 1994. "The Narrative Constitution of Identity". *Theory and Society: Renewal and Critique in Social Theory*. 23 (5): 605–649.

Yakalı-Çamoğlu, D. 2012. "Heroes and Villains in Gendered Narratives of Children". In *Villains and Heroes, or Villains as Heroes?: Essays on the Relationship between Villainy and Evil*, edited by Luke Seaber, 53–77. Oxford: Inter-Disciplinary Press.

CHAPTER 5

Control and Exclusion of Female Bodies in India: Responding to Ground Realities

Veenu Kakkar and Aanchal Kapur

The "Gendered" Birth

Imagine two scenarios in an Indian family.[1]

SCENARIO 1
It's a boy!
The heir to family lineage
It's a boy!
The family status has risen manifold
It's a boy!
He will look after the parents in their old age.

There are celebrations galore – the wife and daughter-in-law has brought good fortune to her marital home: she has kept the honour of the husband's family by birthing a male child. The status accorded to the woman (read: "mother") is because she has borne a son: the prestige of being a boy's mother and not a daughter's mother will remain hers for life. He will bring dowry into the family upon marriage when he grows up. All the elders in the family are pleased and proud to have the much-desired son. They now have a new and higher place in their community and in society.

SCENARIO 2
It's a girl!
There is no one to take the family lineage forward
It's a girl!
The family has been struck by ill-fate
It's a girl!
Family honour (*izzat*) rests on her
She will have to be protected till she is married off.

1 This is a generic example and there are many exceptions to the rule.

 | DOI:10.1163/9789004380233_007

There is no reason for celebration – the wife and daughter-in-law has brought bad fortune to her marital home: the birth of a girl child implies a socio-economic burden. They have a big responsibility to bring up the girl child till a suitable match can be found for her. They will now have to save for her dowry in marriage and this implies a financial burden for life, almost like a recurrent deposit, to ensure that their daughter is protected for all eventualities after marriage. All the elders in the family are silent, sad and (even) angry.

While these scenarios occur after the birth of a child and lay the ground for a lifecycle of discrimination against girl-children and women, in real terms the gender inequalities have been "seeded" before her birth.

Missing Girls

One of the gravest realities that Indian society is dealing with today is gender-biased sex selection. Decreasing sex ratios and increasing numbers of missing girls are reflective of the rising incidence of son preference across the country. This phenomenon is rooted in a male-dominated social and family structure that values sons and the deep-rooted inequality and injustice results in girls being perceived as unwanted.

Female infanticide is a centuries' old practice in India and the first recording of an anomalous sex ratio of India's population, of fewer women than men, came to notice when the synchronous decennial enumeration of people was conducted in the British-occupied parts of India in the late nineteenth century (Visaria 2011, n.p.). Over the last century however, female infanticide and sex-selection have increased to unprecedented proportions.

The deficit of women has increased progressively – the sex ratio[2] has more or less steadily declined from 972 in 1891 to 933 in 2001. The 2011 Census in India shows that the sex ratio has increased by seven points at the national level to reach 940 from 933 in the 2001 Census. However, in the same period there has been a sharp decline in the child sex ratio in the age group of 0–6 years. From 927 in the 2001 census, this child sex ratio has sharply declined to 914 in the 2011 census, indicating a trend towards gender-biased sex selection.

Over the last three decades, the phenomenon of missing girls and women has become a matter of public discourse, research and resistance. Several social, cultural, economic and political factors have been identified as reasons

2 Sex ratio is defined as the number of females per thousand males. It is an important and useful indicator to assess relative excess of deficit of men or women in a given population at that time.

for this problem, including fertility decline. Nobel laureate and leading economist, Amartya Sen, was the first to point out the number of missing women in Asia in the 1990s (Sen 1990, 20). Later in 2001, he raised the issue of "high tech sexism" – the use of newly available ultrasound technology to detect the sex of the foetus. He drew attention to the fact that economic development (or even educational attainment, especially by women) does not invariably reduce women's susceptibility to mortality.

In fact, research evidence now shows that the practice of sex selective abortion[3] is more prevalent among urban educated and high-caste populations (John et al 2008). The 2011 Indian Census indicates that this spread is not only from the urban to the rural landscape of India, but also from less than 10 states (as per the 2001 census) to more than 18 states in the country. Punjab, Haryana, Himachal Pradesh, Gujarat, and Delhi reflect the most alarming figures (Census 2011, n.p.). The extent to which son preference has become cross-cultural and prevalent in communities that previously did not show any tendency to selecting the sex of the foetus makes it a matter of even greater concern today.

It is in this context that we place the work by Breakthrough[4] in the Indian state of Haryana. With a sex ratio of 879 in the 2011 Census as against 861 in the 2001 Census, the state has the worst child sex ratio in the country at 834, though this shows an increase from 819 in the 2001 Census ("Haryana Population Census" 2011, n.p.) and six of its districts appear amongst the ten worst districts for sex ratio. The fact that Haryana is within 100 km of the political capital of India (Delhi) made it a significant entry point to mobilise and advocate for challenging and reversing the trend of daughter-aversion in India. Breakthrough initiated the Gender-Biased Sex Selection (GBSS) programme in Haryana in 2012.

If we go back to Scenario 2 above, we find that the birth of a girl is rarely celebrated; even in her birth the sense of burden is overpowering. Customs and traditions place sons as the sole inheritors of family property (while women's bodies are owned by men as property); they are also accorded the responsibility and expectation of caring for old parents, carrying out funeral rites and perpetuating the family name. While sons constitute a profitable investment, daughters are seen as "*paraya dhan*" (someone else's wealth) who need to be given dowry, only to leave their families once they are married. There is also

3 In working with Breakthrough, we use the term "sex selection" and not "sex selective abortion", for reasons that are elaborated in the chapter.

4 Breakthrough is a global human rights organization working to eliminate violence against women and girls and establish gender equality. See www.us.breakthrough.tv.

the stress of assuring a daughter's safety and protecting her honour in an environment where sexual harassment is rife and women's mobility is severely restricted. People thus resort to any means, including gender-biased sex selection, to avoid having a daughter. The perpetrators of gender-biased sex selection include members of the family, relatives, community, unscrupulous doctors and quacks and the media. The impact of gender-biased sex selection is a violation of women's rights to life, education and work as well as the right to mobility and leisure.

In Haryana, it is believed that when four or five daughters are born to a family, giving them (local) names such as *bhotti, bhatteri, antim, ram bhatterri, maafi* or *kaafi*, all of which signify "enough/no more," will invite divine intervention. People believe that God will get the message and, instead of sending more girls, will send a son. The story is no different in other regions of the country. The reality is that this practice has been replaced by the misuse of technology by families to beget sons instead of daughters. In the process and between the birth of several daughters and sex-selective abortions to produce a male child, the mother's (female) body, her physical and psychological health along with her own sense of worth as a woman is violated in multiple ways.

Patriarchy is the central and defining ideology that sustains individual and social attitudes, behaviour and rituals/practices that discriminate between sons and daughters from conception onwards. It enables a culture wherein those women who bear and rear sons are given incentives in the form of social status in the community and society.[5] Research conducted in India (Breakthrough 2013) identifies a variety of reasons for son preference:

- The high costs of marriage and the practice of dowry for daughters
- Sons are seen as a source of old age support and to carry forward the family lineage
- The inter-generational transfer of resources in favour of sons in the family
- The increasing costs of education and living
- The concern for protecting daughters in the context of the burden of sexuality.

Beyond patriarchy and its associated mindsets, which give men a superior position in society, post-modernist trends are among the causal factors for the phenomenon of daughter-aversion having spread around the country over the past three decades. "Waiting" for the birth of a son after one or two daughters

5 Paradoxically, the government (through conditional cash transfers) has introduced incentives in the form of conditional cash transfers for having girls. There are several schemes and offers to families with daughters, for education, marriage, etc.

was a normal practice in earlier times, however, today, only a son is a "wanted" child. Interestingly, family size tends to be higher for those who have more girls, as some families stop having children when they have a son as their first child. Further, families who plan to have two children most definitely stop after two sons. Behind this decision of each family lies the entrenched social norm that undermines girls (considered a liability) and favours boys (seen as heirs and social security).

Added to the above factors, the increased 'access' (if one may use this word) to sons is the result of new and advanced technologies that can detect the sex of the foetus while in the womb – and the spread of this technology across the length and breadth of the country, across intersectionalities. In a country where the birth of a child was considered sacred and god-given, and abortion seen as 'sin' (especially before it was legalised), we are now witness to mobile vans, clinic kiosks and such facilities (found across some rural but more semi-urban and urban centres, from the remotest to the metro cities) with ultrasound machines for sex detection of the foetus and thereafter, referrals for a sex-selective abortion.

Herstorically speaking, these trends can be located in the small family norm popularised and promoted as part of India's Population (read family planning) Policy in the post-emergency period of the seventies. This policy strongly contributed to the legalisation of abortion in India.[6] Paradoxically, while the right to abortion is pro-women's choice, and there have been several struggles across the world to secure this human right for women, in India and with specific reference to sex-selection, it is often viewed as anti-women. However, the Pre-Conception and Pre-Natal Diagnostic Techniques (Prohibition of Sex Selection) Act (PC & PNDT) of 1994 (Pre-Conception & Pre-Natal Diagnostic Techniques Act 1994) makes it illegal to detect the sex of the foetus, whether or not one opts for abortion after the detection. Along with the service provider, who is seen as an offender under this law, the PC & PNDT Act defines the entire family that goes in for sex determination as offenders. However, as one of the few progressive, women-centric laws in India, the PC & PNDT Act recognises that the pregnant woman undergoing the sex determination test is in fact not a decision maker in the process, and provides for her to be acquitted from the offence unless proven otherwise. And yet, despite the existence of the PC & PNDT Act, there is impunity and the business of sex selection is thriving and growing all over India.

6 Medical Termination of Pregnancy was legalised in India in 1971, but it cannot be used for sex selection, which is detailed within the law.

Gendered Exclusion and Discrimination

> The real challenge with the skewed sex ratio is the strong son preference which results in daughter discrimination and more broadly, discrimination against women from conception to adulthood. (Breakthrough 2013, n.p.)

Through childhood to adolescence and adulthood, from being girls to becoming women, discriminated against in their access to sufficient food and nutrition, opportunities for education and play, and they face restrictions in mobility and decision-making, whether in the family, with respect to paid work, or the external world. They are seen in their gender roles, as unpaid workers and carers for the families' (read male) needs, but are excluded from the ownership of family assets and property.

Parents prefer to invest more in boys than girls and, even though girls are allowed to attain certain levels of education (especially now with free education up to age fourteen), the mindset is that they should be less educated compared to their prospective husbands. In Haryana, where Breakthrough is working, we find that boys are sent to public schools, while girls go to government-run schools. Most girls are asked to leave school when they reach puberty and many of them are married off by sixteen.

We have heard stories of girls being an economic burden for life and therefore, not worthy to be partners in the property share with their brothers: "My sister gets a dowry on her marriage, every festival she is given something either in cash or in-kind – it's almost as a recurring deposit to her for life. In this situation, if she asks for property rights it will mark the end of our brother-sister relationship." Examples of "exchanging a boy for a girl from the same family" are also cited. This takes the form of "*atta satta,*" where a brother will give his sister to any (usually older) man in a family where he finds his bride! There are examples of seventy-year-old men getting married to sixteen-year-old girls in Haryana to bear a son as well as son adoptions from extended family members. All these practices are followed in the name of son preference and to ensure that the property remains in male hands. In discussions with lawyers, evidence shows that most property transfers are done with the complete ignorance of the sister and this is an accepted reality.

As the above narrative shows, through socialisation and its associated norms, the difference between girls and boys is established by the time children grow up. In a similar way to Dikmen Yakalı-Çamoğlu's chapter in this volume, we follow the Foucauldian understanding of power relations producing particular types of (masculine and feminine) identity within a patriarchal discourse. As

Yakalı-Çamoğlu notes, "there are two distinct sets of popular social narratives, one for girls and the other for boys." We see this process unfolding similarly in Indian society. In our interactions with young people in Haryana, we find that young people begin to realise (read accept and follow) their status or position in the family and the kind of roles expected of them from an early age. When asked about family decisions vis-à-vis who will be sent to school if resources are limited, the response is in favour of the son. Just being a male secures certain privileges and age is no factor here. For example, even if a girl is accompanied by a boy who is much younger, she is considered safe when going out of the house: the mere physical presence of a male is equated with a woman's security – and once again this establishes male control over her life and destiny. Through these experiences, young people are able to see the positives and negatives of being a girl or a boy in their adolescent years. Further, the family, community and society reaffirm the discrimination against girls as an acceptable and given social norm.

There is also the reality of early and enforced marriage for many girls across India, though with exceptions in some communities and states. Social customs and practices such as dowry, honour killing and witch hunting are part of the continuum of violence against women and girls.

The sheer physical absence of girls is a stark reminder of the phenomenon of missing girls in the state of Haryana. This is also manifested in the increase of human trafficking from the surrounding states as well as from across the country. These girls are trafficked in the name of "bride-buying": they are treated as sexual slaves and wombs to breed boys for family lineages. They are abused mentally, physically and sexually by multiple men in the family that has purchased them. The continuum of sex selection and the skewed sex ratio does not make visible the implications of not valuing girls and having fewer or no girls; in fact, it contributes to a cycle where women are even more excluded and discriminated against. In the process of reproducing male offspring, these hapless women's bodies are ripped apart by sexual exploitation and (multiple) unsafe abortions. Often bought at a price lower than that of a cow, most of these young women are disowned by their natal families and have no status in their new families. In many cases, there is no legal marriage: they are bought as mere bodies to give birth to sons and many of the women have to go through multiple abortions till they have a male child for the family who has bought them. In several instances, after they have performed their duty to the family that 'bought' them, these women are resold to yet another family and forced to leave even their own male child behind, to be treated in an even more inhumane manner.

Together with the complete lack of attention to their sexual and reproductive health and rights, these female body/selves (bodies, self-esteem and body-image) are completely negated, ignored and exploited to the worst possible levels. The oft-heard adage "from the womb to the tomb" could not be more apt than in this state of affairs.

In our experience, the concept of intersectionality discussed by Tuija Saresma in her chapter later in this section is equally relevant to the interplay of gender, sexuality and class in the state of Haryana. Here there is no question of the notion of love in marriage; the heterosexual relationship is only established to use the female body for producing 'male bodies'. The fact is that the female body is being used as a breeding ground for sons and creating a male-centric world. The use and abuse of women's bodies is rampant in many communities, on the one hand, as wombs and on the other, as sexual bodies to fulfil 'male lust' through the exercise of power to violate women's bodily integrity. In fact, the concept of bodily integrity is completely undermined as the woman fears for her own self and the body she inhabits with every step she takes.

Institutional and Policy Responses

There have been several policy-level and grassroots responses to the problem and practice of sex selection over the past three decades by the government, the judiciary, civil society and the media in India, some of which are mentioned here. The women's movement in India has played a key role in bringing attention to this practice and has led several campaigns to advocate for legal action against sex selection and changing attitudes and behaviour at the public level. Targeted media and communication strategies have been implemented over the years across diverse strata of society, focussing on the issue from different angles, and the state has also initiated various programmes and policies that have aimed at monitoring and legislating against the practice of sex selection (at the state and national level).

The introduction of the Pre-Natal Diagnostic Tests (Regulation and Prohibition of Misuse) Act 1994 (PNDT Act) is one of the most significant state responses to the problem. With an amendment in 2003, this became the Pre-Conception and Pre-Natal Diagnostic Techniques (Prohibition of Sex Selection) Act (PC&PNDT), to include pre-implantation techniques and other elements to closely monitor the practice.

Efforts at advocating for gender-transformative legislation that addressed the ideology of son preference itself, in particular issues around inheritance and social security in old age also brought some positive changes a decade later. The Hindu Succession (Amendment) Act (HSA) of 2005 legislated for daughters to be equal inheritors to ancestral or joint family property. The Maintenance and Welfare of Parents and Senior Citizens Act (MWPSCA), 2007, made it a legal obligation for sons, daughters, and other heirs to provide maintenance to parents and senior citizens from whom they inherit, in proportion to the share of any property inherited (Goel 2016).

Many new central and state-level government schemes have also been introduced to improve the position of women and girls in society through various measures, including countering sex selection. Conditional cash transfer schemes have also been put in place by which parents (of girls) receive incentives to encourage birth registration, immunisation, enrollment in school and delaying age of marriage of their daughters, but have not had the expected success in reducing sex selection.[7]

Along with strengthening the implementation of the PC&PNDT Act in the context of gender-biased sex selection specifically, it is equally important for the Indian government to ensure that other enabling legislation, such as the Dowry Prohibition Act, 1961; the Prohibition of Child Marriage Act 2006; the Protection of Women from Domestic Violence Act 2005; and the Hindu Succession (Amendment) Act 2005, which help address structural gender inequities, are equally and effectively implemented.

Perceptions and Actions at the Grassroots

The context of gender-biased sex selection and gender-based discrimination and the efforts to combat this problem led Breakthrough to initiate focussed interventions to address the practice in Haryana. Our work in Haryana began with a background review on the issue of sex selection and the communication strategies around it at the national level over three decades. The entry into the state began with a social mapping and baseline survey in Haryana, followed by ground-level mobilisation from 2012 onwards. While Breakthrough could provide in-depth research, we recognised that the scale of outreach and impact was only possible through an intensive engagement with the state government.

7 As a critique of the practice of cash transfers, it is important to note that by offering cash incentives to families with girls, the state is, in some ways, agreeing to share in the burden of having daughters and not sons. At the same time, there are some examples of cash transfers, allowing girls to delay their age of marriage by being in school for a longer period due to the allowances available for them.

Our work with frontline health workers, who have regular and direct access to family members, especially women, appointed by the state government, has been significant in creating awareness and discussion on the subject as well as equipping them with simple, effective and practical solutions to deal with the problem of sex selection in Haryana. In our training workshops with these women, a participatory methodology has been applied to enable participants to reflect on the problems at hand. The women have shared that an unsafe environment for women is one of the main reasons that families use to justify sex selection. They have also analysed the implications of a world deprived of girls and drawn linkages between the increasing violence against women (trafficking, sexual exploitation etc.) and the decreasing numbers of girls. In our workshops and interactions with these workers, we have consciously linked women's reproductive health and safety issues to repeated and late-term abortions, and raised questions around women's (independent) decision making, choices and rights over their bodies. The workshops address the diffused and confused messaging vis-à-vis the legality of abortion, together with the illegality of sex-selective abortion. These discussions and understanding (we believe) are crucial to the work of frontline health workers with individuals, families and communities so that they can see the problem in its entirety and build a local environment that says "No to Gender-biased Sex Selection."

Breakthrough regards its work with youth as critical for furthering rights-based change. One of its priorities is the inclusion of men and boys. This led us to conduct several training workshops with young people in colleges across the four districts of Haryana. During the course of these capacity-building processes, we realised that the youth were a different constituency from other stakeholders – they were not interested in any peripheral information; they wanted more in-depth knowledge on issues of safety, security, sexuality, and sexual abuse and we needed to focus on these issues in our engagement with them. They demanded action points for understanding and contextualising their learning and we understood that once they had realised the situation with regard to sex selection, they were capable of being change makers.

Our findings in the field corroborated what has been found by research world wide – that the youth have the capacity to unlearn and learn, and so bring about a change in their behaviour and attitudes. Therefore, Breakthrough initiated a Randomised Control Trial with students in the age group of 12–16 years across 150 schools in Haryana, which included the formation of youth groups called "*Taaron ki toli*" (literally meaning "a gamut of stars"). With a baseline survey to guide us, this programme includes the implementation of a life-skills module on the issue of gender-based discrimination over three years. It will have 18 000 young people go through rigorous training on the issue for three years, after which they will participate in an end-line survey to measure changes in their attitudes, behaviour and knowledge. As the programme gains ground, a buzz of change is starting to be heard: girls only and boys only classes in many of the schools have become "mixed sections"; during class breaks and on the sports field, girls and boys are heard saying that it's a "one and gender equal world." There are examples of girls resisting mobility restrictions, especially those against going to school because of their parents' fear of sexual harassment on the streets: in a walkathon and a bicycle rally organised by Breakthrough, only girls thronged the streets to reclaim their mobility. More and more confident and fearless girls in public spaces are the way forward. Many boys have started to tell us of their decisions to eat with their sisters at home (the normal practice is that girls and women eat only after the boys and men have been fed) so that they can ensure and monitor what their sisters are given to eat, indicating that they are beginning to recognise the gender-based discrimination in their households.

The outreach and inclusion of health workers and young people was possible due to the collaborations and rapport developed by Breakthrough with concerned government departments and agencies at the district and state levels. These included the National Service Scheme (NSS) which operates as an extra-curricular social service option in colleges and has the mandate to enable young people to make a social contribution to their community and social environment. They are taught to understand the community in relation to themselves, identify the needs and problems and be a part of the solutions at the local level. Breakthrough also formalised links with the (nodal) Department of Women and Child Development and the National Health Mission in Haryana, and at the national level, to enhance the impact and reach of our efforts. In fact, the government has adopted some messages and information material from our mass media campaign as part of its *Beti Bachao, Beti Padhao* (Save the daughter, Educate the daughter) campaign in recognition of the efficacy of Breakthrough's work on the subject in terms of content and communication.

With a lot of issue-based and people-to-people learning already completed, in early 2015, Breakthrough decided to begin a campaign on the issue of gender-biased sex selection in Haryana, entitled "Mission Hazaar"[8] in four districts of Haryana: Sonipat, Panipat, Rohtak and Jhajjar. The strategy is aimed at magnifying the impact of our ground-level capacity-building efforts with focussed campaigns every three to six months.

8 The word *hazaar* in Hindi means "one thousand." The title "Mission Hazaar" is thus used symbolically to imply that we aim to achieve a 1000:1000 sex ratio and also open up a thousand equal opportunities.

Addressing the root and structural causes that perpetuate sex selection is integral to our campaign and we are using varying (non-virtual and virtual) strategies to achieve this objective. The campaign highlights and addresses the phenomenon of son preference from the perspective of gender-based discrimination and its links to with the practice of sex selection. It seeks to go beyond the numbers game and open up a discussion on how continued sex selection puts women and girls at risk.

Evidence from a Youth Audit,[9] conducted as part of the Mission Hazaar campaign, highlights the increasing gender difference in family size from the previous to the present generation, with the numbers of boys rising and the numbers of girls falling. Among the previous generation, these respondents mentioned a low ratio of females compared to males – the number of *Maasis* compared to *Mamas* and *Buas* compared to *Chachas*[10] – on the side of their mothers' and fathers' families respectively. These findings show us that sex selection is not just a problem of the present generation, but has a "his"tory (and "her"story) from the past. Respondents mention that there are more boys and fewer girls in their class at school, and this fact is not only related to girls' being denied education but also to the availability of girls to be educated. Beyond classrooms, on the question of the number of women who are seen on the roads or at other public spaces when they go out (for example at playing fields, local grocery shops, cinema halls, farm fields and *panchayat*[11] meetings) – nearly two-thirds point out that they see more men than women in the given public spaces. Despite these statistics, the gravity of 'missing women' is not adequately recognised or acknowledged. With respect to the existing gender biases vis-à-vis women's value and worth, our youth audit shows that 89% of the women in respondent families are engaged in household work, followed by cattle rearing, handicrafts and farming, and are least or rarely found to be doctors/engineers, police women, politicians, *panchayat* members, teachers or sales women, etc.

9 This youth audit or survey was conducted in 2014 with 10000 young students (boys and girls) from schools and colleges in the districts of Haryana where the GBSS project has been implemented. Through questions asked of the youth group, the survey gathered data on the numbers of male and female members in a family (siblings, cousins, paternal and maternal uncles and aunts), girls as compared to boys in classrooms, female family members engaged in different occupations, and the numbers of women and girls seen in public places, workplaces and out after dark. The youth audit was a method to understand and record their experiences of gender-biased sex selection, both as an audience and to mobilise them as partners in the campaign.

10 *Maasi* is the mother's sister, *Mama* is the mother's brother, *Bua* is the father's sister and *Chacha* is the father's younger brother.

11 *Panchayat* is a Hindi word that refers to a local self-governing institution.

Evidence from a research conducted in Haryana and Punjab[12] reveals that a majority of the adult population has a poor understanding (read acknowledgement) of what qualifies as discrimination against women and girls. Forty percent of the adults surveyed were not able immediately to identify any form of discrimination faced by women and girls, although some responses emerged on probing further. These included the following phenomena:

- Girls not being able to finish their school education;
- The lack of mobility in terms of going out to play, work or accessing public spaces;
- The lack of choice in the clothes they wanted to wear.

However, in the same line of thought, they were very clear that the girls cannot disobey the family's wishes and if need be, should give up their education and jobs, thus reiterating the exclusion of women and girls from the rights of education and employment, as well as health and public participation.

The analysis of survey data once again reaffirmed the preference of sons over daughters, as parents and families are concerned about girls' safety and security issues when it comes to their mobility for going to school, work or even community spaces, while sons are considered as a support for parents in their old age and sole heirs of the family.

In the context of field research and findings, the communication content and methodology (including theatre, video vans, training programmes and youth *melas* or fairs) of Mission Hazaar aims at challenging the patriarchal social values of son preference and moving away from blaming or putting the moral onus of sex selection on the woman. For example, we argue that dowry does not ensure that our daughters are protected, and that, instead giving them an equal share in property is the way forward, thus enabling them to exercise agency to resist and cope with the violence while having an asset that provides economic security. We are drawing links between the problem of decreasing numbers of girls to the increasing concern about their safety and (the ensuing) restrictions on their mobility. We argue that having fewer women, combined with their inability to access and be in public spaces (especially after dark) in fact accentuates the chances of violence against them. Instead, the presence of more and more women in public spaces will contribute to changing this scenario for the better. When we ask who commits violence against women, we realise that most perpetrators are boys and men from the victims' families and

12 NR Management Consultants (NRMC), "Baseline Survey of Strengthening Child Rights in the Cotton Farming Districts of Punjab and Haryana Project," Funded by IKEA Foundation to support the work of Save the Children, Pratham Education Foundation and Breakthrough, NRMC, New Delhi, 2014.

communities itself. Therefore it is time to instil in boys and men the value of respecting girls and women, to enable them to defy gendered behaviours and expectations, and agree that such violence against women is unacceptable.

Think about this

- Are women safe in public spaces?
- Do women face sexual harassment on a daily basis?
- Is this the reason that families do not allow women to go out, resulting in lower numbers of women in schools and colleges, public spaces, streets and bus stops?
- Is this the reason why parents don't desire daughters?
- Is this why there are only 834 girls for every 1000 boys in Haryana?

Now, think about this

- More than 90% of women face sexual harassment in their lives.
- When women face sexual harassment, their families and communities blame them instead of the perpetrators of this crime.
- Families decide that it is in their best interest to restrict the movements of women, sometimes with the extreme step of only trying to have sons.
- Isn't it time that instead of practicing sex selection to have sons, we strive for the safety and security of our girls?

Going Forward

Breakthrough has set its eyes on reducing and stopping gender-biased sex selection in Haryana and our work has shown us five strategic paths that we need to follow in order to achieve this goal in a holistic and targeted manner.

First, we recognise that this issue cannot be viewed in isolation from gender-based discrimination. At a discourse level, sex selection has been recognised as a symptom of the problem and not the disease. It is therefore necessary that we look at its inter-linkages with other issues, especially the value of women in our society and the various restrictions and violence that are associated with being women.

Second, this issue needs to be articulated and communicated in women-friendly language – one that is pro-choice and rights-based, is non-threatening to men and boys, does not blame women for being the enemy of their own kind, and considers women beyond their relationships, especially that of being the mother or *janani* (one who gives birth).

Third, we note that the problem of sex-selection requires an intensive engagement with boys and men at different levels to address gender-based discrimination and structural causes of violence against women.

Fourth, and as Breakthrough's field level mobilisation and training programmes have demonstrated, a multi-stakeholder approach is critical for success. Eliminating sex selection needs to be an issue that the masses can relate to, including everyone we engage with. Capacity building, mobilisation and advocacy of young people, frontline health workers, *panchayat* leaders, service providers and key government departments and ministries are all essential to this work.

Fifth, and finally, we understand that our work on gender-biased sex selection needs to be both in-depth in terms of the information and knowledge shared and discussed as well as expansive in terms of the scale for reaching and impacting individuals, families, communities, (medical) service providers, law and enforcement agencies and policies that allow for son preference and daughter aversion in Haryana and other parts of India.

References

Abdul Latif Jameel Poverty Action Lab (J-PAL). 2012–13. *Baseline Survey: GBSS Results Monitoring Report.* India: J-PAL.

Breakthrough. 2013. *Review of Literature and Communication on Sex Selection in India.* New Delhi: Breakthrough. Unpublished.

Goel, Preeti. 2016. "The Maintenance and Welfare of Parents and Senior Citizens Act." *Voice4India.* http://voice4india.org/the-maintenance-and-welfare-of-parents-and-senior-citizens/36/.

John, Mary E., Ravinder Kaur, Rajni Palriwala, Saraswati Raju and Alpana Sagar. 2008. *Planning Families, Planning Gender: The Adverse Child Sex Ratio in Selected Districts of Madhya Pradesh, Rajasthan, Himachal Pradesh, Haryana and Punjab.* New Delhi: ActionAid and IDRC.

NR Management Consultants (NRMC). 2014. "Baseline Survey of Strengthening Child Rights in the Cotton Farming Districts of Punjab and Haryana Project." Funded by IKEA Foundation to support the work of Save the Children. New Delhi: Pratham Education Foundation and Breakthrough. http://www.nrmc.co/index.php/what-we-do/our-projects/16-project-data-base/199-monitoring-and-evaluation-of-strengthening-child-rights-in-the-cotton-farming-districts-of-punjab-and-haryana-project.

Sen, Amartya. 1990. "More Than 100 Million Women Are Missing." *New York Review of Books* 37 (December): 20. http://www.nybooks.com/articles/1990/12/20/more-than-100-million-women-are-missing.

Visaria, Leela. 2011. "India's Sex Ratio: Misplaced Advocacy?" Seminar, n.p. http://www.india-seminar.com/2011/617/617_leela_visaria.htm.

CHAPTER 6

The Concept of Love in Masculinist Blogs: A Strategic Ideal

Tuija Saresma

Theoretical and Conceptual Background

Love is often considered a positive emotion, an ethical, equal relationship and even a radical power that can transgress established social practices and norms (Grossi 2013). Romantic heterosexual love as the dominant discourse of love in Western societies is reproduced throughout contemporary culture. It has been analysed in abundance by critical theorists, cultural studies scholars and feminists, who have repeatedly demonstrated the heavy ideological burden of the romantic ideal of love as bourgeois, heteronormative and conservative.[1] Some feminist critics of love have, however, shown the fluidity of love and its potential as both a modern equaliser of relationships and an institution that produces unequal competition between women and men in the spheres of capitalist structures (cf. Illouz 2007).

Whereas love as a private emotion is limited to bourgeois ideals of romantic love, it seems that the ideal of romantic heterosexual love is, besides reproduced in the private domains, simultaneously increasingly produced publicly in digitised contemporary culture. Assessing the blurring of public and private spheres is important in discussing love as an individual experience and an institutionally regulated form of organising emotional attachment and relationships to others. The private, or intimate, has been understood as a feminine area, whereas public has been the domain of the "free man" ever since the dawn of democracy in Greek Antiquity. Emotions have been perceived as belonging in the private arena, rationality as a public virtue and reason as a feature of men. It is worth noting that the division into public and private spheres continues to be heavily gendered even in mediatised contemporary culture. However, the interconnectedness of private and public spheres in digitised contemporary culture becomes evident in the blogosphere as a limitless repository of discussions and representations of love.

1 See Simone de Beauvoir (1949); Shulamit Firestone (1970); Marilyn Friedman (1994); Carol Smart (1992).

 | DOI:10.1163/9789004380233_008

The idea of romantic love is closely confined to heterosexual behaviour, which is aptly described by the philosopher Judith Butler as *heteronormativity* (1990). In Western culture heteronormativity foregrounds marriage as an institution that, according to anthropologist Edward Westermarck, is universally monogamous, *connects* man and wife and parents and children and *arranges* the relationships of men and women, adults and children as well as social life and sociability, sexuality, working life and wealth.[2] In her critical analysis of marriage, professor of jurisprudence Anu Pylkkänen has shown that in regulating the life of the married couple, marriage functions more effectively in protecting property (of men) than in assuring sexual and bodily integrity and care (for women and children) (2012, 13). As Dikmen Yakali suggests in her chapter in this volume, heterosexual marriage functions as the innate means of patriarchy to reproduce itself as a means to govern women in the spheres of both intimate sexuality and public working life; and that the imperative to marriage leads to compulsory heterosexuality, where the only appropriate way to live in either an intimate or a public sphere is to pair with a representative of the other sex (Veijola and Jokinen 2001, 84–85, 95).

Lauren Berlant's concept of *intimate publics* (2008, x) is useful in analysing the representations of love and marriage, as it denies the dichotomy between private and public domains and shows their intermingling. In contemporary intimate publics, the most private experiences and emotions are often thrashed out publicly in the media and increasingly on the internet. Also, the concept of *semi-public* has been introduced to describe the blurring of the demarcation between private and public in digitised contemporary culture, filtered through the media. Marriage as an arrangement that organises both private and societal relations that deal with emotional attachment, welfare, taxation, succession and transnational family relations also shows the impossibility of separating the levels of social structures and individual emotions and experiences (Pylkkänen 2002, 24). Understood at least in secular Western societies through the romantic ideal of marriage as the arrangement of a (heterosexual) couple who care deeply for each other, but simultaneously mixing with legislation and political economy, love is a thoroughly political concept that has the potential to affect behaviour and mobilise people. As Eva Illouz puts it, "emotions are cultural meanings and social relationships that are very compressed together and [that] it is this compact compression which confers

2 Edward Westermarck (1891, 271, cited in Veijola and Jokinen 2001, 19). Note that marriage organizes not only the life of the married, but also the unmarried 'yet, any more, or at the moment', because it is the underlying presupposition of how to live (Westermarck 1891, 271).

on them their energetic and hence their pre-reflexive, often semi-conscious character" (Illouz 2007, 3).

In everyday understanding, gender is often understood as a bipolar system within which separate and even oppositional groups of men and women differ from and yet complement each other. Instead of the essentialist understanding of gender as an innate characteristic and the dual gender order as a "natural" state of affairs, I understand gender, following Judith Butler, performatively: as something that is constantly produced in our repetitive daily acts (cf. Butler 1990). In this approach, gender as a given premise is problematised: I follow Iris Marion Young in taking gender "not as an element of explanation but rather one of interpretation," and viewing love through a gendered lens, which to Young means "seeing how a certain logic of gendered meanings and images helps organise the way people interpret events and circumstances" (Young 2003, 2).

Besides analysing the relationship between love and gender, and strategic uses of the fluid concept of love, to resist a fluid understanding of gender, I ask how the concept of love is intertwined with notions of gender, sexuality and class. I use intersectionality as my key theoretical concept and as a means to recognise hierarchically organised and constantly negotiated identity positions. Intersectional categories of gender, sexuality and social class, and the understanding of intersecting power relations as mutually constitutive, have become the focus of research in feminist theory during the past decades.[3] Intersectionality as a critical concept refers to the variety of changing hierarchical positions of power that individuals take or are put into (Lähdesmäki and Saresma 2014, 299–313). In this hierarchy, "masculine" is understood as having a higher position than "feminine." Bringing to the discussion other differences, such as social class, age, sexuality and ethnicity or "race," and analysing their interdependence in positioning people in a net of power, is called intersectional analysis. Inspired by intersectionality as a methodological tool, I am not only interested in the gendered representations of love, but the intersectional aspects of love. This means focusing attention on the various and changing social categories of power that function together and simultaneously as building blocks of individual identities and delineate the ways people live their lives relationally, intermingled with others. My aim is to investigate strategic uses of love and the intersections of various identity categories in strategically using love as a means of repression by mapping the various discourses of performing gendered love on contemporary internet (semi-)publicity eagerly spread by so-called masculinists.

3 Crenshaw (1991, 1241–1299), Phoenix and Pattynama (2006, 187–192).

During the past few years there has been a transnational upsurge of a masculinist, explicitly antifeminist movement online. In Sweden there have been internet-based hate campaigns against journalists, authors and researchers that deal with feminist issues. Besides these aggressive campaigns, masculinists in, for example, Sweden, Finland, Canada, Germany and the United States have started to network and promote an antifeminist agenda. Also, more general blogs based on masculinist ideology deal with strong emotions such as love and hate (Holm 2013). I am interested in how love is represented in masculinist texts published on the internet. Blogs are an extremely popular form of self-expression, and the blogosphere has become a new, democratic political arena (with the flip side of being the place for inciting racist, homophobic and misogynist atmospheres) (cf. Keren 2006; Sunstein 2007). It is fruitful to study the blogosphere as a snapshot of the ways of understanding, representing and performing gender in contemporary culture.

Masculinism, also referred to as men's rights activism, is "grounded in political, economic and social power relations between men as a class and women as a class" (Blais and Dupuis-Déri 2012, 25). Based on the idea of the gender order as a fixed given biological fact, it refers to patriarchal ideology, "combats feminism and the progress women have achieved" in contemporary society and is a constituent of antifeminism (Blais and Dupuis-Déri 2012). The word masculinism carries a variety of negative connotations, such as the implicit idea that masculinism is a form of antifeminism and is as legitimate as its feminist counterpart (Blais and Dupuis-Déri 2012, 23). As a result, I would like to state at the outset that I am using the concept in a critical sense, denying the idea of gender equality as a zero-sum game.

Unlike masculinists, and contrary to much of the existing research in the area of social psychology that deals with heterosexual love relationships, the aim here is not to document male-female differences (Peplau and Gordon 1985, 258). Instead, following philosopher Luce Irigaray, I comprehend the difference between genders not as essential, but as an ethical difference. Difference is not something that should be trivialised, belittled or eliminated, but something that functions as the basis for respectful distance and fruitful dialogue of genders. When the difference between genders is understood as ethical, it becomes impossible to define women and men as the negation of or simply complementary to each other (Irigaray 1992, in Veijola and Jokinen 2001, 21). A respectful gender difference is, however, impossible in our culture, where "the space between woman and man is loaded with duties, rights, appeal, lust, owning and consuming" (Veijola and Jokinen 2001, 22).

Love, like other emotions, is socially constructed: it cannot be separated from the socio-cultural meanings that determine the way they are experienced and expressed (cf. McCarthy 1994; Lupton 1998; Sennett 2012). When analysing the affective expression of the masculinists, I am interested in affects and emotions as socially constructed and performed, instead of taking them as individual psychological traits, and I wish to emphasise the intersubjective aspects of emotions: they are not only individually experienced or intrinsically situated in any one person, but are always experienced in relation to others (Ahmed 2004, 2). To be more specific, I investigate the social effects of emotional expressions and the societal context of affective rhetoric and strategic uses of love. In doing this, I wish to deconstruct the idea of love as a utopian, exclusively positive emotion by critically analysing the ways the representations of love are used for reactionary, submissive goals in the masculinist blogosphere. In emphasising the fluidity of the uses of love, I ask how the concept of love is reframed and used as a rhetorical means to legitimise an unequal distribution of power between genders. Inspired by multidisciplinary cultural studies and feminist studies, my hypothesis is that love as a fluid and elastic concept is used strategically. In late modern society, where the dichotomous gender order and rigid gender roles have undergone dissolution (about the blurring of gender norms and positions, see Angela Tumini's chapter in this volume), love is used by masculinists as a repressive concept. Drawing simultaneously from the understanding of love as an emotion that arouses positive responses and from heteronormative and misogynist ideologies, the ideal of love is used by masculinists strategically to reposition women and men in the traditional gender order.

Reading Masculinist Blogs on the Internet

Love is discussed endlessly in television, pop lyrics, cinema, women's magazines and self-help literature – and in blogs and dating sites on the internet. Love has always been represented in novels and the film industry, and the contemporary self-help literature industry echoes the ideal of an enduring relationship and pure love. The spread of social media has nevertheless encouraged all kinds of representations of love to flourish. Representations of love range from seemingly sweet and innocent love quotes and sugary pictures of red hearts and kissing bunnies to the porn industry's objectifying photographs and videos that commercialise love to make a profit.[4] There are sites promoting, for example, LBGT rights or gender-neutral marriage, but there is also a loud group of people advancing anti-immigrant, homophobic and antifeminist ideologies,

4 For example, "Love Quotes" (Brainy Quote 2014).

whose understanding of love is, as I suggest, traditional and repressive towards all groups of people other than white heterosexual men.

Masculinism is a movement that focuses "primarily on masculinity and the place of white heterosexual men in North American and European societies" and is "concerned with the alleged domination of women in both the public and private spheres" (Blais and Dupuis-Déri 2012, 23) in contemporary culture, where women have entered the arenas of education and working life, and where the LGBT movement has contributed to making the boundaries between previously firm gender stereotypes more porous. This has led to challenging traditional assumptions about heterosexual relationships and a weakening of traditional gender roles; thus, intimate life has been democratised (Weeks 2007) and the man is no longer the self-evident head of the family (Peplau and Gordon 1985, 258). This poses a challenge to men, some of whom experience as a major threat the situation where, unlike Parson's concept of the functional family of the 1950s, "the husband's instrumental leadership in the family [being] fundamentally tied to his nearly exclusive role as breadwinner" is questioned, and where the wife's offering to the nuclear family has spread beyond mothering and homemaking to economic contribution (Parsons 1955, in Peplau and Gordon 1985, 268). I hope to show how masculinists, as advocates of the conservative gender order, use the positive connotations of love to promote their agenda of seeking to restore the traditional patriarchal gender order from the 1950s when gender roles were clearly separated: men as breadwinners were the head of the family, while women as their wives served as housewives and homemakers, taking care of the children and keeping the home tidy and cosy so that both the husband and the kids would feel comfortable and "the family would be harmonious and well-balanced." Thus, in the nuclear family, idealised in the "cult of home," the duty of the wife and mother was to fill the private sphere with care and love (cf. Hytönen and Rantalainen 2013).

Besides nostalgic yearning for the imagined "lost paradise" of the 1950s (which actually never existed in real life),[5] the most prominent themes of masculinist thinking, such as the need for men to have regular sex with women; pop evolutionary psychology; problems with fatherhood, visitation rights and maintenance allowances; men's health issues; the allegedly distorted statistics on domestic violence and equal pay,[6] are summarised on the Angry Harry site, which claims to be "one of the best-known websites frequented by those

5 See Saresma 2014a (in Saresma and Jäntti 2014, 249–284).
6 See Saresma 2012 (in Harjunen and Saresma 2012, 13–34); Saresma (2014b, 46–53).

concerned with Men's Rights and by MRAs" (Angry Harry, n.p.).[7] The site positions itself, striving for irony but simultaneously deadly serious, as longing for "[t]he good old days. When men were men, and when women were, as ever, complaining" (Angry Harry, "Housework" n.d.).

Focusing the investigation on a narrow case, the Angry Harry site as explicitly heterosexual and "white," means there is no discussion of other ethnicities or sexualities at the outset. However, during the analysis, special consideration will be directed at reading the fractures of this white heterosexual narrative. With the help of intersectionality as a methodological tool, I wish to demonstrate how identity positions, such as sexuality and class, intersect with gender in discussions dealing with love. In my analysis, I use intersectionality as the critical recognition of hierarchically organised and constantly negotiated identity positions (Lähdesmäki and Saresma 2014). My aim is to analyse how the categories of gender, sexuality and class function *together* and produce each other performatively when discussing love (cf. Karkulehto et al 2012, 17–28). As an exception to many intersectional investigations that emphasise the mutual working of subordinating identity categories, for example, the oppression of poor uneducated Latina women in the United States (as discussed by Crenshaw 1991), my particular interest here focuses on the "unmarked categories of power," that is, the subject positions of white middle-class Western heterosexual men (Choo and Ferree 2010, 129–149).

When choosing to analyse the Angry Harry site, I followed Sara Ahmed's views on the influentiality of texts: when circulating in public, texts arrange and organise us by situating "others" as the "sources of our emotions." The emotionality or affectivity of texts has to do with the way the texts move us, and also with how emotions are performed in the texts (Ahmed 2004, 1 and 13). Analysing the representations of love found on a masculinist site, known for its affective, black-and-white rhetoric, misogyny – reflecting the deeply-rooted cultural misogyny that Veenu Kakkar and Aanchal Kapur discuss in their chapter in this volume – and even hate speech towards feminists (cf. Sveland 2013), I aim to analyse the understanding of love from another angle, and to uncover the representations of love that do not deal with the positive connotations of nurturing affection and care.

My method of reading is a narrative discourse analysis that enables studying the performativity of writing and the functions of linguistic choices (as propounded by Laclau 2005). More specifically, this rhetorically-inspired close reading can be described as the "methodology of intentional misreading," based on

---

7 MRAs is an abbreviation of Men's Rights Activists.

the feminist critique of ideology (for example, Spivak 1987). This is a form of close reading that deliberately interrupts the narrative (Veijola and Jokinen 2001, 34). By teasing out the meanings between the lines, I reach towards what lies behind the foreseeability of these texts, through their familiarity and recognisability. As methods, the teasing and interruptive misreading mean that the researcher does not allow the dominant ways of reading to guide the interpretations, but that she leads the reading herself, asking her own questions. This method of teasing out and deliberately misreading as a form of deconstructive reading means asking disruptive and subversive questions rather than merely accepting the conclusions explicitly drawn by the text. In reading the Angry Harry site I ask: What actually is meant by love as it is understood and used by the Angry Harry bloggers? Is love gendered in the blogs? What is said about women and men and about their relationship? How are the expressions of love articulated as a subtext of the expressions of hate, resentment or subordination? How do masculinists use the ideal of love in their re-articulations of love? In other words, I am interested in the socially constructed and shared understanding of ideal love and the ideology behind its representations.

Four Thematic Constellations Masculinists Use in Discussing Love

The Angry Harry site contains essays by the writer himself, the most popular of which are "Why Governments love feminism" and "The psychological difference between men and women," as well as links to essays published elsewhere, such as "Are domestic violence statistics bogus?" by Wendy McElroy (2014), or "The women brainwashed by therapists to believe their parents abused them" by Amanda Cable (2014). The page is structured as a blog, showing the most recently updated essay right at the top of the site.[8]

In the left column of the page there is an "MRA corner" and links to, for example, the *A Voice for Men* site and radio show, the *Page for Men* site with its rude pictures of half-naked girls in suggestive postures and a YouTube clip headed "The real reason there aren't more female scientists,"[9] while in the right column glowing comments from the readers of the site are posted. Rhetorically, the site follows all the principles of populist language that relies on emotive expressions, strong polarisations and simplifications and stereotypes. It uses vague expressions and colourful metaphors and is based on juxtaposing various groups of people and constructing competing groups of "us" and "them."

8 The site can be found at http://www.angryharry.com/index.html.

9 http://www.avoiceformen.com/; http://www.pageformen.com/.

Another central aspect of populist rhetoric is that it eagerly perceives threats, faults and enemies everywhere (Lähdesmäki and Saresma 2014).

To find representations of love on the Angry Harry site, I used the "search" command on the page and found five essays that had "love" in the heading. They were: "Mike Tyson – Women just love violent men" (from now on referred to as "Violence"); "Feminism pros and cons: Why governments love feminism" ("Government"); "Women love Manga and masculine voices" ("Manga"); "Do men love to bash pregnant women?" ("Bashing"); and "Do women love to do housework?" ("Housework"). Romantic love as a "pure relationship" (cf. Giddens 1992) was not in the focus of any of the writings; instead love was described as either a feeling women cannot help but have towards violent men (Angry Harry, "Violence" 2014); a feeling Western governments have towards feminists as their allies in creating "as much disharmony as possible between men and women in order to fund their own empires" (Angry Harry, "Violence" 2014); a strong attraction of women to Manga comics as a representation of their fantasy of being raped and loving it (Angry Harry, "Manga" 2014); or an ironical note about research on domestic violence that (allegedly falsely) reports that 17% of pregnant women have encountered domestic violence (Angry Harry, "Bashing" 2014). Thus, "love" seemed to be a divergent concept that often had an opportunistic undertone.

Reading these texts by teasing out the meanings of love in them, I found four thematic constellations of discourses that intertwine and overlap in the masculinist understanding of love. Each of these constellations is present in one or more of the five essays analysed here. After introducing them and looking at the intersecting differences behind the most obvious difference, namely gender difference, I will discuss their role in constructing ideal love in masculinist thought.

A *The Fundamental Difference*

For Luce Irigaray, the genders should not be comprehended only in relation to each other. Instead, the idea of radical gender difference enables thinking about difference and dissimilarity without reducing woman and man to counterparts of each other (cited in Korsisaari 2006, 177–178). Contrary to this philosophical ideal, the starting point of Angry Harry is that men and women are profoundly different and thus act differently. Gender is conceived as a fundamental biological difference and a congenital difference in feminine and masculine behaviour. The masculinist understanding of genders is postulated in "evolutionist psychology":

> … the need for human beings to adapt to a hostile environment in prehistoric times resulted in men and women having different but

> complimentary roles and attitudes, a balance that unfortunately has been upset by feminism since the 1960s. (Blais and Dupuis-Déri 2012, 24)

The simplified pop version of evolutionist psychology means a few things for Angry Harry. One of these meanings is that men's "hormones and sexual urges will drive them [toward being what women find attractive]" (Angry Harry, "Violence" 2014, 3). Besides the obvious reference to sexual desire, a fundamental difference is also seen in attitudes towards housework. The reason women do more housework than men is, bluntly put, the natural gender divide: "it is part and parcel of women's wily natures to be concerned more than men about the look of things" (Angry Harry, "Housework" 2014, 4), which probably has to do with the fact that "many female mammals and birds have something within their brains akin to a nesting instinct" (Angry Harry, "Housework" 2014, 4). A woman interfering with this 'natural law' of imbalance in the share of housework "is unconsciously seeking a divorce" (Angry Harry, "Housework" 2014, 4).

Although binary gender difference is presented on the site as the normal state of affairs and a biological fact, the dual gender order with men at the one end and women at the other is implicitly supported by the presupposition of heterosexuality. For Judith Butler, "women" and "men" are fraught categories that do not exist independently, but are always tied with other facets of identity, such as class, ethnicity, and sexuality (Butler 1990). The argument of intersectional feminists and queer theorists that sexuality intersects inseparably with gender is supported by the famous claim of Adrienne Rich in her article on compulsory heterosexuality (1980): that heterosexuality needs homosexuality to stabilise its existence, and yet, in the contemporary gender order, the lesbian existence is compulsorily denied or hidden. Thus, the idea of the fundamental difference between the two genders is used here in an intersectional manner, invoking the "natural" sexual order, namely heterosexuality. Moreover, the assumed gender difference, emphasising the different behaviour of genders – women as easily directed by their inherent emotionality, men as "serious" and rational, as the ancient division has it – is used as the basis of social and economic arrangements. Marriage is a perfect example of this social hierarchy produced by gender divisions that contain implicit emotional divisions, producing emotional hierarchies, which in turn implicitly organise moral and social arrangements, as Eva Illouz (2007, 3) aptly explains. This assumption of the hierarchically organised emotional division of genders is implicit in the emphasis on biological difference between genders.

B *The Household as an Exchange Economy*

The following description evocatively states the masculinist understanding of the place of women in society that is, indeed, straight from the 1950s white suburban ideal:

> But there is nothing more arousing for a man than to peer over the top of his newspaper in order to observe closely his woman scuttling around, hither and thither, vacuuming the carpet, dusting his furniture and cleaning the windows – her pretty negligee rising and falling tantalisingly to the sensual rhythms of her labours. (Housework, 4)

In the citation above, the woman is described as an intellectually immature sexual object, almost parallel to furniture, whose task is to keep the home tidy and to look desirable. In the ideology so well captured in this (perhaps intentionally) ironical statement, women get protection and shelter from their husbands in exchange for sexual and domestic services. In my earlier readings of texts by Finnish masculinists, namely a blog by media celebrity Henry Laasanen (Saresma 2014a and 2017) and an essay collection by poet and essayist Timo Hännikäinen (Saresma 2016), I found similarities in the emotionless tone of their texts: positive feelings such as love are not discussed, but instead, the idea of hetero-sex as an exchange of commodities, inspired by neoliberalism, penetrates the texts. This is not only a characteristic of masculinist ideology, but more broadly a feature of what Max Weber called the spirit of capitalism, which has been conceptualised in the commercialisation of intimate life as described by Arlie Hochschild (2003).

Although this citation from the Angry Harry site uses affective expressions in depicting a harmonious heterosexual idyll, it perpetuates the idea of women trading sexual services for protection and economic upkeep that is widely circulated in masculinist texts (Saresma 2014a and 2017). The tendency to see women in need of protection follows the patriarchal logic in which "the role of the masculine protector puts those protected, paradigmatically women and children, in a subordinate position of dependence and obedience" and legitimates authoritarian power to the man as the head of the family (Young 2003, 2). The logic of masculinism, as Iris Marion Young has it, "associates with the position of male head of household as a protector of the family, and, by extension, with masculine leaders and risk takers as protectors of a population" (Young 2003, 3).

The idea of men and women as classes originally emerged in the theorisations of feminist thinkers such as Zillah Eisenstein, who understood gender as a social class. In her theorisation, men and women as classes are organised hierarchically: men dominate, while women are subordinated (1995, 196–217). The principal means of controlling and governing the lower class is economic exploitation, through which women are forced to be housewives, raise children and serve men without pay. Thus, marriage – although validated with love – is based on economic subordination and sustains the personal and universal dependency of women on men (Veijola and Jokinen 2001, 93).

In Angry Harry's opinion, on the contrary, Western women have done well, as they "live as the most pampered, the most protected, the most catered for and the most over-indulged organisms ever to have existed on the planet" ("Housework" 2014, 2). Thus economic issues are discussed explicitly under the ideal of heterosexual love – although the underlying assumption that the readers of the blog are middle-aged and the internalisation of the Western ideal of the nuclear family are not discussed. However, feminists now pose a threat to marriage as the natural way of arranging relationships.

C *Feminism as a Threat to Marriage, Family and Society*

Masculinist texts utilise an affective tone, often slanted by anger and resentment (Saresma 2014a and 2017). This is evident in Angry Harry's texts as well, as can be seen in this excerpt:

> Feminist hysteria, disinformation and intimidation all ensure that women in this society are held responsible for very few of the many negative things they, themselves, cause to happen. ("Violence" 2014, 4)

The feminist threat is rhetorically produced as a counterpoint to the paradise-like, harmonious society, which is created when men and women fulfil their social roles, described by affectively appealing to its positive aspects:

> […] imagine a society – a somewhat idealised society – wherein the women are happy to spend their days being closely associated with their homes and with their children, while the young men and the fathers are reasonably happy to troop off to the workplace […]. ("Government" 2014, 1)

However, the setting loses its balance because "the main aim for feminists is to create as much disharmony as possible between men and women" ("Government" 2014, 3), leading to divorce, which leads to "a whole cascade of social problems [because] the youngsters [are] not having fathers around" ("Government" 2014, 5). Marriage and its erosion also causes "hatred towards men and a fear of men" ("Government" 2014, 7), not to even mention that "vulnerable people [besides children, the elderly and the sick] are either abandoned to waste away on their own, or they are put into care homes and hospitals" ("Government" 2014, 6). All this is caused by the alliance between feminists and the government – "the perfect hammer for smashing up people's relationships" ("Government" 2014, 16) – that forces families to break up by encouraging women to divorce, "breaking apart the relationships between men and women and men and children," encouraging "excessive immigration" and by enacting "laws to do with hate speech and with 'offending people' " which "distance people from each other" ("Government" 2014, 15).

Constructing feminism and feminists as a threat follows, as Iris Marion Young has it, the logic of masculinist protection that often constitutes the "good" men who protect their women and children, in opposition to other "bad" men who are liable to attack. In this logic, virtuous masculinity depends on its constitutive relation to the presumption of evil others. Here, those others are not (ethnically, socially or in other ways) other men, but feminists. There is, thus, a correlate dichotomy between the "good" woman and the "bad" woman. To cite Young:

> Simply put, the "good" woman stands under the male protection of a father or a husband, submits to his judgment about what is necessary for her protection, and remains loyal to him. A "bad" woman is one who is unlucky enough not to have a man willing to protect her, or who refuses such protection by claiming the right to run her own life. In either case, the woman without a male protector is fair game for any man to dominate. There is a bargain implicit in the masculinity protector role: either submit to my governance or all the bad men out there are liable to approach you, and I will not try to stop them. (Young 2003, 13–14)

On the Angry Harry site, feminists as bad women are positioned as a threat to those good women who want to stay at home, pampering their husbands and children. Power and subordination are thus brought up in the blogs under the disguise of heterosexual love, and the worst threat seems to be the equal rights of women to go to work and to earn their own salary. Intersecting power hierarchies of gender, economic situation, social status and education are in operation *par excellence* here.

D *The Defence of Male Violence*

In three out of the five essays analysed here, Angry Harry argues, somewhat surprisingly in the context of discussing love, for a close link between sexuality and violence. In all these essays violent and aggressive men are described as the subjects of female fantasies: "Mike Tyson would click his fingers at one of the gorgeous young women in the queue, and she would be the one honoured with his bed for the night" ("Violence" 2014, 1). The alleged female worshipping of "arrogant, loud-mouthed, muscular, boundary-breaking men" who "perform aggressively and rudely" ("Violence" 2014, 2) leads to male violence, because "men, statistically speaking, will drift toward being whatever it is that women find attractive" ("Violence" 2014, 3). Based on this evolutionary claim, a shift of perspective is executed:

> [...] instead of simply blaming men for their propensity toward violence, one might take notice of the fact that significant numbers of women encourage it, and get turned on by it. ("Violence" 2014, 4)

A similar logic of making excuses for male violence is found in the essay about Manga, the main argument of which is a generalisation based on the claim that rape fantasy expressed in Manga comics is popular among Japanese women: "many women just love the idea of being abused. They *love* it" ("Manga" 2014, 2).

The argument goes as follows: Gradually, men learn to behave according to "women's ubiquitous rape fantasies," using "aggression as a means of making women feel good" ("Manga" 2014, 3), but this turns out to be dangerous because, in Angry Harry's world, there are women like Little Miss Victim or Vengeful Alice. They also have fantasies about rape, but for some reason after intercourse they change their mind regarding the enjoyment caused by aggressive sexual behaviour and charge the innocent man with rape ("Manga" 2014, 3–6).

In the essay dealing with bashing pregnant women, pregnancy changes the power relations of the heterosexual relationship, for now "her partner not only ceases to be the centre of her universe, he quickly turns into not much more than an implement for achieving her aims. Most of the animal kingdom seems to operate in this fashion" ("Bashing" 2014, 1). The argument continues:

> As a result, [men] often feel very insecure and threatened by [pregnancy]. Further, they often feel that they have been duped, and lied to, because of the dramatic changes in their partners' attitudes toward them – hence the violence. ("Bashing" 2014, 2)

Besides justification of domestic violence conducted by men – "the more men are disempowered within their relationships, the more will men and women tend to end up reacting toward each other with aggression" ("Bashing" 2014, 9) – the essay tries to prove that statistics on domestic violence lie, hiding of course, the power hierarchies of gender and physical ability.

Conclusions and Discussion

The four thematic constellations introduced above indicate the various strategic uses of love in masculinist thought. The last quote above proves their intertwining, bringing together the evolutionary psychological explanation, the crisis of men and the breakdown of the traditional heterosexual partnership, and the erosion of the patriarchal idea about the man as the head of the family, all wrapped up in a package of affective rhetoric. In an exemplary way, the citation describes the change in the status of white middle-class heterosexual male in contemporary culture.

Advocating the traditional gender order, masculinists use the concept of love to promote the repressive ideas of misogynist and antifeminist ideologies. My hypothesis was that love is used as a justification of the restoration of the traditional, patriarchal gender order, within which the white heterosexual Western male dominates, subordinating people of any other gender, sexuality or ethnic background. This did not happen quite as expected. Indeed, love was actually mainly discussed outside the context of heterosexual romantic relationships. For Angry Harry, using the concept of love is a stylistic choice, a tool for creating tension between men as the victims of modernisation and destructive feminists. Thus, it is not a numinous force that can elevate us above the mundane, but rather a notion loaded with irony.

In my previous readings of renowned Finnish masculinists, I found similarities in the texts of a blogger and a poet: positive feelings such as love are not discussed, but instead, there is the capitalist, neoliberal idea about hetero-sex as an exchange of commodities (Saresma 2014a, 2014b and 2017). My analysis of the representations of love in the texts by Angry Harry supports my previous findings, although love as a theme is more explicitly dealt with here. In Angry Harry's blog, too, love is a commodity that is bought, sold and traded. And yet, when scratching the surface of the site, performing love is at the very core of the blog. It is done by juxtaposing men and women, reinforcing a traditionalist view of gender roles, and in the context of a narrow understanding of love as heterosexual and monogamous. Patriarchal ideology holds, as "love" is used to tie women to their roles as wives, mothers and homemakers. However, intersectionality adds another layer to the interpretations: it is not only gender, but also the heteronormative white bourgeois way of strategically using love as a means to make women stay at home by appealing to their "inner nature" as pampering parents.

Furthermore, what is worth noting is that love is obviously not only a genre for escapist entertainment directed at teenage girls and women. Men also seek love, although it has been suggested by Jorgen Lorentzen that "love is not at all an important part of heterosexual men's lives," who "work hard to embody the masculine ideal, to be admired for their physical, financial and political strength, which will guarantee them a certain kind of love from people who fit into and enhance their masculine image" (2007, 190–198). For de Beauvoir, these "serious men" "reproduce their patriarchal versions of love in all forms of intimate relationships" (Mundy 2015, 187). The argument finds support in other texts, such as in Anthony Giddens' idea of men behaving according to the pre-modern family system, even though as a culture, we have moved to a different mode of organising family relations, whereas women have adopted the post-modern mode, where intimate relations and reflecting one's emotions have become indispensable (Giddens 1992).

All in all, the advocates of the traditional gender order use the positive connotations of love to promote the repressive ideas of misogynist, antifeminist and heterosexist ideologies on the internet. It is noteworthy that this understanding of love as a pure, altruistic and noble emotion is not limited to masculinists. Feminist thinkers such as Adrienne Rich have argued that the very notion of love as idealized perpetuates female subordination. Albeit the discussion analysed here is only a narrow and fragmentary example of the subordination of women in the name of love, the influence of the masculinist movement is becoming more pervasive on the internet, in addition to traditional print and digital media. Thus, the masculinist reconceptualisation of love as a gendered concept that is ideologically loaded as an adjunct to male conquest of women is worth studying. And yet, while studying the fixed uses of love, it should not be forgotten that love as a fluid concept also includes the potential of optimism, change and transformation that is capable of challenging the rigid norms and repressive regulations of established institutions such as heterosexual marriage (Berlant 1998).

References

Ahmed, Sara. 2004. *The Cultural Politics of Emotion*. Edinburgh and London: Edinburgh University Press and Routledge.

Berlant, Lauren. 1998. "Intimacy: A Special Issue." *Critical Inquiry* 24 (2): 281–288.

Berlant, Lauren. 2008. *The Female Complaint. The Unfinished Business of Sentimentality in American Culture*. Durham: Duke University Press.

Blais, Melissa and Dupuis-Déri, Francis. 2012. "Masculinism and the Antifeminist Countermovement." *Social Movement Studies* 11 (1): 21–39.

Butler, Judith. 1990. *Gender Trouble. Feminism and the Subversion of Identity*. New York and London: Routledge.

Choo, Hae Yeon and Myra Marx Ferree. 2010. "Practicing Intersectionality in Sociological Research: A Critical Analysis of Inclusions, Interactions, and Institutions in the Study of Inequality." *Sociological Theory* 28 (2): 129–149.

Crenshaw, Kimberlé. 1991. "Mapping the Margins: Intersectionality, Identity Politics, and Violence against Women of Color." *Stanford Law Review* 43 (6): 1241–1299.

De Beauvoir, Simone. 1949. *Le Deuxième Sexe*. Paris: Gallimard.

Eisenstein, Zillah. 1995. "Constructing a Theory of Capitalist Patriarchy and Socialist Feminism." *Critical Sociology* 2/3: 196–217.

Friedman, Marilyn. 1994. *What Are Friends For? Feminist Perspectives on Personal Relationships on Moral Theory*. Ithaca: Cornell University Press.

Firestone, Shulamith. 1970. *The Dialectic of Sex: The Case for Feminist Revolution*. New York: William Morrow.

Giddens, Anthony. 1992. *The Transformation of Intimacy: Sexuality, Love and Eroticism in Modern Societies*. Oxford and Cambridge: Polity Press.

Grossi, Renata. 2013. "Romantic Love – a Feminist Conundrum?." http://thefeministwire.com/2013/feminist-critiques-of-love/.

Hochschild, Arlie Russel. 2003. *The Commercialization of Intimate Life: Notes from Home and Work*. Los Angeles: California University Press.

Holm, Malin. 2013. "Men who hate women – Online. Mapping the Swedish Anti-Feminist Movement in the New Media." Draft paper prepared for the 2013 ECPG Conference, Barcelona, Spain.

Hytönen, Kirsi-Maria and Rantalainen, Keijo (eds.). 2013. *Onnen aika: Valoja ja varjoja 1950-luvulla* [*The Time of Happiness: Lights and Shadows in the 1950s*]. Jyväskylä: Atena.

Illouz, Eva. 2007. *Cold Intimacies: The Making of Emotional Capitalism*. Cambridge: Polity Press.

Irigaray, Luce. 1992. *J'aime à toi: Esquisse d'une félicité dans l'histoire*. Paris: Éditions Grasset and Fasquelle.

Karkulehto, Sanna, Saresma, Tuija, Harjunen, Hannele and Johanna Kantola. 2012. "Intersektionaalisuus metodologiana ja performatiivisen intersektionaalisuuden haste" ["Intersectionality as a Methodology and the Challenge of Performative Intersectionality"]. *Naistutkimus – Kvinnoforskning* 25 (4): 17–28.

Korsisaari, Eva Maria. 2006. *Tule, rakkaani! Naisen ja miehen välisestä etiikasta kirjallisuuden rakkauskuvauksissa* [*Come, My Love! On the Ethics between a Woman and a Man in the Literary Depictions of Love*]. Helsinki: Teos.

Keren, Michael. 2006. *Blogosphere: The New Political Arena*. Lanham: Lexington Books.

Laclau, Ernesto. 2005. *On Populist Reason*. London: Verso.

Lupton, Deborah. 1998. *The Emotional Self. A Sociocultural Explanation*. London: Sage.

Lorentzen, Jorgen. 2007. "Love and Intimacy in Men's Lives." *Nordic Journal of Women's Studies* 15: 190–198.

Lähdesmäki, Tuuli and Saresma, Tuija. 2014. "Re-framing gender equality in Finnish online discussion on immigration: Populist articulations of religious minorities and marginalized sexualities." *NORA – Nordic Journal of Feminist and Gender Research* 22 (4): 299–313. DOI: 10.1080/08038740.2014.953580.

McCarthy, E. Doyle. 1994. "The Social Construction of Emotions: New Directions from Culture Theory." *Sociology Faculty Publications* 4. http://fordham.bepress.com/soc_facultypubs/4.

Mundy, Leo. 2015. "The Question of Men in Love: A Beauvoirian Response to Jorgen Lorentzen." *NORA – Nordic Journal of Feminist and Gender Research* 23 (3): 187–202.

Parsons, Talcott. 1955. "The American Family: Its relations to Personality and to the Social Structure." In *Family, Socialization and Interaction Process*, edited by T. Parsons and R. F. Bales, 3–33. Glencoe, Ill.: Free Press.

Peplau, Letitia Anne and Gordon, Steven L. 1985. "Women and Men in Love: Gender Differences in Close Heterosexual Relationships." In *Women, Gender, and Social Psychology*, edited by E.V. O'Leary, R. K. Unger, and B. S. Wallston, 257–291. Hillsdale, NJ: Lawrence Erlbaum.

Phoenix, Ann and Pattynama, Pamela. 2006. "Intersectionality." *European Journal of Women's Studies* 13 (3): 187–192.

Pylkkänen, Anu. 2012. *Vaihtoehto avioliitolle: Seksuaalisuudesta yhteistalouden sääte-lyyn*. Tampere: Vastapaino.

Rich, Adrienne. 1980. "Compulsory Heterosexuality and Lesbian Existence." *Signs* 5 (4): 631–660.

Saresma, Tuija. 2012. "Miesten tasa-arvo ja kaunapuhe blogikeskustelussa." In *Sukupuoli nyt! Purkamisia ja neuvotteluja [Gender now! Deconstruction and negotiation]*, edited by Hannele Harjunen and Tuija Saresma, 13–34. Jyväskylä: Kampus Kustannus.

Saresma, Tuija. 2014a. "Maskulinistiblogi feministidystopiana ja kolonialistisena pastoraalina" ["The masculinist blog as a feminist dystopia and a colonial pastorale"]. In *Maisemassa: Sukupuoli ja kansallisuus suomalaisuuden kuvastoissa [In the landscape: Gender and nationality in Imageries of Finnishness]*, edited by Tuija Saresma and Saara Jäntti, 249–284. Jyväskylä: Nykykulttuurin tutkimuskeskus.

Saresma, Tuija. 2014b. "Sukupuolipopulismi ja maskuliininen standpoint-empirism" [Gender populism and standpoint empiricism]. *Sukupuolentutkimus – Genusforskning* 2: 46–53.

Saresma, Tuija. 2016. "Kauna Timo Hännikäisen kokoelmassa *Ilman* – esseitä seksuaalisesta syrjäytymisestä" [Resentment in Timo Hännikäinen's collection *Without* – Essays on Sexual Displacement]. In *Tunteet ja tuntemukset suomalaisessa kirjallisuudessa [Emotions and Affects in Finnish Literature]*, edited by Anna Helle and Anna Hollsten. Helsinki: SKS.

Saresma, Tuija. 2017. Fictitious Memories of the Nostalgic Past: Racialised Gender Melancholy in the Manosphere. In Maja Mikula (ed.), *Remembering Home in a Time of*

Mobility. Memory, Nostalgia, and Melancholy, 151–165. Cambridge: Cambridge Scholars Publishing.

Sennett, Richard. 2012. *Together. The Rituals, Pleasures and Politics of Cooperation*. London: Allen Lane/Penguin Books.

Smart, Carol. 1992. *Regulating Womanhood: Historical Essays on Marriage, Motherhood, and Sexuality*. London and New York: Routledge.

Spivak, Gayatri Chakravorty. 1987. *In Other Worlds: Essays in Cultural Politics*. New York: Routledge.

Sunstein, Cass. R. 2007. http://Republic.com 2.0. Princeton: Princeton University Press.

Sveland, Maria. 2013. *Hatet. En bok om antifeminism*. Stockholm: Leopard Förlag.

Veijola, Soile and Jokinen, Eeva. 2001. *Voiko naista rakastaa? Avion ja eron karuselli*. Helsinki: WSOY.

Weeks, Jeffrey. 2007. *The World We Have Won: The Remaking of Erotic and Intimate Life*. New York: Routledge.

Westermarck, Edward. 1891. *The History of Human Marriage*. London and New York: McMillan.

Young, Iris Marion. 2003. “The logic of Masculinist Protection: Reflections on the Current Security State.” *Signs: Journal of Women in Culture and Society* 29 (1): 1–25.

PART 3

Aspects of Love and Gender for Transgender People

CHAPTER 7

What Would Jesus Do? Transgender and Transsexual Narratives of the Relationships between Religion and Education

Andrea Mathews

Introduction

In today's world, gender identity has become more fluid. After following the social networking site – Facebook, which in February 2014 changed its gender options for its users to offer 50 categories of gender identity – the editors of Sydney University's newspaper decided to post a survey on its Facebook page which included as many non-binary options as they thought would be relevant to the question, "what is your gender?" By doing this, the newspaper's editors felt they were making the survey as inclusive as possible. Their reasons for doing this resulted from a high court battle regarding a person who won the right not to be legally obliged to declare a gender identity (Blair 2014). This shows that society's conceptions of gender are changing, implying and reinforcing arguments that gender is now seen by many as fluid, rather than fixed.

These examples illustrate the trend in postmodern society to challenge traditional, established categories. Traditional categories only included two gender identities of femininity and masculinity that opposed each other in a neat gender binary, but since movements and events such as the Stonewall riots (1969)[1] and the feminist movement of the 1960s and 1970s, these rigid categories have begun to face challenge and subsequently have become more flexible; it is now apparent that once-stable identities have become questionable, changeable and optional.

There has been much research about gender identity, largely stemming from a binary viewpoint of what is means to be *feminine* and what it means to be *masculine*. In recent times, there has been a growing wealth of research

1 After a series of events demonstrating police discrimination to homosexual customers, June 28 (1969) saw angry and hostile retaliations by these customers aimed at police in protest against their harassment. At a popular gay bar in Greenwich Village – the Stonewall Inn – a riot broke out and as word spread throughout the city about the demonstration, others joined them in an attempt to experience civil rights on the basis of their sexuality. This riot lasted for days and as a result of the significance of this event, the LGBT movement was born.

 | DOI:10.1163/9789004380233_009

about gender identities that might not fit these binary categories and as a result, might fit somewhere on a *continuum*, or *spectrum* of gender identities. People who challenge these binary identities are often referred to as transgender. Identifying as transgender is not easy to explain and is often considered by many to be an umbrella term to acknowledge the varying degrees of gender expression that go beyond the traditional binary of "feminine" and "masculine." For example, Feinberg's expression of identity may cause confusion for some if such an umbrella concept did not exist; at the start of his seminal text, *Trans Liberation*, Feinberg's self-introduction is "I am a masculine, lesbian, female-to-male cross-dresser and transgenderist" (Feinberg 1998, 19). Feinberg comments that an identity such as this presents a pronoun challenge for those outside of this umbrella, but permits people to express identities beyond the confines of a gender binary.

Identifying as transgender is a subjective experience and although people may identify themselves as sharing a particular identity, it does not mean their experiences will be similar. Individual definitions of transgender do vary, but for the purposes of this chapter, I will be using Whittle and Turner's definition: "people whose appearance and behaviour does not conform to the cultural "norm" for the gender into which they were born" to encompass any gender-variant identity beyond the traditional gender binary identities (2008, 26).

The varying definitions and explanations of what it means to identify as transgender could result in a lack of definitive identification, which has possibly slowed the acceptance of the transgender identity in today's society. Although legislation in England and Wales states that the transgender identity is protected against any form of discrimination, without a true understanding of their own identity, transgender people are unlikely to be their true selves. While there has been progress in some areas of society in acknowledging and even celebrating this gender diversity, some institutions still remain which are progressing at a slower pace and one of these institutions is the education system.

Official numbers of transgender pupils attending a school cannot be ascertained. There are various reasons why it is difficult to establish data on existing transgender pupils: one is that the identity is so diverse that the way one pupil defines it could be different from another, making it difficult for schools to document their student demographics accurately. Whittle et al (2007) believe there is another reason why people who openly identifying as transgender cannot be quantified in education – bullying (Whittle, Turner and Al-Alami 2007). They found that transgender pupils who form their new identity whilst at school are highly likely to experience bullying and harassment. What is alarming here is that the bullying does not just come from other students, but teachers too. Whittle et al's survey of 874 transgender self-identified participants shows that 64% of transgender men and 44% of transgender women have experienced harassment, bullying, or both, from their teachers and other pupils. Whittle et al claim that these rates are much higher than for pupils who are gay or lesbian. A lack of awareness, education and skills potentially makes this an enormous problem for a transgender child and often, hiding their true identity is a way of coping and staying safe. Some transgender pupils feel there is no other option but to drop out of education. This is reinforced by Whittle et al's research demonstrating that although transgender pupils do return to their education at a later date – when they will be called "second chancers" – they have a high rate of school drop-out at level two. Coinciding with this, Adebowale et al reported that the current growth rate in the number of transgender people in England and Wales is 15% since the previous year, but these figures refer to adults (Adebowale, Devane and Kelsy 2014). Taking all this into account, children may not declare their true identity out of fear of the social pressures they might face, such as worrying what family members will think or how the school will react.

How is this Situation Complicated in Schools of a Religious Character?

Conducting research with transgender people who have either attended a school of a religious character – sometimes called a faith school – or those who educate transgender pupils attending such schools has shown that their general educational experience may have a negative impact on their transitioning. Whittle et al's (2007) transgender respondents reported that all they wanted was to be "normal" and be treated the same as their cisgender female and male peers, but the community they wanted to join had a disjointed perception of normality. Sometimes their view of normality came from their peer groups, their families and even the religions[2] they followed (Whittle, Turner and Al-Alami 2007).

Prior to the 1960s, religious education (R.E.) in schools was defined as religious instruction (R.I.), allowing schools to *train* their pupils into religious

2 It is necessary to draw attention to the fact that when I refer to schools of a religious character and their influence, I am referring to schools following Abrahamic religions, and in particular, Christianity. It appears that some other religions do acknowledge, and even celebrate transgender; but in Britain, the main religions influencing education are Abrahamic religions, particularly Christianity.

doctrines. If a child did not conform to the norms expected from that particular religion, the threat and punishment of eternal damnation was alluded to. At that time, religion was not questioned by society and conformity to religious laws was widespread. If a child did question her/his gender identity during this time, it would be perceived as the child stepping away from her/his "God-given" identity, and this was frowned upon.

The religious nature of schools has changed over time; the political and social movements of the 1960s and 1970s questioned the rigid approach of religion and subsequently had an effect on how religion was taught in schools. Instead of creating a society based on Christian values, R.I. was rebranded as R.E. and pupils, rather than being *told* how to live, were allowed and encouraged to develop their own views based on Christian content. Issues concerning morality and ethics became key parts of the R.E. curriculum, whose content now included issues of human rights and citizenship and the celebration of equality and diversity was endorsed. In today's society, faith schools based some of their religious teaching on Gospel values rather than scripture. But what impact has this had on the transgender child? And, what do schools mean by diversity?

All institutions in society have policies in place addressing equality and diversity. All, I suspect, contain phrases declaring their intentions, such as "…ensuring individuals or groups of individuals are treated fairly and equally and no less favourably, specific to their needs, including on grounds of race, gender, disability, religion or belief, sexual orientation and age," but no matter how well-intentioned the policy, if the people in institutions lack understanding, they are meaningless and inequality and discrimination will persist (University of Edinburgh 2016). My research shows is that although faith schools intend to be inclusive and accepting, and although their school encompasses Gospel values such as hope and justice, their lack of *understanding* of transgender is actually damaging.

The Catholic Education Service (CES) (2008), in its response to the introduction of the Sex and Relationships Education (SRE) review (2008),[3] claimed that when studying SRE in Catholic schools, children should be taught that, in his creation, God has made each and every person unique. Further to this, the CES guidance notes on the Equality Act (2010) recognise that the Act asserts that it is unlawful for anyone to use religion to discriminate against another person. This is a remarkable opportunity to accentuate inclusivity towards transgender pupils and to celebrate and demonstrate

3 The Sex and Relationships Education Review was implemented in schools in England and Wales as a way to 'prepare' children for sex education. Rather than focusing on sexual relationships, the review advised that children and young people should be taught the skills and values needed to progress throughout their lives.

that within a classroom, not everyone is the same and that differences do exist (cf. "Equality Act" 2010).

Nevertheless, for Wilchins (2004), crossing gender boundaries in education, and even more so in a faith school, is still a source of shame. She believes that people are socialised into gender templates and any characteristics that do not fit them are excluded. An example of this is provided by Mollenkott (2007), who states that some LGBT pupils who, when declaring a new identity, will still meet with resistance, particularly in faith schools whose doctrines are reinforced by scripture. Wilchins calls this "fascism of meaning" (Wilchins 2004, 38) where people and/or institutions force LGBT people to live in an impossible gender or face the consequences. One of Hunt and Jensen's (2007) respondents – a pupil attending a Catholic school – declared that if a person was not a natural heterosexual, they would: "… go to hell because the Bible condemns it … It's horrid, you just want to go and cry at some of the remarks made by teachers. It's just not fair" (Hunt and Jenson 2007, 10).

Nevertheless, in 2015 the then British Education Secretary, Nicky Morgan, quoted the Prime Minister, David Cameron, to justify instructing schools to prioritise established religions over atheism (Swinford 2015). This means that faith schools are allowed to use religious teachings to impress on pupils what is considered to be morally acceptable. Yet this poses a problem. Yip (2010) claims that by its very nature, religion is perceived as traditional; Abrahamic religions in particular allow little scope for any amendment in their dogma, and although some branches of these religions do accept change, progression and diversity, religion is still very much about social control.[4] If faith schools follow this line of thinking, then the acceptance of transgender pupils will not progress and these pupils are likely to remain isolated and victimised.

Several research texts claim that mainstream religions accept transgender identities, emphasising Christian claims such as:

> "We are created in the very likeness of God" (Genesis 1 v26);
>
> "There are varieties of acts, but it is the same God who activates all of them in everyone" (1 Corinthians 12 v6);
>
> "In God there is neither male or female, for you are all one in Jesus Christ" (Galatians 3 v28).

4 Both Yip (2010) and Hardy & Rafaelli (2003) comment on the nature of religion being conservative and unlikely to change.

The interpretations of these Biblical quotes can easily show God not being bound by gender and can support the argument that all types of gender and sexualities are made and accepted by God. With such philosophy in mind, surely this is a positive start for cementing the inclusivity of transgender pupils and of being well on the way to meeting Ofsted's new inspection assessment criteria of the Behaviour and Safety of Pupils.[5] However, as previously mentioned, faith schools today are more likely to be teaching Gospel values in their religious education rather than liturgy, meaning that children are less likely to hear such inclusive quotations.

Interview Data

Among all the themes arising from this research, the delivery of Gospel values in Christian education was one of the strongest. When I interviewed practitioners from a mixture of four faith schools, one Arch Diocesan Director for Church of England schools in the north of England and three Christian transgender participants aged 22, 59 and 70, Gospel values were strongly and positively commented on. All respondents believed that Gospel values were necessary for life, and in particular, that they should guide education and be evident and strong in the school's ethos. Gospel values include justice, respect, love and dignity of the person (The Gathering Church 2013). Using Gospel values in today's schools could be a substantial benefit to transgender children; learning about justice and respect, for example, are ways in which a school can work towards the inclusion of children who are different. Embracing these teachings in the Gospel values of love and dignity can help children to accept each other more readily. To demonstrate this, when asked how Gospel values impact on the inclusion of transgender pupils the Diocesan Director of Church of England Education in the North of England showed the overt nature of Gospel values in the school environment, saying:

> I go into lots of schools these days and I see the values up on the walls and a number of schools actually take a value for half of a term and they make it the focus of their assemblies and you know, work done in R.E ... and so on, erm, so you'd go in ... I was in a school on Tuesday ... and you know,

5 In inspections of schools in England and Wales, the inspection body – OfSTED – measures different components of schools with a view to grading their effectiveness. How well children behave and how safe they feel (Behaviour and Safety of Pupils) is one aspect of a school's inspection.

> the value for this half term is forgiveness, so you know, in huge letters behind the erm, you know, the podium in the hall ... that was there and then in the entrance area, they'd got a sort of, forgiveness tree and er, very colourful, but er, all the children in the school – it's a primary school – had written little examples which were leaves on the tree and that was there for this half term ... And next half term it may be ... it may be justice ... It may be peace, you know? ... Whatever it is, and even if you're not specifically talking about the maintenance of, you know, including transgender in with homophobic attitudes, and so on, you know for this illustration, even if you're not specifically talking about it, I would expect that the attitude is that everybody is a child of God and everybody is to be treated and valued as an individual in their own right to come through very, very strongly.[6]

The advantage of being taught Gospel values in Christian schools from the start of a child's education is that they become familiar and an integrated part of that child's learning and understanding of inclusivity. However, schools do not teach Gospel values in a statutory and standardised manner, thus posing a number of issues. For example, just because Gospel values were evident and dominant in these schools does not mean they would automatically affect all children positively, making them unequivocally welcoming of their transgender peers. Just as a child being baptised into a faith does not mean (s)he will practise that faith, so Gospel values learned in school may not be practised; they may be learned as a curriculum subject without understanding the *lived experience* of enacting them in daily life. The resulting possibility is that pupils may exclude the transgender child. The subjective and flexible manner in which Gospel values are taught means that their experience is variable, with the potential for some children to feel loved and accepted and some not having the opportunity of this. To place this in context, a transgender child in one UK faith school may have a very different experience of what it means when taught about love and respect compared another transgender child learning about love and respect in a faith school in a different location.

I conducted a number of interviews in the course of my research, but there are three in particular that stand out. First of all, I would like to comment on my interview with a 22-year-old FTM called "Danny." He possibly had the most extensive and wide ranging experience of what it was like to be transgender in a school of a religious character. He himself had attended such a school as a

6 Interview with the Diocesan Director of Church of England Education in the North of England.

primary school pupil; he was raised in a family where his father is a minister of a church attached to a school; he works in educational settings as a trainer of LGBT issues in schools; he currently works at a LGBT youth group; and is a student worker at a university chaplaincy. He found that faith schools varied in their acceptance of transgender pupils. Some found transitioning fairly easy, where the child was allowed to use her/his preferred name, pronouns and toilets, while in other faith schools, the child's true gender identity was not encouraged.

"Danny" also noticed that these schools seemed to place more emphasis on parents' wishes and interests than the child's. For example, it was the parents who gave permission – or not – for any LGBT training to go on in the school, and also whether the child could attend such training, regardless of what the child wanted or needed. This was also evident in the second and third interviews with two head teachers of faith schools.

One reason why conservative religious parents may oppose LGBT workshops in their child's school could be that they were raised in society at a time when religion was more static and conservative in terms of gender than it is in the twenty-first century. This means that they would have been raised with the religious belief that life has been pre-planned by God and to question this, or even change any part of it would be considered blasphemy. "Danny" commented that:

> ... I do volunteer work as well for [a LGBT youth group], and I go to schools to tell my personal story as part of their training, erm, and there's been two faith schools we've gone to ... er, both Catholic, [pause] yeah, both Catholic, erm, to train teachers, and both of the schools have said, "Oh well, maybe we should take up your training for pupils," but then there have been several members of staff who've said, "Oh well, we can't do that unless we, like well, tell their parents and allow them to get taken out of class, and most of them probably won't go to it anyway" ...

This could present difficulties for a transgender pupil. At a time when (s)he is uncertain and questioning her/his gender identity, having such lessons and workshops in school could help the child to come to terms with her/his gender identity. These workshops – even if they are with the child's cis peers – may prove to be a convenient substitute for the child having to ask questions and drawing attention to her/himself at a time when (s)he does not value such attention. More conservative religious parents who do not understand – or know about – their child's ambiguous gender identity may reject the opportunity for their child to learn about and accept diversity. This could be detrimental for the transgender child, leaving her/him with limited avenues to explore for guidance and reassurance regarding her/his true gender identity.

The second interview was with the head teacher of a Catholic secondary school in the North of England. He described his school as a Catholic organisation where *everybody* was included. Although he had a transgender child in his school, he did not have any explicit policies in place to address gender issues and staff had not been trained in the growing diversity of gender identities. Instead, he felt the sex education policy, general bullying policy and the school's homophobic policy was enough to cover any gender-related issues. He firmly believed that his school lived by, acted out and embraced Gospel values whereby diversity and inclusion were at the core of the school's ethos. I asked what he meant by that and he replied that the school has three Down's Syndrome children, as well as pupils with disabilities, and that as a head teacher, he conducts an assembly on homophobia. To his mind, this head teacher believed that because other vulnerable minority groups were evident in his school, the school could generically be viewed as inclusive. However, one can question this claim on the grounds that the school does not have policies relating to gender variance and there is no training for staff in these matters.

The head teacher followed this up with, "we like to celebrate difference in every way." I was curious about this, so I asked him, considering he had a transgender pupil in his school, if gender identities such as transgender were in fact celebrated. He stated that they were not but on reflection, he did accept that this group of people could be talked about more explicitly, but still he persisted that his school was inclusive and whenever I raised any issues to do with transgender, he immediately reverted back to either homosexuality or homophobia. I tried to explain that homosexuality was not the same thing as being transgender and was met with this response; "Most schools are at the point, at the moment … more explicit about homophobia … and homophobia is the most current stage where schools are at." He acknowledged that in schools of a religious character, understanding of gender identities was limited and commented quite flippantly that "… maybe transphobia will be the next big thing."

In addition to the teachings within a faith school, two of the head teachers commented on the effect the clergy attached to the school might have on transgender children. Both the Catholic Education Service and the Church of England share the view that the whole school has a responsibility to ensure children are educated into the Church's teachings and values, meaning that the local Church leader will often be seen in the school talking to staff and children and possibly leading some lessons, and in this instance, both schools have at least one local religious leader attached to them (Church of England 2015). However, in my interviews with the head teachers of a

Catholic secondary school and a Church of England secondary school, they acknowledged that some clergy were variable in their suitability for the children in their schools. For example, when I (I: Interviewer) asked the head teacher of a Catholic secondary school (HCS) about the role of the clergy in his school and the relationship they might have with their transgender pupil, he commented that there are a number of clergy attached to the school and depending on the issue, they deliberately select a priest who is suitable for the occasion:

HCS: Erm, most priests that I know are pastorally very sensitive to these issues.
I: Yeah. And do they know about this young [transgender child]?
HCS: No.
I: ... Is that for any reason ...?
HCS: Erm, yes. It would be respecting the lad's privacy really ... but I know in terms of discussion around gender and homosexuality ... that on a pastoral level ... most of our priests are very accepting of that situation and understand the Church's teaching ...
I: Yeah. You say "most." Are there some that perhaps aren't? (both HCS and I laugh)
HCS: They might not be ... They may not be the priests we'd feel comfortable with inviting in.
I: Ok. So you get to choose who you want to bring?
HCS: Yeah ... But as a secondary school, erm, some priests are more predisposed to understanding young people ... and when it comes to being with them and celebrating liturgy and so on ... there are certain clergy we'd go to first.

This could suggest that the Christian ethos of the school was more important than the school's agenda towards the child; if the school dictated to the clergy through the school's equality and diversity policy, training or provision how the child should be treated then it should not really matter which priest was involved with the child, but in this instance it clearly did. This amplified the need for *all* staff to be trained about transgender issues as the treatment of children in this school is clearly variable and could hold detrimental consequences for the transgender child.

A school's Christian ethos can be positive for a transgender child who might have experienced discrimination and exclusion in other parts of her/his life. Using Gospel values such as respect and love may be one of the reasons why a transgender child enrols at such an institution. This was highlighted by the head teacher at a Catholic secondary school, who commented that vulnerable pupils often *choose* to enrol at this school because of the reputation of being inclusive:

> Not from a Catholic background at all. Erm, approached me and our school to say, erm, to describe what their lad was like, and I said, "absolutely no problem," you know? ... "The values here will support you and your boy ... in terms of, you know, becoming who he was meant to be."... So it was an active choice for us, in terms of what they could see in terms of our values ... The, [short pause] the Catholic Church very much respects the rights of the primary educators and you know, whenever we've had anyone come to us with a difference, our response was, "what do you need? How can we help?", not, "this is what we'll do."

The third interview was with a head teacher of a Church of England secondary school who had considerable experience as a head teacher and a leader of a Church of England Church. He also commented, just like "Danny," that parents' wishes were held in more esteem than children's and made it clear that the school's religious teachings were designed so as not to upset the parents. He claimed that their syllabus was designed to ensure "we aren't doing things to offend Christian parents." So, if being transgender violated any Christian teachings in *any* way, it was not acknowledged or taught. By his own admission, he had very limited transgender knowledge, let alone experience of transgender pupils in his school. He was very keen to let me know that he had had pupils who had questioned their sexuality and that they were treated in a non-judgemental and "normal" way. However, like other schools, none of their equality, diversity and bullying policies includes transgender and gender-related issues. It is *assumed* that being transgender is a feature of sexuality, and it is not. A transgender person *does* have a sexuality, but that is in addition to her/his gender identity, in the same way as a child who does not question her/his gender identity.

In comparison to Gospel values being explicitly demonstrated in the school's physical environment, the actual practice of them became more questionable in the interview with this head teacher. For example, I asked him how a transgender child could be included into the Christian ethos of this school and he replied:

> ... Erm, so, it's difficult to say in that ... we don't have any one in that position, but it is a danger because we're not actively looking and aware, that we don't know if we have anyone in that position.

It could be argued that most, if not all schools do not *actively* look for pupils who are different and/or vulnerable. In most cases, other institutions who have had dealings with a vulnerable child will pass on the necessary information to the school concerned in preparation for their time there. If this is not done, the necessary provision for their inclusion will not be made. However, "not actively looking" for such children may also be interpreted to mean that unless a transgender child is directly brought to the attention of the school – and in most cases, as previously seen, this is unlikely – the school does not actively or formally make provision for the child; this is very much like the solipsistic view that if the problem does not exist it cannot be dealt with. This shows that even though Gospel values demonstrate love and acceptance, in this instance, religious values actually become a barrier for inclusivity. As all head teachers have to abide by relevant equality legislation, there is an additional problem in faith schools as Christian ideologies in education have given rise to a range of views. For example, some of these head teachers were more liberal in their religious practices than others – the head teacher of the Catholic secondary school was a more liberal practitioner than the head teacher of the Church of England secondary school. However, this range of Christian expression also exists amongst pupils. All of this makes the inclusion of transgender pupils in faith schools variable.

In addition, although talking about homosexuality, the Head teacher of a Church of England secondary school – himself a practising Christian – had difficulty understanding why a person would change what was God-given:

> … I struggle with the whole homosexuality thing, I do and I'm not totally with it, in terms of I've not got the clearest of, erm, I'm not totally sure if it's a good idea to be totally clear on it anyway …

This head teacher, like many other people when they are not fully aware of something and "backed into a corner" reverted back to type; his habits and previously held values came to the forefront of his behaviour. This head teacher was in his late 50s and had been a Christian all his life. Being raised in a conservative Christian doctrine with an unreserved acceptance of liturgy may lead him to find changes in a person's identity incomprehensible. Such entrenched ways become an additional problem because he is a head teacher and responsible for guiding young people in their way in the world to make their own self-discoveries. Comments and behaviour such as these may be obstacles for the child being accepted in society, and particularly within institutions associated with religion. This head teacher is also an executive head teacher and, due to his outstanding leadership, has been placed in charge of three separate underperforming schools to raise their standards. However, no matter what dynamic and inclusive policies may be in place in these schools, if the practitioners are not prepared and knowledgeable on vulnerable groups, such as transgender children and their need for inclusivity, then their treatment and behaviour towards these children becomes unclear and the head teacher's strong leadership comes into question.

It is clear from some of the comments mentioned in my interviews that some faith schools are not fully prepared for inclusivity towards transgender children. This could be explained by their evolutionary approach to change. Thatcher (1999) believed that changes in education are usually influenced by changes in wider society, but the conservative nature of religion frequently means that it does not handle change well; if change does happen in faith schools, this usually takes place after secular schools. An example of this arose in May 2014 when the Archbishop of Canterbury, Justin Welby, reported his concerns about the number of instances of *homophobic* bullying that occurred on young people and its impact. This concern led to the Church of England publishing a document specifically for Church of England schools in 2017 entitled *Valuing All God's Children – Guidance for Church of England Schools on Challenging Homophobic, Biphobic and Transphobic Bullying* (Church of England 2017). One reason these schools may struggle to be inclusive is because their change and acceptance is *slow* – these schools are just coming to terms with homosexuality, and transgender identity appears not to be something they are prepared for yet. Moreover, no document of this size or status has been commissioned about transgender pupils in faith schools. As with other groups in history experiencing discrimination, such as women and homosexuals, societal acceptance has been slow and gradual: the Church of England's recent advice on homophobic bullying is a case in point. In today's society, homosexuality has now begun to be more acceptable and visible, but it has not been easy. It appears that a similar pattern is now emerging with the acceptance and inclusion of transgender people. It could be argued that the visibility and increasing acceptance of homosexuality may have paved the way for people who identify as transgender to come out. However, it must also be argued that such an evolutionary approach is dangerous in schools. Today's society has moved on significantly and with the progressive contribution of social media to daily life, children are able to see examples of people from different backgrounds and need educating about such social groups. An example is Johanna Schorn's research into how transgender people are represented in the media (2014). Given that young people in contemporary society are actively involved with media representations, false or discriminatory images can contribute to their socialisation, and if not corrected through institutions such as schools, this ignorance can "perpetuate the false and damaging stereotype" (Schorn 2014) of transgender people.

It may seem that any training offered to faith schools on transgender issues may prove difficult to pin down in the immediate future. Schools such as these have additional personal ideologies to contend with in their daily running; very often, challenging such ideologies can meet with resistance and offence. As such schools operate on a religious ideology that does not alter at the same pace as wider society, it might be that the best solution in the immediate future is to incorporate examples of transgender people when teaching about Gospel values, such as respect and love, and to do this from the moment a child begins education. The leaders in the schools must also be proactive in ensuring what they need to know and do to include transgender pupils in their school without compromising its religious ethos. As the number of Christian churches advertising themselves as fully inclusive is growing in England, (for example, Metropolitan Community Churches), it may be useful for a relationship to be established between the Church and the school – here, the active practice of inclusion means people are able to practise Christianity without fear of reprisal. This could be a perfect opportunity for schools of a religious character to learn about true inclusion without compromising their Christian ethos.

Conclusions

Ellis and High (2004, 213–25) emphatically state that one reason why faith schools are not as inclusive as they believe is that teachers are ill-equipped to deal with any child who is uncertain about her/his gender and/or sexuality and, as a result, shy away from the issue. In all my interviews with head teachers of faith schools, none said they had invited training for themselves or their staff regarding gender identity issues – there had been some training on sexuality, but none on gender. Their lack of conviction and confidence in this matter is often picked up by children through the hidden curriculum. Even though teachers may not overtly display their agitation when confronted with a transgender child, the fact that they do not fully understand the uncertainty these children face regarding their identity may be relayed to the child or their peers.

This was reinforced by "Danny's" remarks regarding an INSET training day he delivered at a school, where a teacher was asked how he would react if there were a transgender person in his class. His response was he "would tell them to stop being ridiculous ... they couldn't be a girl ... because they had boys' bits."

Comments such as these give the impression of a lack of understanding that a person's gender identity could in fact be altered based on the belief that the person has been born into the wrong body. Comments such as these immediately present barriers to a transgender child's inclusion in this religious school, thus contradicting the CES's (2008) comments about children being taught that God has created each person unique.

References

"About Us." 2015. *Catholic Directory*. http://www.catholicdirectory.org/aboutus.asp.

Adebowale, Victor, Ciaran Devane and Tim Kelsy. 2014. "NHS England Review of NHS Citizen and the NHS Citizens Assembly at the AGM." *NHS England*. https://www.england.nhs.uk/wp-content/uploads/2014/10/item5-board-1114.pdf.

Althaus-Reid, Marcella and Lisa Isherwood. 2009. *Trans/Formations*. London: SCM Press.

Blair, Tony. 2014. "University Gender Identity Survey Offers a Mind Boggling 57 Different Options but None Are Simply Male or Female." *The Daily Telegraph*, 22 April. http://www.dailytelegraph.com.au/news/nsw/university-gender-identity-survey-offers-a-mind-boggling-57-different-options-but-none-are-simply-male-or-female/story-fni0cx12-1226892403442.

Church of England. 2017. *Valuing All God's Children: Guidance for Church of England Schools on Challenging Homophobic, Biphobic and Transphobic Bullying*. https://www.churchofengland.org/sites/default/files/2017-11/Valuing%20All%20God%27s%20Children%27s%20Report_0.pdf.

Ellis, Viv and Sue High. 2004. "Something to Tell You: Gay, Lesbian or Bisexual Young People's Experiences of Secondary Schooling." *British Educational Research Journal* 30 (2): 213–25.

"Equality Act 2010." 2010. *The Stationary Office Limited*. http://www.legislation.gov.uk/ukpga/2010/15/contents.

"Equality and Diversity." *The University of Edinburgh*. http://www.ed.ac.uk/equality-diversity/about/equality-diversity.

Feinberg, Leslie. 1998. *Trans Liberation – Beyond Pink or Blue*. Boston: Beacon Press.

Guasp, April. 2012. *The School Report: The Experiences of Young Gay People in Britain's Schools in 2012*. Stonewall. http://www.stonewall.org.uk/documents/school_report.pdf.

Hardy, Sam and Marcela Raffaelli. 2003. "Adolescent Religiosity & Sexuality: An Investigation of Reciprocal Influences." *Journal of Adolescence* 26: 731–39.

Herman, Joanne. 2009. *Transgender Explained for Those Who Are Not*. Indiana: Authorhouse.

McCarthy, Richard. 2009. "Facilitating Dialogue on Religion and Sexuality Using a Descriptive Approach." *New Directions for Student Services* 125. http://www3.interscience.wiley.com/browse/?type=JOURNAL.

"Ministerial Education and Development." *The Church of England*. https://www.churchofengland.org/clergy-office-holders/ministry/ministerial-education-and-development.aspx.

Mollenkott, Virginia. 2007. *Omnigender: A Trans-Religious Approach*. Cleveland: OH: Pilgrim Press.

"Review of Sex and Relationship Education (SRE) in Schools." 2013. *External Steering Group*. http://webarchive.nationalarchives.gov.uk/20130401151715/http://www.education.gov.uk/publications/eOrderingDownload/SRE-Review-2008.pdf.

"School Inspection Handbook." *Ofsted*. https://www.gov.uk/government/uploads/system/uploads/attachment_data/file/391531/School_inspection_handbook.pdf.

Schorn, Johanne. 2014. "Taking the 'Sex' Out of Transsexual: Representations of Trans Identities in Popular Media." Unpublished Paper presented at the GL4 conference, Mansfield College, Oxford, UK, 24–26 September.

Swinford, Steven. 2015. "Schools must teach children that Britain is a Christian country." *The Telegraph*, 27 December. https://www.telegraph.co.uk/news/religion/12070607/Schools-must-teach-children-that-Britain-is-a-Christian-country.html.

Thatcher, Adrian. 1999. *Spirituality and the Curriculum*. New York: Cassell.

"Who We Are: The Gospel & Our Core Values." *The Gathering Church*. http://www.thegatheringchurch.com/sermon-series/who-we-are/.

Whittle, Stephen, Lewis Turner and Maryam Al-Alami. 2007. "Engendered Penalties: Transgender and Transsexual People's Experiences of Inequality and Discrimination." *The Inequalities Review*. https://www.west-info.eu/transgender-lgbt-homosexuality-uk-sexual-identity/the-equalities-review/.

Whittle, Stephen and Lewis Turner. 2008. "Sex Changes? Paradigm Shifts in 'Sex' and 'Gender' Following Gender Recognition Act?" *Sociological Research Online* 12 (1). http://www.socresonline.org.uk/12/1/whittle.html. DOI: 10.5153/sro.1511.

Wilchins, Riki. 2004. *Queer Theory, Gender Theory*. Los Angeles: Alyso.

Yip, Andrew. 2010. "Special Feature: Sexuality and Religion/Spirituality." *Sexualities* 13: 667–670.

This chapter in no way attempts to vilify schools of a religious character. It does appear that on the whole, their intentions of living out Gospel values are honourable and well-meant, but their experience, training and knowledge is evidently lacking.

CHAPTER 8

Merging Queer Lines and Straight Ties: Love in Indonesian Transgender Family Intimacies

Sylvia Tidey

What Is Love?

We can think of love as a moral experience that is "singular and particular and must be sustained by means of a fidelity to the life trajectory established by its founding evental demand" (2013, 201). In this chapter I want to describe one such moral experience that stands out in its singularity and particularity. I want to address the romantic relationship between an Indonesian transgender woman (waria), Esperanza, and her *gay* boyfriend, Rai. In particular, I will focus on how expectations of and responsibilities to family impact the possibility of fidelity to the shared life trajectory Esperanza and Rai have embarked on. In short, in this chapter I ask how the queer lines of nonheteronormative romantic relationships relate to the straight line of heteronormativity in Indonesia.

This chapter is based on ten months of fieldwork I conducted in 2013 in Bali, Indonesia. This fieldwork forms part of a larger research project on how waria manage, not just to survive or live, but, rather, to live happily in the shadow of a life-threatening illness that disproportionally affects waria.[1] Politically, I am interested in what kinds of lives, or what kinds of possibilities for being otherwise (Povinelli 2011), are available for those who seem to live outside of what counts as an Indonesian heteronormative "normal". Bracketing – though not dismissing – for the time being issues such as stigmatization, discrimination, violence, and suffering, I wish to study waria life as lived experience, as being-in-the-world, and pay particular attention to hopes, dreams, desires, and fantasy. I hoped to find ways of living that challenged hegemonic conceptions of the good life, and most notably its espousal of marriage and reproduction. Perhaps, in an extreme sense, I was hoping to find a radical refusal of the framing

1 According to the Indonesian AIDS mailing list (AIDS-INA – aids-ina.org) approximately 14% of waria nationwide are infected with HIV. Although waria make up a relatively small part of all Indonesians infected with HIV, they are, after injecting drug users, the key population that is most affected by HIV.

 | DOI:10.1163/9789004380233_010

of the political field in terms of what Lee Edelman calls reproductive futurism, meaning "terms that impose an ideological limit on political discourse as such, preserving in the process the absolute privilege of heteronormativity by rendering unthinkable, by casting outside the political domain, the possibility of a queer resistance to this organizing principle of communal relations" (2004, 2). Put differently, I hoped to find a kind of queer ethics outside of the dictates of kinship and reproduction. What I found, however, was the pull of the heteronormative, a tenacity of what waria described to me as the "normal" (*normal*). This surprised me somewhat because most of the people I spoke with – including waria themselves – often referred to waria as "not normal" (*tidak normal*). Nevertheless, the "normal" figures prominently in living happily – even in the lives of those who may be considered to lead what Judith Butler has called "unlivable" lives (2004, xv).

With this in mind, I now turn to how this concept of the "normal" permeates and informs the romantic ties that waria maintain and create. I address configurations of transgender, kinship, and love in the non-West by discussing the often-fraught relationships between waria and their relatives. Popular themes that have emerged in relation to transgender kinship configurations centre on topics such as same-sex marriages and the construction of non-biological new kinship formations.[2] Although psychological literature points to the importance of the influence of "old" kinship formations on transgender well-being, not much ethnographic attention has been paid to the unfolding of transgender lives in relation to their embeddedness in heteronormative kinship networks – in particular from viewpoints outside psychology and the West.[3] To address this lacuna, I want to provide an account of the everyday lived romantic experiences of transgender women in the non-West by addressing the precarious waria-family relationships in Indonesia and the role the "normal" plays in their maintenance. As such, this chapter provides a complementary contemporary contrast to Kelly Gardiner's chapter on performances of gender and experiences of queer love in seventeenth century Paris.

My methodological and analytical approaches draw on interpretive phenomenology. As Desjarlais and Throop state, "a central goal of phenomenological description is to destabilize those unexamined assumptions that organize our preprereflective engagements with reality" (2011, 87–102). It favors a "bracketing" of assumptions and prioritises attending to lived experience.

2 See, for example, William L. Leap (2004); Kath Weston (1997 [1991]); Timothy J. Biblarz and Evren Sayci (2010).

3 See, for example, Stephen Erich et al. (2008); Rupert Raj (2008); Robert Wallace and Hershel Russell (2013).

Rather than analyzing waria negotiations of the "normal" in terms of my understandings of gender and love, I therefore, aim to attend to the experiential dimension of such negotiations to challenge these understandings. This chapter is based on over thirty formal interviews and countless informal conversations I had with waria in Bali, Yogyakarta, and Jakarta during 2013. In particular, I will draw on the interviews, conversations, and participant observation I conducted with a dozen or so waria who gather daily around a housing project (*kos-kosan*) adjacent to a beauty salon in South Denpasar, Bali.[4]

Waria, the *Normal* and Straight Lines

As anyone who has spent any time in Indonesia can no doubt confirm, waria are a far more visible part of society than transgender women are, for instance, in Europe or the United States (perhaps with the exception of Hawai'i). The term waria is a combination of the words *wanita* (woman) and *pria* (man). It was coined in the early eighties by the then minister of Religious Affairs after the Indonesian council of Ulamas objected to the term "wadam", a combination of the words "Adam" and *wanita* that had been in use since the late sixties to describe transgender women (Oetomo 1996, 262). Not all Indonesians know the term waria. Far more common terms Indonesians use to refer to waria in everyday speech are *banci*, somewhat equivalent to the word "sissy", and its ruder form *bencong*. Most Indonesians use these words as umbrella terms to describe gay men (*gay*), effeminate men, and transgender men, whereas the *gay* Indonesians and waria I met tend to refer to themselves using the more specific terms of *gay* and waria.

Waria, and other non-normatively gendered Indonesian subjects, have become increasingly visible in Indonesian public discourse in recent years. The swift transition to democracy Indonesia underwent since the 1998 fall of Suharto's New Order regime has fueled transgender visibility in two, conflicting, ways. On the one hand, an influx of international funds has facilitated a scaling up, interconnecting, and professionalisation of what until then had been a dispersed collection of grass-roots, community-based, LGBT organisations (cf. Blackwood 2008; Hadiwinata 2002). Freedoms of speech and protest, furthermore, have allowed for an articulation of rights and recognition in the public sphere in ways previously unimaginable. On the other hand, non-heteronormatively gendered citizens have been at the center of post-Suharto

4 In order to protect the privacy and anonymity of my interlocutors, I use names other than the ones they use with their waria friends or their family members.

moral anxieties. In recent years, several conservative Islamic organizations have spoken out against transgender women, while the hardliner Islamic Defenders Front (FPI) attacked various transgender and LGBT meetings.[5] The government has also revised its Penal Code to put restrictions on homosexual sexual intercourse (Blackwood 2007).

This is not to say that transgender women, or waria as they are now commonly known, were an obscure and unknown part of Indonesian society before their current public visibility. Tom Boellstorff notes that transgender women, in some form, were already noted in Batavia (colonial Jakarta, the capital of Indonesia) in the 1830s; in Surabaya in the 1850s; and in Bali in the 1930s (2004, 163–165). Older transgender women I spoke with told me how in their youth in 1940s Java and 1970s Papua neighbors and family members would already call them by the terms *banci*, which as mentioned is a word still used for effeminate men, or *wadam*, an amalgam of *wanita* (woman) and "Adam". Transgender women have thus occupied recognizable subject positions throughout the Indonesian archipelago for a long time. However, the recent deployment of waria in government policies, media, and non-governmental organizations designates a fixity to this subject position that I found to be at odds with the everyday experiences, and in particular with futural imaginings, of many actual waria.

Although it is not uncommon in Indonesia to encounter waria, waria are not considered "normal". It is this "normal", or *normal* in Indonesian, that I want to address here. The Indonesian *normal* is not unlike the English word "normal" but, nevertheless, comes with some particular heteronormative connotations with regards to expected life trajectories that deserve specific attention.[6] The *normal* can describe any common, expected way of being in the world, while its opposite *tidak normal* (not normal) describes any digression from the everyday, the common, and the expected. To act in a way that is *normal* means to act properly in the way one is expected to. Nevertheless, the *normal* pertains in particular to the heteronormative moral obligation to get married heterosexually and to reproduce. The expectation that every Indonesian should at some point get married and have children constitutes a "triple compulsion of religion, tradition, and nation" (Boellstorff 2005, 109). Given this particular frame of what counts as *normal*, old spinsters, single

---

5 See, for instance, "Islam Tak Kenal Jenis Kelamin Waria" [Islam Does Not Know the Sex Waria] (2010); "Muhammadiyah: Waria dan Homoseksual Berlawanan dengan HAM" [Muhammadiyah: Waria and Homosexuals Are at Odds with Human Rights] (2010); Jamison Liang, "Homophobia on the Rise" (2010).

6 See also Boellstorff (2004); Boellstorff (2005); Richard Stephen Howard (1996).

parents with children, divorcées, and childless married couples (as I can personally attest) are far less *normal* than, for instance, abusive parents or unfaithful husbands (Brenner 1995, 35). In this context it is not surprising that not only *normal* Indonesians but also waria themselves would routinely describe waria to me as *tidak normal*.

In this sense, I would suggest, the Indonesian *normal* is not unlike the "straight line" that Sara Ahmed addresses in *Queer Phenomenology: Orientations, Objects, Others*, in which she aims to bring phenomenology into dialogue with queer studies (2006). Similar to the Indonesian *normal*, the straight line is made up of not merely gender identification and sexual orientation, but also of marriage, family, and reproduction. What makes Ahmed's conception of the straight line particularly helpful in my attempt to highlight the role of temporality in transgender living is the foregrounding of the phenomenological question of orientation. Orientation has been a central means for phenomenologists to get at an understanding of what it is like to be in the world as embodied beings, whether through a Husserlian intentionality (Husserl 2002 [1931]) or a Heideggerian "Being-toward" (Heidegger 2008 [1962]). Orientation thus has an aspect of "towardness" or directionality, which can have a spatial connotation as an orientation toward objects and others, or, as I suggest in this chapter, a temporal connotation as an orientation toward futures.

Before taking this idea of orientation to entail the casual possibility to orient ourselves in any way we would like, Ahmed cautions us that "the body gets directed in some ways more than others" and that in many ways we tend to follow the line that is followed by others (2006, 15). Being oriented in a certain way, toward the straight line, is neither accidental nor "natural". To stick with the example of the straight line of the Indonesian heteronormative *normal*, much long-term work and effort in institutional, discursive, and intersubjective familial realms lies behind the commonsensical and obvious appearance of what I call the straight line of the *normal*. For example, a particular notion of the heteronormative nuclear family, known as the "family principle" (*azas kekeluargaan*) has been a fundamental part of Indonesianness since the very conception of the Indonesian nationalist project in the early 20th century.[7] It has become so engrained in everyday modern Indonesian society that "the traditional family is now merely customary while the Indonesian family is an effect of the nation" (Siegel 1998, 87). What counts as properly gendered, *normal*, citizenship reverberates in education, the

7 See David Bourchier (1997); Suzanne A. Brenner (1998); Mary Steedly (2013, 203–207).

military, civil service, and the media.[8] Indonesians are thus born into a world already oriented in such a way that makes following the straight line of the *normal* commonsensical and not requiring reflection.

Besides commonsensical, everyday corrections toward the straight line of the *normal*, waria receive disapproval from their digression from the *normal* in many other ways. Certain Indonesian religious organizations have issued fatwas on waria (Safitri 2013, 98–99); venues for prayer refuse to allow waria in; murders of waria go uninvestigated. Furthermore, in their everyday moving through space and interacting with others waria face constant insults, name-calling, mocking, and even physical violence. In short, the world waria are born into and face is one that continuously reinforces an orientation toward the straight line of the Indonesian *normal* in various ways that are both unreflective and deliberate.

Such worlds can be unsettling and disorienting to those of us who, like many waria, feel uncomfortable on the straight line. Ahmed states that moments of disorientation are vital and might provide opportunities to reorient and ground oneself again (2006, 157). Feelings of disorientation stemming from compulsive heterosexuality, heteronormativity, or the Indonesian *normal* might provide an opportunity to create queer lines (queer in the sense of "oblique"), lines that go in a new direction and challenge the status quo. These moments of queer reorientation hold the promise and possibility for creating new kinship formations or, perhaps, of challenging "reproductive futurism" (Edelman 2004) altogether. But for many of my waria interlocutors, any kind of queer reorienting is always done without veering off too far from the *normal*. Despite failing to be proper *normal* children, moral subjects, and citizens, instead of opting out of their kinship ties altogether, some waria and their parents manage to rework the terms that stipulate what counts as proper kinship – what counts as *normal*. Therefore, I ask how the "straight lines" of the Indonesian heteronormative *normal* merge with the "queer lines" of waria desire and family intimacies.

Bodywork and Temporality

One way in which straight and queer lines merge in waria life trajectories is in what some waria imagine to be the temporary character of their waria lives. Early on in my fieldwork, and contrary to what I expected, I discovered that it was a misconception to think that waria necessarily always intended to *be* waria for the rest of their lives. Many waria I met (but by no means all) told me

8 See Suzanne Brenner (1999, 13–37); Saya S. Shiraishi (1997); Julia I. Suryakusuma (1996).

how they planned to "become normal again" (*jadi normal lagi*) at some point in the future. For instance, Delilah, a waria in her early twenties, who participated in waria beauty pageants, regularly showed off her acquired feminine shapes, and often exchanged kisses with her boyfriend for all to see, told me: "When I am thirty, I will become normal again. Yeah, I just want to go home, find a girl to marry, and have children. I'll just become a normal man again" (*jadi laki-laki normal lagi*). She smiled at my surprise over this statement and said that this, meaning her waria life, was fine for now, but that when she'd turn thirty she would be bored with this life and would want to go home. Claudia, a waria outreach worker from a local LGBT HIV prevention and care organization, similarly put a time limitation on her life as a waria. On several occasions she told me that when she would turn forty she would cut off her hair, leave her high-heeled shoes behind, move out of the room she rented by herself, and move back into her parental home to be with her family. She planned to give up sex work and, instead, make money selling small foodstuffs and household necessities. She referred to this either as "becoming normal again" or as "becoming gay again" (*jadi normal lagi; jadi gay lagi*) because she felt more comfortable living at home when she could as least visibly pass as a *normal* man.

Many other waria talked in similar terms of their imagined future life trajectories: after a certain age they wanted to go home (*pulang*), find a wife and have a few children. For many waria I came to know during my fieldwork, their becoming waria was enacted as a temporary suspension of the normal, such that a return to the Indonesian heternormative *normal*, or the straight line, remained an ever-present possibility. This construction of gender as a temporary suspension of the *normal* stands in stark contrast with, for example, much biomedical work that assumes an essence or temporal stability at the heart of gender and that in many places still underlies eligibility for gender reassignment surgery.[9] Yet, for waria, becoming waria never closes off into being waria but, rather, always remains a process of becoming that could, at some point, shift into a process of becoming *normal* again.

Bodywork forms a particularly salient experiential realm of waria life in which this potential openness to a future *normal* comes to the fore. Bodywork and maintenance plays a significant role in the everyday lives of waria. Nevertheless, the kinds of bodywork and maintenance most waria engage in leave open the possibility of a future return to the straight line of the Indonesian *normal*. Idrus and Takeo note that waria "do not experience their bodies as fixed biological entities, but as 'projects' they can manipulate with pharmaceutical

9 See, for instance. David O. Cauldwell (2006); Richard von Krafft-Ebing (2006); Heino F.L. Meyer-Bahlburg (2010).

products and cosmetics" (2010, 796). However, few of these pharmaceutical products and cosmetics have permanent effects. Based on their work in the Eastern Indonesian city of Makassar, Idrus et al describe in great detail the kinds of pharmaceuticals and cosmetics waria use to cultivate their bodies around particular ideals of feminine body shape and white skin. In order to decrease muscle tone and, more importantly, to grow breast tissue, Makassarese waria experiment with a variety of oral and injected contraceptive hormones. They furthermore use a wide range of creams, exfoliating products, and cosmetic covering products – often in combination with each other – to whiten their skins (Idrus and Takeo 2010, 796).

Like the waria in Makassar Idrus and Takeo describe, the Balinese waria I worked with similarly prize having a white skin and use a wide variety of creams, facials, masks and even Vitamin C injections to achieve this. They also combine oral and injected contraceptive hormones to grow breast tissue and acquire an overall softer, more feminine body shape. Unlike the waria they describe, who mostly want to cultivate breasts, the waria in Bali also want shapely buttocks like the ones Jennifer Lopez and Beyoncé, American pop stars whose posters hang in almost every waria bedroom, possess. In order to get a more "guitar-like shape", as they put it, they sew padding into their skirts, pants, and leggings or wear pre-made padded underpants. They also desire shiny, long, straight hair and spend significant amounts of time and money on treating their hair with shampoos, hair masks, sprays, and other beauty products. Some waria grow out their own hair, whereas others rely on regular hair extensions to obtain the desired length. Bodywork and maintenance thus play a significant role in the everyday lives of waria.

Nevertheless, the kinds of bodywork and maintenance many of them engage in leave open the possibility of a future return to the straight line of the Indonesian *normal.* As Claudia said of her breasts while discussing hormone injections with me: "they disappear, they disappear by themselves. If you have an operation they can't disappear, with an injection they can. No injection means they won't get bigger, they'll get back to normal (*biasa*). This is how it goes, from big to small". Keeping in mind Claudia's desire eventually to move back into her parental home, the fact that the effects of the contraceptive hormones she is injected with are temporary matters to her. If we recall, Claudia thinks that in order to move back home she should at least be able to pass visibly as a *normal* (or gay) man. Her breasts should therefore be able to go, as she puts it, "from big to small". These examples of bodywork with temporary effects thus support the construction of waria life as a temporary suspension of the *normal,* after which the queer line waria traverse for a while merges with the straight line of the Indonesian heteronormative *normal* again. I now want to consider how this plays out in configurations of transgender, kinship and love. If love entails fidelity to a trajectory one embarks on, but waria trajectories are imaged to be temporary, can a love between lovers coexist with a love for family?

Esperanza and Rai

Esperanza and Rai, a young couple consisting of a waria and a *gay* man, seemed to pose an exception to the incompatibility of queer lines with straight ones, or the non-commensurability of kinship bonds with waria romantic relationships. As mentioned earlier, when I started my fieldwork I was interested in seeing if or to what extent waria lives in some way could offer digressions from the straight line or could hold possibilities for an "otherwise" – in whatever shape or form (cf. Povinelli 2011). During the first stage of my fieldwork period, potential possibilities for being otherwise or for veering away from the straight line of the *normal* appeared to coalesce around Esperanza, a waria I had not yet met but whom other waria talked about frequently.

Esperanza's unusual family background already suggested a digression from the Indonesian heteronormative *normal*. Weeks before I ever met Esperanza, Claudia, a close waria friend of Esperanza, took me to the house where Esperanza's mother lived, along with two of Esperanza's unmarried siblings as well as a married sister, her husband, and children. The reason Claudia took me there was because she wanted to convince Esperanza's younger sibling, Desi, to start ARV medication for an HIV infection that had already advanced into AIDS. Desi, like Esperanza, was a waria and often sold sex on the streets at night. Furthermore, as I learned during our visit, Esperanza also had a younger *tomboi* sister.[10] Out of six children, so Claudia said, three were "not normal".

Besides coming from a seemingly non-gender conforming family, Esperanza's romantic situation also seemed to veer away from the straight line of heteronormativity. Esperanza was in a relationship with Rai, a former waria sex worker who used to go by the name of Amanda but who, as he said, "became a man again" after he and Esperanza met and fell in love. By "man" he meant a homosexual man, a *gay*.[11] When I met them they shared a small but relatively comfortable house with their two little Pomeranian dogs. Many waria live with

10 For a discussion on how positioning of Indonesian *tomboi* in local gender regimes and how *tomboi* differ from the English term "tomboy", see Blackwood (2008, 483).

11 For an elaboration of the various local, national, and global layers that converge in the Indonesian gay subject position, see Boellstorff (2005).

boyfriends, whom they refer to as "husbands", and in this sense Esperanza and Rai's relationship is unremarkable. However, whereas most waria-boyfriend relationships centered around active waria desire for the young, sexy, teen bodies of the young heterosexual men (*brondong*) they court and these men's passive acceptance of the favours (sexual or monetary) and gifts, such as food, clothes, and other consumer items that waria bestow upon them, the relationship Esperanza and Rai maintained centred around something else. As Rai said during an interview I had with them,

> As for me and Esperanza, I take responsibility for this. I am no longer on the streets, not like before, I only hang out now. I don't need to hurt Esperanza. This is my commitment (*komitmen*). I don't have to bother with those, those who judge us even though they are worse than I am. Those who have a wife but are still on the streets or those who have a wife and still have a *brondong*. As for me and Esperanza, we have a commitment. That is what I guard/preserve. (Rai, interview with author 2013)

In short, Esperanza and Rai, a self-identified waria and a former waria turned gay man, focused on mutual "responsibility/accountability" and "commitment" to ground their relationship, thereby challenging the kind of gendered imbalance that characterises both "normal" relationships of the straight line and the relationships waria tend to have with their *brondong*.

As I described in the previous section, most waria engage in types of bodywork and maintenance with temporary effects, and which thus hold open a future "becoming *normal* again". The bodywork and maintenance Esperanza engaged in, however, reflected her commitment to a more permanent orienting away from *normal* masculinity. Besides engaging in the kinds of bodywork with temporary effects as described in the previous section, Esperanza was the only waria I met during my fieldwork who had undergone bodywork with permanent effects. In early 2013 she underwent breast enhancement surgery in a clinic in Thailand during a three-day layover from Germany where she worked as a sex worker. Unlike the breast tissue that other waria built up with their regular regimen of oral and injected contraceptive hormones, Esperanza's breasts would not disappear if she stopped her bodywork and maintenance routines. She also started silicone injections in her hips, butt, and thighs in order to achieve an hourglass shape similar to that of her idol, Beyoncé. Esperanza thus seemed resolved to disassociate herself from the Indonesian heteronormative *normal* permanently.

Yet, particular conceptions of the *normal*, and in particular a continuation of existing familial ties, figure prominently in Esperanza's present and in her imagined future, which surprised me given the unorthodox composition of her family. This, for instance, came to the fore in an interview I had with Esperanza, during which she described the way in which she and her mother navigate the topic of her breast enhancement surgery. Esperanza intended to keep the fact that she had undergone this surgery a secret from her mother, while still visiting her regularly. This is puzzling because her impressive double D's formed a very visible presence on her slender torso. How did she think she could keep them a secret? What did she mean by hidden? And what does keeping her breasts "hidden" or a "secret" enable?

E: So when I came *back* [sic] to Indonesia, I still kept it a *secret* [sic] from my mother.
S: But – I'm sorry yeah – they are so big, how can you keep them hidden? From your mother or other people?
E: My mother was suspicious at first because I was not driving my motorbike. But I just wore a jacket all the time.
S: You couldn't drive a motorbike because you were still in pain?
E: It still hadn't healed. So after seeing me like this for a long time – I had a wound here right – my mother asked. Maybe her thinking was that I maybe had an operation yeah.
S: What did you wear so all of this couldn't be seen?
E: Just a scarf.
S: So how did your mother find out about the surgery? Did she hear it directly from you?
E: No, not directly from me. Maybe some *banci* or someone else told her that Esperanza had an operation. It had already happened, what can you do (*gimana lagi*)?
S: Did you ever talk with your mother about this?
E: No, silent. Just like that, Sylvia.
S: Until now … still silent?
E: Still just silent (*diam-diam aja*). (Esperanza, interview with author 2013)

When Esperanza talked about keeping her breast enhancement surgery a secret or hidden she does not mean a literal hidden, as in covering her formidable chest. Keeping it a secret or keeping it hidden, instead, points to a keeping silent; not talking about her breast enhancement. In a similar vein, she never told her mother about her living as a waria. A neighbour told her mother but she and her mother never talked about it. Keeping something hidden is not about seeing. Rather, it is about speaking. As long as Esperanza and her mother did not talk about Esperanza's breast enhancement surgery and what it entails for a more general digression from the straight line and stayed silent, it did not matter. What remains unspoken and undiscussed does not exist in a socially relevant way – in the everyday familial structures of the *normal*.

Remaining existent in this socially relevant way to her mother and other family members mattered to Esperanza and she did her best to maintain a place within the family. For example, she directed a sizeable part of her earnings from her work abroad to her mother. She used the money she earned in Australia and Germany not only to pay for her breast implants and the little house she shared with Rai and the dogs: she also used it to buy the house in which her mother and several siblings lived. Furthermore, she covered the costs of setting up a little *kios* (a stall from which to sell small foodstuffs and household items) attached to the house for her mother and opened a special savings account for her. She also extended this generosity to some of her siblings, for instance by paying for her younger *tomboi* sister Dewi's education. Dewi was about to graduate from senior high school and would be the first sibling to attend college. But Esperanza did not help all of her siblings financially. She explained: "As for my siblings, I only take care of Dewi, and Tommy and Desi. The others, they are already their husbands' responsibility, not mine". Her felt responsibility only extended to those siblings who were not married (to men).

When I asked Esperanza why she did these things, she answered "because I want them to be happy, so my mother is content, so my younger siblings are content. Like that". These explanations Esperanza gives for her various (financial) investments in her family highlight her admirable motivations, such as a desire for their happiness, care, responsibility, as well as her commitment to securing a better future for her family, whether in the form of savings accounts and a *kios* in order to achieve financial stability, or in the form of a college education in order to open up future job opportunities. In spite of the obvious yet undiscussed permanent digression from the straight line of the Indonesian heteronormative *normal* that her breast implants suggest, Esperanza remains invested in her family. Instead of choosing "new" families in a more permanent traversing of a queer line, she stays connected to her "old" kinship ties. Put differently, even from a queer line the *normal*, and in particular a continuation of existing familial ties, figure prominently in Esperanza's present and future.

If family ties endure Esperanza's traversing of a queer line through a mutual keeping silent and a constant flow of financial support, how does Esperanza's relationship with Rai resist the continuous pull of the *normal*? The emphasis

Esperanza places on care, responsibility, and a desire for her family's happiness when explaining her reasons for supporting her family financially downplays the extent to which she intends to secure a future with them for herself as well. Her investments in her family's future are also investments in her own future. Having bought the house for her mother meant that she would have a home to return to if – or when – needed, for instance, in the event of an end to her relationship with Rai.

Although I initially viewed Esperanza and Rai's relationship as an intriguing veering away from both the heteronormative and waria-*brondong* "normal" and admired the way they valued commitment and responsibility, I underestimated the extent to which their relationship could withstand the demand placed on them by the *normal*.[12] The commitment and responsibility they emphasized in their relationship would not supersede the commitment and responsibility of the eventual unavoidable *normal* – at least not according to Rai. Rai made this clear one afternoon during a conversation about their possibilities for a future together. Rai told me that Esperanza had met his mother on one occasion, which was something Esperanza had asked for several times but which Rai found pointless. He said

> I don't want this [relationship, meeting the parents] to get too much inside, in the end it will be devastating. It is just different with a woman, or with my wife later or kids. Only then will I involve my parents, my family. That is different. She [Esperanza] was definitely self-centered (*egois*), hard-headed. She wanted to meet my parents. What for? I said, like that. You won't gain anything from meeting my family, you will never have my family and my family will never be able to accept/receive you, how can they? (Rai, interview with author 2013)

In spite of the commitment and responsibility that Rai prized in his relationship with Esperanza, he placed a higher value on his family and all that it implied. He described what he and Esperanza were doing as self-centered, something he accused Esperanza of when he said: "Now, this thing that we are doing is just our own egoism". The relationship they have was just for them and was just for now. "Later" was for his parents, his family and a "woman", a "wife later or kids". Eventually the *normal* will claim Rai and Esperanza, whether willingly or reluctantly.

12 In this regard, we should keep in mind that the heteronormative *normal* permeated their queer relationship in various ways, for instance when Rai gave up his waria persona, Amanda, to become more like a man.

The refusal of reproductive futurism, which is captured in the Indonesian heteronormative *normal*, and which Esperanza and Rai seemed to promise, turned out to be temporary. If the relationship between a waria and a former waria who became a *gay* man and who plans to get married offered an otherwise, it is an otherwise that will not last. So where does that leave love?

What's Love Got to Do with It?

In this chapter I have explored configurations of transgender, kinship, and love in Bali. I have shown how waria life, viewed as embarking on a queer line in Sara Ahmed's sense of the word, is inextricably tied to the straight line of the Indonesian heteronormative *normal*. I drew on various examples of bodywork that waria engage in to illustrate how waria leave a potential future return to the *normal* open by rarely engaging in types of bodywork that have lasting, permanent effects. I discussed the relationship between two nonheteronormative Indonesians, Esperanza and Rai, to enquire to what extent they might offer a more permanent digression from the straight line of the *normal*. Yet, as I have shown, the *normal* has a strong hold over queer lines. The *normal* is maintained in kinship relations through silences, such as Esperanza and her mother's keeping silent about her breast enhancement surgery, financial contributions, such as Esperanza gives to her mother and siblings, and in intentions to get married heterosexually, as Rai plans to do. In short, I hope to have shown how the Indonesian queer line never veers far from the straight line of the *normal* and, in time, is expected to merge with it again.

The story of Esperanza and Rai is most likely not one that ends in a happily ever after, at least not in an ever after they share with each other. We can therefore, I suggest, view them as real-life counterparts to the similarly gender-transgressive literary couples Deirdre Byrne describes in her chapter in this volume. Just as the romances between Aomame and Tengo or Katniss and Peeta ultimately inspire a sense of pessimism because their gender rebellion cannot overcome the heteronormative consensus reality, so too does the romance between Esperanza and Rai cast a sense of doom since their queer digression ultimately fails to overcome the pull of the Indonesian heteronormative *normal*. In the opening paragraph of this chapter I referred to a description of love that holds love to be a moral experience that is "singular and particular and must be sustained by means of a fidelity to the life trajectory established by its founding evental demand" (Zigon 2013, 201). Love, in this sense, is closely tied to exactly that which Esperanza and Rai cannot fulfil, namely fidelity to a particular life trajectory. Their romantic relationship, their love, is, like so many aspects of waria life, expected to be merely temporary. If love entails fidelity to a trajectory, can we speak of love when the trajectory is only traversed for a while? And if this is love, can we reconcile ourselves to its looming end, since the life trajectory they are committed to, due to the "founding eventual demand of love", is a temporary queer one that will turn back to the straight line eventually – when there is a "wife later or kids" (Rai, interview with author 2013). Can we settle for a love that is temporary or do we want a love that conquers all – including the *normal*?

References

Ahmed, Sara. 2006. *Queer Phenomenology: Orientation, Objects, Others*. Durham and London: Duke University Press.

Biblarz, Timothy J. and Evren Savci. 2010. "Lesbian, Gay, Bisexual, and Transgender Families". *Journal of Marriage and Family* 72: 480–497.

Blackwood, Evelyn. 2007. "Regulation of Sexuality in Indonesian Discourse: Normative Gender, Criminal Law, and Shifting Strategies of Control". *Culture, Health, & Sexuality* 9 (3): 293–307.

Blackwood, Evelyn. 2008. "Transnational Discourses and Circuits of Knowledge". *GLQ: A Journal of Lesbian and Gay Studies* 14 (4): 481–507.

Boellstorff, Tom. 2004. "Playing Back the Nation: Waria, Indonesian Transvestites". *Cultural Anthropology* 19 (2): 159–195.

Boellstorff, Tom. 2005. *The Gay Archipelago: Sexuality and Nation in Indonesia*. Princeton and Oxford: Princeton University Press.

Bourchier, David. 1997. "Totalitarianism and the 'National Personality': Recent Controversy about the Philosophical Basis for the Indonesian State". In *Imagining Indonesia: Cultural Politics and Political Culture*, edited by Jim Schiller and Barbara Martin-Schiller, 157–185. Athens: Ohio University Press.

Brenner, Suzanne A. 1995. "Why Women Rule the Roost". In *Bewitching Women, Pious Men: Gender and Body Politics in Southeast Asia*, edited by Aiwha Ong and Michael G. Peletz, 19–50. Los Angeles and Berkeley: University of California Press.

Brenner, Suzanne A. 1998. *The Domestication of Desire: Women, Wealth, and Modernity in Java*. Princeton: Princeton University Press.

Brenner, Suzanne A. 1999. "On the Public Intimacy of the New Order: Images of Women in the Popular Indonesian Print Media". *Indonesia* 67: 13–37.

Butler, Judith. 2004. *Precarious Lives: The Powers of Mourning and Violence*. London and New York: Verso.

Cauldwell, David O. 2006. "Psychopathia Transexualis". In *The Transgender Studies Reader*, edited by Susan Stryker and Stephen Whittle, 40–44. New York and London: Routledge.

Desjarlais, Robert and C. Jason Throop. 2011. "Phenomenological Approaches in Anthropology". *Annual Review in Anthropology* 40: 87–102.

Edelman, Lee. 2004. *No Future: Queer Theory and the Death Drive*. Durham and London: Duke University Press.

Erich, Stephen, Josephine Tittsworth, Janice Dykes and Cheryl Cabuses. 2008. "Family Relationships and Correlations with Transsexual Well-Being". *Journal of GLBT Family Studies* 4 (4): 419–432.

Heidegger, Martin. 2008 [1962]. *Being and Time*. New York: Harper & Row Publishers, Inc.

Hadiwinata, Bob S. 2002. *The Politics of NGOs in Indonesia: Developing Democracy and Managing a Movement*. London and New York: Routledge.

Howard, Richard Stephen. 1996. *Falling into the Gay World: Manhood, Marriage, and Family in Indonesia*. PhD dissertation, University of Illinois at Urbana-Champaign.

Husserl, Edmund. 2002 [1931]. *Ideas*. London and New York: Routledge.

Idrus, Nurul Ilmi and Takeo David Hymans. 2014. "Balancing Benefits and Harm: Chemical Use and Bodily Transformation among Indonesia's Transgender Waria". *International Journal of Drug Policy* 25 (4): 789–797.

"Islam Tak Kenal Jenis Kelamin Waria" [Islam Does Not Know the Sex Waria]. 2010. *Nahdlatul Ulama Online*. http://www.nu.or.id/post/read/22848/islam-tak-kenal-jenis-kelamin-waria.

Krafft-Ebing, Richard von. 2006. "Selections from *Psychopathia Sexualis* with Special Reference to Contrary Sexual Instinct: A Medico-Legal Study". In *The Transgender Studies Reader*, edited by Susan Stryker and Stephen Whittle, 21–27. New York and London: Routledge.

Leap, William L. 2004. " 'Marriage', 'Family', and Same-Sex Marriage: Are We Addressing the Right Questions?". *Anthropology News* 22.

Liang, Jamison. 2010. "Homophobia on the Rise". *Inside Indonesia*. http://www.insideindonesia.org/homophobia-on-the-rise.

Meyer-Bahlburg, Heino F. L. 2010. "From Mental Disorder to Iatrogenic Hypogonadism: Dilemmas in Conceptualizing Gender Identity Variants as Psychiatric Conditions". *Archives of Sexual Behavior* 39 (2): 467–476.

"Muhammadiyah: Waria dan Homoseksual Berlawanan dengan HAM" [Muhammadiyah: Waria and Homosexuals Are at Odds with Human Rights]. 2010. *Republika Online*. https://www.republika.co.id/berita/breaking-news/nasional/10/05/03/114004-muhammadiyah-waria-dan-homoseksual-berlawanan-dengan-ham.

Oetomo, Dédé. 1996. “Gender and Sexual Orientation”. In *Fantasizing the Feminine in Indonesia*, edited by Laurie J. Sears, 259–269. Durham and London: Duke University Press.

Povinelli, Elizabeth A. 2011. *Economies of Abandonment: Social Belonging and Endurance in Late Liberalism*. Durham and London: Duke University Press.

Raj, Rupert. 2008. “Transforming Couples and Families: A Transformative Therapeutic Model for Working with the Loved-Ones of Gender-Divergent Youth and Trans-Identified Adults”. *Journal of GLBT Family Studies* 4 (2): 133–163.

Safitri, Dian M. 2013. “The Politics of Piety in the Pondok Pesantren Khusus Waria Al-Fattah Senin-Kamis Yogyakarta: Negotiating the Islamic Religious Embodiment”. In *Islam in Indonesia: Contrasting Images and Interpretations*, edited by Jajat Burhanudin and Kees van Dijk, 91–107. Amsterdam: Amsterdam University Press.

Shiraishi, Saya S. 1997. *Young Heroes: The Indonesian Family in Politics*. Ithaca, New York: Southeast Asia Program Publications.

Siegel, James. 1998. *A New Criminal Type in Jakarta: Counter-Revolution Today*. Durham: Duke University Press.

Steedly, Mary. 2013. *Rifle Reports: A Story of Indonesian Independence*. Berkeley: University of California Press.

Suryakusuma, Julia I. 1996. “The State and Sexuality in New Order Indonesia”. In *Fantasizing the Feminine in Indonesia*, edited by Laurie J. Sears, 91–119. Durham and London: Duke University Press.

Wallace, Robert and Hershel Russell. 2013. “Attachment and Shame in Gender-Nonconforming Children and Their Parents; Toward a Theoretical Framework for Evaluating Clinical Interventions”. *International Journal of Transgenderism* 14 (3): 113–126.

Weston, Kath. 1997. *Families We Choose: Lesbians, Gays, Kinship*. New York and Oxford: Columbia University Press [1991].

Zigon, Jarrett. 2013. “On Love: Remaking Moral Subjectivity in Postrehabilitation Russia”. *American Ethnologist* 40 (1): 201–215.

PART 4

Fluid Gender, Fluid Love in Postmodernity

CHAPTER 9

Fictions of Love: Writing About 17th-Century Ideas of Gender and Love

Kelly Gardiner

Introduction

> When I was younger – then – I didn't understand the difference between desire and love. How could I? Desire was the only thing I had known, and it felt so strong, so consuming, that I thought – I assumed – especially after a few bottles of wine – that feeling must be the romantic love of the ballads and the stories.
>
> But it wasn't. I see that now. Don't get me wrong. Desire can be a fine thing. Desire is enough, sometimes. It will send armies to conquest, inspire the poets – pathetic lot that they are – make friends aim pistols at each other in the Place Royale.
>
> It was enough for me. For years.
>
> […] I've had few friends but loyal. I've had many romances – are you keeping some kind of tally, Father, in that book of yours? Double it. I can't be bothered to tell you of the boring fucks and the odd momentary madness.
>
> I've had great love. Felt it. Lived it. Lost it. Truly great love, Biblical love, a romance worthy of a thousand books, of an opera, of a broken heart.
>
> There is passion in all of it, even in the anger, even in the curses and spitting fights and long nights staring into the embers.
>
> Passion isn't a sin. Passion is God-like. But so human. Passion is the link between all of those things – desire, love, friendship, sin – between all of us. (Gardiner 2014, 276)

That is the voice of my interpretation of Mademoiselle de Maupin (also known as Julie d'Aubigny), a seventeenth-century swordswoman, cross-dresser and opera singer who became a celebrity in Paris and Brussels in her lifetime, infamous for relationships with powerful men and women, and a symbol of transgressive desire in the centuries since her death. Most famously, the nineteenth-century version of her, in Théophile Gautier's *Mademoiselle de*

 | DOI:10.1163/9789004380233_011

Maupin, recreated her as the essence of Romanticism, of mysterious gender, of fluid sexuality, of beauty, and of idealized love.

In writing a new fictionalized interpretation of her life and character, I needed to understand: in a pre-Freudian world view, before twentieth-century sociological and political frameworks of sexual and gender identity, before feminism, before queer theory, how might the real woman have seen herself? And how might people around La Maupin have perceived her? What or whom did they imagine her to be? How can we account for the popular acclamation of some cross-dressing and/or same-sex oriented women (and men) in an era when others were severely punished?

Saint, Sinners and Celebrities

Although Butler, Foucault and Laqueur, among many others, have highlighted the possibilities of and slippages between performances of gender and sexuality in the early modern era, there is no doubt that penalties were severe for women's crimes such as wearing male clothing. But were cross-dressing women seen as unprecedented? As monstrous? As, perhaps, desirable? Dekker and Van de Pol (1989) have catalogued contemporary trials of women who dressed and sometimes passed as men, some of whom were in lesbian relationships, and note that many women saw themselves as part of a legitimate European tradition. The celebrity of women such as La Maupin, highwaywoman Moll Cutpurse, pirates Anne Bonney and Mary Read, and later female soldiers such as Hannah Snell, who disguised themselves as men, was only part of that tradition: it also consisted of theatrical cross-dressing, wearing male costume for special events such as festivals, and a long line of legendary and romanticised women from history and literature.

When these women's contemporaries cast around for examples to help them place lesbian, cross-dressing, martial, or indeed even intellectual women, in a context which justified or provided meaning for their actions and their lives, the usual iconography of sainthood was not easily applied to these often outlandish personalities. Instead, contemporary texts most often referred to three identifiable precedents: from ancient Greece, the Amazons and Sappho; and France's own warrior maid, Jeanne d'Arc.

This is a lineage which appears at first glance to be sporadic, but echoes through history. These connections, as we shall see, also thread through opera, theatre and literature, and are evident in later portrayals of La Maupin. This is a literary and historical tradition to which La Maupin had access. It is the context in which she has been placed, perhaps unconsciously, by many of her biographers, and may help us to understand how such a remarkable figure was celebrated in her lifetime. This lineage in turn questions the concept of the exceptional queer or the lone proto-feminist struggling to survive without peers, without context, without precedent.

Amazons and Poets

The term most often applied to La Maupin is "Amazon." This is not surprising: she was famous as a duellist, and these legendary figures are the eternal symbols of warlike women. Amazons, who are now known to be real historical figures, rather than mythical or imagined (Mayor 2014), were associated in art and in story with goddesses: Artemis/Diana the virgin huntress and the warrior maiden Athena/Minerva (Warner 1976). Marina Warner has traced the "web of imagery associated with the power of women since antiquity" (2013, 184) linking the Amazons to the medieval French heroine, Jeanne d'Arc.

On the other hand, women of independent or artistic mind or of "lesbian-like" sexuality (Bennett 2000, 1), including La Maupin, have often been, throughout history, likened to another figure of antiquity: Sappho. As one of the first and greatest poets in the western tradition, Sappho defined love and desire and, in a sense, the idea of Sappho has, ever since, been integral to our definitions of sexuality, and love, and transgression (Reynolds 2003). This underlines Bridget Sandhoff's suggestion, in her chapter in this volume, that, "Desire, lust, and longing fall under the most dangerous aspect of love, *eros*, or in other words, mindless sexual desire" (2018, 35), and Sappho's celebrations of *eros*, as well as her life, were seen as both unconventional and sublime. As Sandhoff argues, Roman society later institutionalized a kind of love devoid of *eros*, through the convention of the arranged marriage, while male Roman writers such as Ovid tried to subvert the idea of such staid marital love through romantic poetry of heterosexual longing and lust. In this world view, the transgressive love of women such as Sappho, revered poet though she was, or seemingly uncontrollable warriors such as the Amazons, is doubly dangerous.

Perhaps it is not surprising, then, that one of the most important origins of the mythical Sappho which was familiar to early modern readers was Ovid's lament, in his version of her voice, in *Heroides* (Ovid 2004). This later version of Sappho is a former lesbian, now distraught and abandoned; desperately in love with the low-born and heartless ferryman, Phaon, she is about to fling herself from the cliff top.

> … daughters of Lesbos whom I loved and
> For whose love I am ashamed, stop there,
> Do not come near my shell's music.
> Phaon has destroyed what you once held so dear […]
> He was my genius. It left with him. (Ovid 2004, 140)

As Joan DeJean argues: "Nowhere in Sappho's passionate cry from the heart as Ovid imagines it does he draw the line between fact and fiction; nowhere does he indicate that, in her case alone of all the characters in the *Heroides*, is he dealing with a historical rather than a legendary figure. In short, Ovid never discloses that he is presenting a fiction of Sappho, enshrining the original woman writer as a male myth" (1987, 795).

Ovid converted the Sappho of history, the Muse admired by Plato, into something paradoxically new, an imagined character that is also, at the same time, a blend of history and mythology. In the absence of her own words, most lost by the ninth century while Ovid's were not, it was a heterosexual Sappho whose lovelorn voice sounded throughout Europe in many languages, and was echoed by countless writers for many hundreds of years. Conversely, the word "Sappho" became a slander that could be applied to any woman who forgot her place or whose desires centred on other women.

This discursive process is perceptible in the biographies of La Maupin; these are subjective, often imagined, stories which act as revisions of the contemporary reception of her flamboyant persona, and influence portrayals of her to this day. As is the case with La Maupin, there are myriad portrayals of Sappho: in countless paintings, on stage, in opera, on television, in B-grade lesbian movies. Her words have been reinterpreted by generations of poets, from Sir Philip Sidney to Robert Lowell. She is evident in Gautier's *Mademoiselle de Maupin* and in every portrayal of La Maupin. It does not matter that we now know Sappho lived into old age: she is visible in dozens of paintings of a woman so overwhelmed with emotion – with that uncontrollable *eros* – that she flings herself from the metaphorical cliff top. Ovid's "fictions of Sappho" became fictions of a whole range of women in literature and in imaginative works ever since.

But La Maupin was part of a generation that acknowledged women as intellectuals: discussing literature and politics in salons, composing music, writing memoirs and the new form, novels; even a libretto, in the case of Madame de Saintonge's *Didon* (first performed in 1693, starring La Maupin). These "notorious women" (DeJean 1991, 67–86) argued for divorce and property rights, and wrote about love, beauty, sexuality, faith; and many were explicitly conscious of being a part of a timeless literary tradition. In letters (often read aloud in the salons) and privately published or circulated works, well-read women, such as Madame de Sévigné, engaged in spirited discussion about theological, political and philosophical topics of the day and reflected upon their own approaches to love, scripture, beauty, the arts, and nature. Others debated issues of equality and gender between themselves and with male writers and philosophers. The rhetorical works of Madeleine de Scudéry, including *Les Femmes Illustres* (*Illustrious Women,* published in 1642), were published under the name "Sapho" and greatly admired by other intellectual women of Paris, including Madame de Sévigné – the circles that also celebrated La Maupin.

Even between themselves, these women made conscious references to their predecessors in the lineage of intellectual women and also martial heroines from antiquity. The philosopher and essayist Marie de Gournay published several works on the topic of women, including *L'égalité des hommes et des femmes* (*The Equality of Men and Women,* published in 1622) and *Les grief des dames* (*The Ladies' Grievance*, published in 1626). In England, writers such as Katherine Philips (under her pen name, Orinda) and Aphra Behn were acclaimed for often coded but clearly Sapphic poetry and plays. The remarkable Margaret Cavendish published commentaries on nature, philosophy and science, and wrote fiercely Utopian works such as *The Blazing World* (published in 1666), which has, amongst its many motifs, the ideals of Platonic love between women, female virtue and courage.

These women proudly claimed the intellectual mantle of Sappho for themselves or had it applied to them.

Female Bridegrooms and Chevaliers

At the same time, especially in France and England, a new iconography sprang up, linking the Amazons of old and the more recent Jeanne d'Arc with the heroic women who had led men into battle during the civil wars that wracked both countries in the middle of the seventeenth century (DeJean 2003, 117–147). Although not canonized until 1920, Jeanne was reimagined as an emblem of Catholic faith, of purity and virtue, of French nationalism, and sometimes all three, woven into the Amazonian ancestral chart. Her portrayals over time, like those of Sappho and La Maupin, range from hagiographic to hostile, but the fact of her and all she came to represent resonate through French history in particular, and compounded the iconography of the Amazons into a new and often romantic symbol consequently applied to many real women who came after her.

These women were linked, too, to the goddesses of the classical era. Fictional narratives of Warrior Maidens were also common in Europe during the sixteenth and seventeenth centuries. Twenty-five novels or fictional autobiographies on the topic were published in Dutch alone between 1600 and 1815, and many works were translated from and into Italian, Spanish, French, Dutch and English (Dekker and Van de Pol 1989), while on the English stage Shakespeare and others were confounding gender perceptions with characters that shifted between performative guises.

This, again, was in part due to the renaissance of interest in the ancient tales and the creative reimagining of Ovid's *Metamorphoses* (2002) into contemporary settings. Itoitz Rodrigo Jusué creates a "genealogy of *impossible love*," tracing the later manifestations of Ovid's story of the cross-dressing Iphis and the gender metamorphosis which allows her to marry her true love, Ianthé. As Jusué argues:

> Stories as live discourses not only capture the social and cultural reality from which they arise, they also have the power to rewrite, criticize, change, reinforce and reproduce social realities. (2015, 118)

Just as *Heroides* defined perceptions of Sappho, *Metamorphoses* profoundly influenced early modern conceptions of romance, gender and indeed sexuality. These were stories familiar to every literate European, and which were recreated on stage, in music, in public readings, and in popular literature after the introduction of the printing press to Europe. Much of the composer Lully's work, like that of his contemporaries Handel and Gluck, was based on *Metamorphoses* and later works influenced by it, especially the French romance *Amadis de Gaule* (based on the Spanish epic *Amadis de Gaula*). Consequently, those early Baroque operas – in which La Maupin appeared – created worlds brimming with fantasy, heroics, divine intervention and the possibility of metamorphosis.

Warner has noted a marked change in the portrayals of Amazonian figures, particularly in these romantic epics: she argues that the warrior woman is no longer fearsome but desirable, now an object of chivalrous love (2013, 198). Emma Donoghue suggests that cross-dressers – whether on stage, on the page or in real life – are often admired, as well as vilified, because their existence can "celebrate desires fleeting or ambiguous, but no less powerful for that; they are fantasies, games, speculations, outrageous travesties of the real and the natural" (2010, 18).

Valerie Traub goes even further, arguing that early modern England was the specific site of "a *renaissance* of representations of female homoerotic desire" (2001, 245–263). Harriette Andreadis, too, identifies the development of a "Sapphic discourse" in literature and on stage in seventeenth-century England, in particular, "often with Sappho as primary icon and embodiment of transgression" (2001, 51). These developments included the work of women writers, intellectuals and artists, but are also evident in the creative reworkings of the idea of Sappho and women like her by male poets such as John Donne.

Donoghue traces the strands of overt and subtextual portrayals of lesbians in literature throughout history, and argues that both classical and early modern texts firmly embedded the idea of the "female bridegroom" and Amazon traditions in literature and, by extension, in the popular imagination. In the first tradition, a female wanderer (or *picara*), dressed as a man, is accidentally betrothed to another woman – just like Iphis in *Metamorphoses*. The second tradition positions the cross-dresser as a noble warrior woman, a new Amazon, defending either her people or her family. The female bridegroom appears repeatedly in literature and, as we shall see, on stage, and in many cases provided an opportunity for public depictions of both cross-dressing and same-sex attraction, even when doubled and doubled again, as it was later in Gautier's *Mademoiselle de Maupin*.

The female bridegroom – from Iphis to Viola in *Twelfth Night* and finally to Villanelle in Jeanette Winterson's *The Passion* – not only captures the imagination but also quite often gets the girl. Or girls. As Susan Lanser, writing of the Sapphic picaresque literature of the eighteenth century, notes:

> If those women who are courted by cross-dressed suitors unwittingly engage in same-sex behaviours, the unquestioned success with which the protagonists not only fool but magnetically attract other women testifies to the fluidity both of gender and desire. (2001, 251–268)

The same might also be said of the breeches roles in later opera and theatre works, in which a soprano or mezzo-soprano performs a male character, or cross-dresses as a male to further the plot. The popular *travesti* characters of Molière and many others created both suspense and playfulness, using the masquerade of masculinity as a pretext for humour, sexual innuendo, and peeking at women's ankles in public – or, in England, men dressed as women, dressed as men. In writing of the English cross-dressing phenomenon of the Elizabethan and Restoration stage, Tracey Sedinger connects the performance of cross-dressing as a coded theatrical experience steeped in knowing, unknowing and desire:

> The crossdresser stages a moment of rupture, when knowledge and visibility are at odds, when difference cannot be defined solely by recourse to the visual. It is this failure that produces erotic pleasure. (1997, 68)

This moment of rupture, though, is also one of familiarity – and hilarity. French audiences familiar with Rabelais and the carnival tradition, like English audiences familiar with *As You Like It* or Aphra Behn's *The Rover*, were able to enjoy being provoked, entertained and mocked by a character who included them in their joke, but was, at the same time, both shocking and desirable.

Beaumarchais, who surely knew of La Maupin, wrote in his stage directions for *The Marriage of Figaro* that the amorous young page, Cherubino, "can only be played [...] by a young and very pretty woman" (Blackmer and Smith 1995, 10). In Mozart's version, the outrageous flirt Cherubino is performed by a soprano or high mezzo-soprano. These forms of play, of ironic gender performance, of cross-dressing as the signifier of a rupture in the signifying order, also recognise the essential transgression of theatre and masquerade.

While cross-dressing did not occur in French Baroque opera practice (La Maupin cross-dressed off-stage), I suggest that the desire she evoked resonates even now with opera-goers acting as spectators to the performance of transgression in opera. Here is Cixous describing the experience of watching a woman sing the role of the king in Rossini's *Tancredi*:

> I divine what is more than a woman, what is more than a man, but above me everything sparkles and dazzles me and merges into a single person with athletic aspirations, rather tall for a woman, yes, she seems to me to be a woman, but set naturally in the bearing of a man, like my pearl in turquoise.
>
> What do you call a person who looks rather more like a woman with dark blue eyes, an icy look in appearance, burning inside, who is large and imposing like the night, and stars nuzzle up against her full breast, closing their eyes in love, who fights like a hero, would give up her life like a mother, and who sheds tears of impatience and grief, and who dreams of destiny only as love, and who takes fortresses more easily than a kiss, and her voice is so deep and warm and moist it sounds like the sea of human tears, and every woman not bound by cords of marriage who hears it feels the burning need to immerse herself in it? (1991, 164)

Marble and Metaphors

In *The History of Sexuality Volume One*, Michel Foucault suggests that there was a great deal of fluidity around concepts of sex, and slippage between the ideas of sexuality and especially sexual "deviance" up to the eighteenth century, so that only after that time was the idea of a "sex" able to be seen and used as "a unique signifier and a universal signified" (1978, 154). Once a sex had been defined as a category, then things that were not that sex could also be defined, "dominated" and regulated. Once a norm had been established, behaviours and pleasures and relationships that deviated from that norm could also be defined and, in some cases, legislated against.

Thomas Laqueur, in *Making Sex: Body and Gender from the Greeks to Freud*, argues that prior to the eighteenth century:

> Gender choice was by no means so open to individual discretion, and one was not free to change in mid-stream. But [Foucault] is right that there was no true, deep essential sex that differentiated cultural man from woman. But neither were there two sexes juxtaposed in various proportions: there was but one sex whose more perfect exemplars were easily deemed males at birth and whose decidedly less perfect ones were labelled female. The modern question about the "real" sex of a person made no sense in this period, not because two sexes were mixed but because there was only one to pick from and it had to be shared by everyone, from the strongest warrior to the most effeminate courtier to the most aggressive virago to the gentlest maiden. (1990, 124)

If we accept the conclusions of Laqueur, it seems that women such as La Maupin were seen by others as bettering themselves by performing as men, rather than as 'imposters' in a male realm, as later writers (such as Bram Stoker) described her. Catherine Craft-Fairchild has suggested that under the one-sex model described by Laqueur,

> female transvestism could be regarded as a natural effort to "move up" the chain-of-being, [but] with the advance of a two-sex model [later in the eighteenth century] it became both unnatural and subversive. (1998, 177)

In *Cross Dressing, Sex, and Gender*, Vern Bullough suggests that it was seen as possible for gender to be insecure or changeable, noting admonitions against men engaging in "womanly pursuits" for fear of becoming womanish, or the risks of women indulging in manly exercise. In an earlier study of the saints' lives, though, Bullough notes that female saints who dressed as men were idealized, while men who wore women's clothes were vilified:

> In theory transvestism may well have been prohibited by the medieval church, but in practice the church did not seem to be too concerned about cross-dressing, providing it took certain socially desirable forms

> and was rigidly circumscribed. Under such conditions, in fact, it was institutionalized. […] A female who secretly wore men's clothes was not considered abnormal. That a female might desire to be a male, in fact, seemed to be a healthy desire, a normal longing not unlike the desire of a peasant to become a noble. This did not mean that either women or peasants were allowed to cross the status lines in great numbers but that the desire to do so was accepted as a norm. (1974, 1392)

But the idea of tolerance of women who dressed or behaved as men is contested: firstly, due to the many trial records of female cross-dressers who were treated as criminals by civic authorities or the Inquisition (Dekker and Van de Pol 1989); and secondly, by some feminist theorists who refuse to accept binary models (whether derived from Aristotle or Foucault) as the basis for broader historical understandings of gender and sexuality. Is it possible that slippage between discursive categories existed within a milieu that also constrained and punished movement between classifications of gender (and race) that appeared to be biologically determined?

Daston and Park point out the seemingly contradictory view taken by authors concerned with medical and legal implications of hermaphrodites and transvestites (conflated, along with other "transgressions," by seventeenth-century writers):

> The new emphasis on female sodomy ["the woman who sleeps with women"] signals another even greater source of sexual anxiety: the male concern with female pretensions to masculine status and prerogatives that is so visible in the popular literature and to some extent in the ritual practice of the period. This concern also crystallized in disapproval of female cross-dressing. At least in the context of hagiography, medieval writers had often spiritualized female transvestism as a metaphor of saintly aspiration […] In the sixteenth and early seventeenth centuries, it became an obsessive theme in the works of male authors and a figure signifying the monstrous pretensions and actions of ordinary women – the "new hermaphrodites" of *Hic Mulier: or the Man-Woman,* the famous English pamphlet on female crossdressing. (Daston and Park 1995, 431)

Donoghue (1993) argues that many of the so-called medical books of the era were vernacular texts, written for the general public, often designed to titillate rather than explain, and that these pre-Enlightenment theories seemed not to build upon one another but to flower randomly and often contradictorily.

She notes the transposable references to the concepts of the hermaphrodite and the *tribade* (lesbian) in much of the literature, and a dependence on folklore and the philosophies of classical authors, rather than empirical research as it was understood in later centuries. Stephen Greenblatt also suggests that no one text or tradition can explain early modern attitudes to sexuality, but that "taken as a whole, a culture's sexual discourse plays a critical role in the shaping of identity" (1988, 75). "It is conceptually and politically vital," writes Belinda Johnston, "for feminist readers of the Renaissance to avoid a reading of the body that treats it as biologically, rather than discursively, determined" (2001, 82). These approaches call into question, in particular, Laqueur's study of the medical and philosophical literature, rather than a broader cultural discourse, as a basis for understanding contemporary views of "deviance" and the gendered body.

Outside Europe's medical and legal circles and the folklore of monsters, there was also a widespread intellectual fascination with the idea and existence of hermaphrodites (the term used at the time to describe intersex people), again influenced by Ovid's *Metamorphoses,* along with the significant discoveries of classical statues of hermaphrodites (just as contemporary sculptors were inspired by the ancient marble representations of Amazons at war, including, most famously, the Parthenon frieze and martial goddesses like Athena). While the term was still used as a slander against people of any gender, artists in particular focused on the concept of the hermaphrodite as a symbol of the perfect union of two halves, of spiritual perfection, even of alchemical processes, representing a couple that joins to become one being like Hermes and Aphrodite. The painter Niccolò Grassi (1683–1748) perceived the hermaphrodite as the very definition of love: "that love is perfect whose knot binds and conjoins two lovers completely, such that, having lost their proper appearance, the two become some third thing" (in Turner 1993, 77).

Later, in the nineteenth century, the idea of the hermaphrodite as a sacred third sex or truly complete being finds its echo in Gautier's fictional interpretation of *Mademoiselle de Maupin*: "I am neither of one sex or the other," says the character Madeleine de Maupin: "I am of a third sex, which as yet has no name; higher or lower, more defective or superior" (1951, 319).

Rosemary Lloyd suggests that Gautier is:

> Attempting the creation of a modern myth in which beauty, poetic inspiration and love can coincide only in a being who is both Apollo and Aphrodite, appealing to both sexes and exciting both the senses and the intellect. (1986, 29)

Mademoiselle de Maupin is based on the essence of La Maupin rather than events in her life. Gender is a literal and metaphorical performance in the novel, a masquerade multiplied: the character Madeleine first appears disguised as a chevalier called Théodore, who then cross-dresses to play Rosalind dressed as Ganymede (who attracts the gaze and unwitting admiration of Phaebe, who is in turn loved by Sylvius) in a performance of Shakespeare's play *As You Like It*. It is the same knowing performance of gender(s) and sexuality as we experience on stage in *As You Like It*; through Mozart's *The Marriage of Figaro* or Strauss's *Der Rosenkavalier*. Gautier places his Mademoiselle de Maupin firmly in the literary traditions of the Amazon and the female bridegroom – in this case a cavalier. Gautier overtly recognizes, too, the erotic possibilities of the cross-dresser as personified by this fictionalized version of Mademoiselle de Maupin, and explores the soft edges between infatuation, desire, and love.

It became one of the most-often banned books in history, and the figure of La Maupin became a rallying cry for the Aesthetic movement; an inspiration for writers and artists from Oscar Wilde to Marcel Proust to James Baldwin; a connection between the ideal youth and philosophy of the ancients and a modern world of gaslighting and radical movements; a trigger for cultural and political debates about gender and sexuality into the twentieth century; and an icon of forbidden sensuality and romance that endured for decades.

Performing Subversion

So if the Amazons defied external expectations of gender and perhaps love, if Sappho defined passionate love for the classical world and yet subverted its rules about whom to love, if Jeanne d'Arc positioned herself as the virginal crusader embodying the warrior maiden tradition; then La Maupin, although no maiden, brought all these ideas together.

While she is consistently described as a subversive figure, she can be viewed within a performative tradition that defies but also enacts tropes active in the communal imagination. On one hand, many biographers admired her panache, her great skill with the sword and on stage, and portray her as a wild, spirited creature, entertaining the crowds and flouting convention. On the other, the truly transgressive nature of her life is often obscured. Her great love affair with the Madame de Marquise La Florensac, described with something like admiration by contemporary diarists, was written out of her life story by most later biographers who refused to admit that her final, "Sapphic," romance was successful and loving – and respected.

Like Marianne Schleicher, I accept Judith Butler's theory of performativity, which argues that "subversive agency requires that individuals work for cultural changes from within their culture by participating in the rule-regulating practices such as rituals and other repetitive acts as a testimony to their loyalty toward culture and non-threatening intentions" (2018, 12). This suggests that the historical figure of La Maupin has been re-written and positioned as the tolerable – and indeed entertaining – face of transgression, perhaps because of her theatrical persona combined with the long association between the stage and cross-dressing as a literal performance of gender slippage. This operates in the same way as camp and drag were celebrated, but not accepted, in later centuries; one could argue that this same framework underlies the concept of tolerance and the current debates over same-sex marriage as an institutionalised performance of non-threatening queerness.

I suggest that La Maupin became, for her generation and many after, a symbol of an interconnected iconography and history, broadly acknowledged within the culture or sub-cultures: a chevalier, an artist and a rebel; a woman in male clothes who fought like a man, sang like a woman and performed as an Amazon in real life; a romanticised Sappho who loved women and men, a goddess and a fairground folly – all in one sublime and queer figure.

This is the rich and palimpsest-laden tradition in which I wrote, and I chose to approach the woman and her life differently from any earlier portrayal. Informing this new, metafictional La Maupin are the complex and inter-related identities of sexuality and gender developed in the centuries since her death, and since Gautier's ground-breaking interpretation of her; specifically, feminist and queer theories and their interrogation of the intersections of gender, sexuality, love, power and cultural representation. The narrative self-consciously addresses the many previous readings of her life, and – invisibly – the lives of women like her and especially Sappho, and is presented as a form of performativity in text.

What I do is knowingly perform a version of her, on the page, in first person *recitative* passages in a constructed voice that is overtly modern and consciously anti-authentic. These are juxtaposed with third-person chapters intended to reflect the gaze of male and female spectators, and to examine the many ways in which she was viewed by those around her during her life and since. The character of La Maupin that *Goddess* projects is an imagined pre-Enlightenment gender performance, conscious of the threads of a cultural and historic lineage but convinced of her own exceptionalism and celebrity status.

I do not transgress. I transcend. I fly, with coronet and sceptre, over the heads of mortals. I amaze them. They worship at my bare feet, gaze up at me tentatively, as if the glory of my eyes might blind them.
Ah! The wonder of it!
The squalor. (Gardiner 2014, 29)

References

Andreadis, Harriette. 2001. *Sappho in Early Modern England: Female Same-Sex Literary Erotics, 1550–1714*. Chicago: University of Chicago Press.

Bennett, Judith M. 2000. "'Lesbian-Like' and the Social History of Lesbianisms." *Journal of the History of Sexuality* 9 (1–2): 1–24.

Blackmer, Corinne, and Patricia Smith. 1995. *En Travesti: Women, Gender Subversion, Opera*. New York: Columbia University Press.

Bullough, Vern L., and Bonnie Bullough. 1993. *Cross Dressing, Sex, and Gender*. Philadelphia: University of Pennsylvania Press.

Bullough, Vern L. 1974. "Transvestites in the Middle Ages." *The American Journal of Sociology* 79 (6): 1381–1394.

Cixous, Hélène. 1991. *Coming to Writing and Other Essays*. Cambridge US: Harvard University Press.

Craft-Fairchild, Catherine. 1998. "Cross-dressing and the Novel: Women Warriors and Domestic Femininity." *Eighteenth-Century Fiction* 10 (2): 171–202.

Daston, Lorraine, and Katherine Park. 1995. "The Hermaphrodite and the Orders of Nature: Sexual Ambiguity In Early Modern France." *GLQ: A Journal of Lesbian and Gay Studies* 1 (4): 419–438.

DeJean, Joan E. 1987. "Fictions of Sappho." *Critical Enquiry* 13 (4): 787–805.

DeJean, Joan E. 1991. "Notorious Women: Marriage and the Novel in Crisis in France (1690–1715)." *Yale Journal of Criticism* 4 (2): 67–85.

DeJean, Joan E. 2003. "Violent Women and Violence against Women: Representing the 'Strong' Woman in Early Modern France." *Signs: Journal of Women in Culture and Society* 29 (1): 117–147.

Dekker, Rudolf M., and Lotte van de Pol. 1989. *The Tradition of Female Transvestism in Early Modern Europe*. London: Macmillan.

Donoghue, Emma. 1993. "Imagined More Than Women: Lesbians as Hermaphrodites, 1671–1766." *Women's History Review* 2 (2): 199–216.

Donoghue, Emma. 2010. *Inseparable: Desire between Women in Literature*. New York: Alfred A. Knopf.

Foucault, Michel. 1978. *The History of Sexuality. Volume One: An Introduction*. New York: Pantheon.

Gardiner, Kelly. 2014. *Goddess*. Sydney: Fourth Estate.

Gautier, Théophile. 1951. *Mademoiselle de Maupin*. First Australian Edition. Sydney: Dymock's Book Arcade.

Greenblatt, Stephen. 1988. *Shakespearean Negotiations: The Circulation of Social Energy in Renaissance England*. Oxford: Clarendon Press.

Johnston, Belinda. 2001. "Renaissance Body Matters: Judith Butler and the Sex That Is One." *International Journal of Sexuality and Gender Studies* 6 (1–2): 77–94.

Jusué, Itoitz Rodrigo. 2015. "Queer Love: Love Policies, Possible Love and Tolerance." In *Past and Present: Perspectives on Gender and Love*, edited by Kelly Gardiner and Sina V. Pfister. Oxford: Inter-Disciplinary Press, 2015. Ebook.

Lanser, Susan S. 2001. "Sapphic Picaresque, Sexual Difference and the Challenges of Homo-adventuring." *Textual Practice* 15 (2): 251–268.

Laqueur, Thomas. 1990. *Making Sex: Body and Gender from the Greeks to Freud*. Cambridge: Harvard University Press.

Lloyd, Rosemary. 1986. "Rereading Mademoiselle de Maupin." *Orbis Litterarum* 41 (1): 19–32.

Mayor, Adrienne. 2014. *The Amazons: Lives and Legends of Warrior Women across the Ancient World*. New Jersey: Princeton University Press.

Reynolds, Margaret. 2003. *The Sappho History*. Basingstoke: Palgrave Macmillan.

Sandhoff, Bridget. 2018. "Romancing the Sexes: Representations of Marital Love in Etruria." In this volume.

Schleicher, Marianne. 2018. "Vulnerable Genders, Vulnerable Loves: Genealogies in Jewish Religion." In this volume.

Sedinger, Tracey. 1997. "If Sight and Shape Be True: The Epistemology of Crossdressing on the London Stage." *Shakespeare Quarterly* 48 (1): 63–80.

Traub, Valerie. 2001. "The Renaissance of Lesbianism in Early Modern England." *GLQ: A Journal of Lesbian and Gay Studies* 7 (2): 245–263.

Turner, James. 1993. *Sexuality and Gender in Early Modern Europe: Institutions, Texts, Images*. Cambridge: Cambridge University Press.

Warner, Marina. 1978. *Alone of All Her Sex: The Myth and the Cult of the Virgin Mary*. London: Pocket Books.

Warner, Marina. 2013. *Joan of Arc: The Image of Female Heroism*. Oxford: Oxford University Press.

CHAPTER 10

Conditions of (Im)Possibility: True Love in Haruki Murakami's *1Q84* and Suzanne Collins's *Hunger Games* Trilogy

Deirdre C. Byrne

Introduction

This chapter explores the representation of gender and true love in two novels: Haruki Murakami's *1Q84* and Suzanne Collins's *Hunger Games* trilogy. Each of these multi-volume texts presents the reader with a heterosexual couple who, in the time-honoured tradition of romantic fiction, overcome obstacles individually, join forces to overcome obstacles together, and end up falling in love. This plot structure is ubiquitous, as Riva H. Tuchakinsky notes:

> Romantic images of love are prompted by a variety of media texts: romantic novels, Hollywood films, advertisements, and so forth. These texts construct love as an external power, utilizing myths such as "love at first sight" that is destined to "conquer all obstacles". (Tuchakinsky 2002, 182)

As Tuchakinsky observes, the plot of such texts presents heterosexual romantic love as a version of fate or destiny; it is an external force that is more powerful than the protagonists. This view of love is perhaps most famously presented in Shakespeare's *Romeo and Juliet*, which figures the lovers as "star-crossed" (Shakespeare 1999, 3). "The stars" in *Romeo and Juliet* are symbols of the irresistible forces of destiny, genetics and social programming. The lovers are products of their destiny, both in terms of their family circumstances and in terms of their love attachment. In this chapter I will explore one aspect of the narrative of romantic love, namely gender ideologies, which gives rise to lovers' belief that they are the products of fate.

Tales of romantic love – undoubtedly one of the most popular narrative patterns – are conditioned by specific contextual understandings of gender roles and gender performances, but they also help to shape such views, so that there is a relationship of mutual influence in the way gendered identities are constructed in literature and performed in social environments. Maria Pia Lara, in *Moral Textures: Feminist Narratives in the Public Sphere*, argues that there is a

 | DOI:10.1163/9789004380233_012

direct link between discursive representation of gendered identities and moral action in the social sphere when she writes:

> My understanding of "symbols" emphasizes the public character of meaningful articulation, which points clearly not to their psychological operation but to how they allow meanings to be incorporated into action. (Lara 1998, 7)

The symbols associated with romantic love include irresistible attraction between the lovers and the inevitability of the outcome of their relationship: either a felicitous union or a tragic separation through death or disagreement. Lara believes that there is a two-way relationship of cause and effect: narrative can provide a space, not only for the depiction of moral and gendered identities, but for their formation. In my view, then, romantic fiction provides not only escape or wish-fulfilment (as Janice Radway argues (1991) that it did for the Smithton women), but also an important modality for shaping gender performances. If this is so, then the gender roles contained in fictional narratives can affect social understandings of these roles and their performative aspects.

The stereotypical plot structure of the romantic narrative can be summarised as recounting the way two people overcome interpersonal and social obstacles to achieve romantic union. The success of this plot structure depends on a dichotomous understanding of the way women and men, respectively, are expected to behave. In this dichotomy, men enact emotional distance and individual achievement, while women promote compassion, intimacy and relationship.[1] Wood's (2001) study on violence in intimate relationships notes that there is an "established gender narrative (male dominance and female submission)" and Floretta Boonzaier also mentions the "standards of adult womanhood or femininity as incomplete unless partnered by a man" (Boonzaier 2006, 146). The corporeal equivalent of male dominance and female submission is seen in the binary opposition where men display bodily strength and firmness, while women manifest physical weakness. Upon examining this opposition in more detail, it resolves fairly quickly into a gendered version of the Cartesian mind-body split. Men are associated with rationality (the mind), while women are associated with emotion, the body and the irrational. Men's superior physical strength, when seen against women's supposed weakness,

1 For example, Svetlana Alexievich's book, *War's Unwomanly Face*, describes woman's nature as inherently compassionate: "All that we know about Woman is best described by the word 'compassion'" (Bausells 2015).

is another attribute of masculine rationality: women's greater embodiment is seen as the consequence of their greater physicality. The "hardness" and power of the ideal male body derives from the fact that the male body is a tool of the mind, while the weaker female body intrudes upon the workings of the mind (as in classical misogynistic views of hysteria),[2] forcing acknowledgement of its corporeality.

The necessity of a gendered mind-body split in order for romantic love to function dates back to classical Greek philosophy, in texts such as Plato's *Symposium*, where men and women are portrayed as severed halves of a composite-sexed being that is both male and female (Plato 2013). In this view, females and males need to find and reunite with the amputated halves of themselves in order to experience ontological wholeness. The *Symposium* may be challenged on several counts, notably the numerical: in order for a perfect union to occur between all heterosexual couples, there would need to be exactly the same number of women and men alive at any one time.

The gendered mind-body split, and its foundational role in the myth of romantic love, has been challenged in several texts, such as Chaucer's *Wife of Bath's Prologue* and *Tale*; Shakespeare's *The Taming of the Shrew*; and many others throughout the history of literature. Likewise, it has been analysed and critiqued in depth by feminist literary critics and theorists, including Virginia Woolf in *A Room of One's Own*, Carolyn Heilbrun in *Writing a Woman's Life*, and Janice Radway in *Reading the Romance: Women, Patriarchy and Popular Fiction*. Nevertheless, I contend that the archetype of a physically strong, rational man finding emotional fulfilment with a weaker woman who possesses remarkable emotional intelligence is current in popular western culture and exerts controlling gender-normative power over both men and women. Judith Butler points to the social need for stable gender identities in *Gender Trouble: Feminism and the Subversion of Identity* when she writes: "persons' only become intelligible through becoming gendered in conformity with recognizable standards of gender intelligibility" (Butler 2008, 23). Butler's "recognizable standards" are produced by what she calls "regulatory practices", by which social subjects are constructed to fit pre-existing gender norms, including the binary division that associates men with the mind (cognitive rationality) and women with the body, including irrationality and emotion. Butler goes on to explain that " 'Intelligible' genders are those which in some sense institute and maintain relations of coherence and continuity among sex, gender, sexual practice, and desire" (Butler 2008, 23). Butler's relevance to my reading of the narratives of love in *1Q84* and the *Hunger Games* trilogy lies in her recognition of the

2 See, for example, Sandra M. Gilbert and Susan Gubar (2000).

importance of gender conformity for social stability and reproduction. While marriage is, pre-eminently, a mechanism for ensuring that social structures are perpetuated, in my view its successful maintenance relies on men subscribing to and enacting the ideals of masculinity as "real men", while women are coerced into behaving as "real women". My chapter will explore how these gendered ideals and the power dynamic they create and police are challenged in *1Q84* and the *Hunger Games* trilogy.

These twenty-first-century texts pose similar questions of the dominant order of gender and sexuality to the film *Nathalie*, directed by Anne Fontaine and discussed, in this volume, by Angela Tumini. As Tumini explains in her chapter, "Anne Fontaine's *Nathalie*: Un-Gendered Spaces and Fluid Desires", "*Nathalie* destabiliz[es] the structures of mainstream cinema where the action, the gaze and vocal discourse usually belong to men". Fontaine's film, in a similar vein to the trilogies by Murakami and Collins, expresses scepticism towards normative gender performances. This might appear to be a feature of late twentieth-century culture, were it not for Kelly Gardiner's salutary reminder, in her chapter, "Fictions of Love: Writing about 17th-Century Ideas of Gender and Love" in this volume, that gender nonconformity, although a modern term, has roots stretching from the Sapphic tradition to seventeenth-century France in the figure of the cross-dressing swordswoman and opera singer nicknamed La Maupin: "a romanticised Sappho who loved women and men, a goddess and a fairground folly – all in one sublime and queer figure". Gardiner's use of the term "queer" is key to her version of La Maupin, because the woman herself, Gardiner demonstrates, interrogates and queers our understanding of gender and sexuality.

1Q84 and the *Hunger Games* trilogy differ from other philosophical and literary challenges to the gendered mind-body paradigm because they belong to anti-realist genres. Abandoning the realist impulse opens up the imaginative possibility of creating worlds that are different from our consensus reality, in a manner that is reminiscent of Darko Suvin's definition of utopia: "Utopia is the verbal construction of a particular quasi-human community where sociopolitical and individual relationships are organized according to a more perfect principle than in the author's community" (Suvin 1979, 49).

Murakami's *1Q84* presents two worlds. One is a realistic description of late twentieth-century Japan; the other is parallel to our own, but mysteriously diverges from our world in certain unsettling ways. Murakami is acknowledged for his penchant for writing novels in which "a highly detailed", realistic setting is invaded by something "too strange to believe" (Strecher 1999, 267). This unexplained strange element causes the secondary world, which the protagonist Aomame dubs "1Q84", to exhibit traces of its own non-congruence: its night sky sports two moons instead of our customary one; and its rules of causality diverge from ours in including magical foundations and supernatural beings at the sources of mysterious events. Collins's phenomenally successful *Hunger Games* trilogy belongs squarely in the genre of YA (Young Adult fantasy). Charlotte Burcher writes of YA that a "generous approach to the genre includes any work that contains magic or other elements that cannot be understood by the rules of reality" (Burcher et al 2009, 227). Both narratives depart significantly from consensus reality, and, I shall argue, from gender norms as well, although they both ultimately culminate in traditional romantic happy endings.

1Q84

The lovers in Murakami's *1Q84* trilogy are Aomame and Tengo Kawana. Murakami alternates them as viewpoint characters in successive chapters, prefiguring their eventual romantic union. The entire novel of more than 1400 pages can be seen as an elaborate intrigue in order to bring them together and as a literary conceit alluding to the difficulty of arriving at romantic union. Tengo and Aomame met once as ten-year-old children, at primary school. Aomame's family are Jehovah's Witnesses, while Tengo is the only son of an NHK (television licence) fee collector. In one archetypal moment, Aomame grips Tengo's hand, and this moment changes both of their lives forever. The moment of holding hands – a memory to which the narrative returns repeatedly – is a typical exaggerated "love at first sight" moment, where the two lovers meet and realise that they are destined to be together. It is prefigured by two significant facts regarding the children's gender performances. First, Tengo is announced as the class genius in mathematics – a subject in which boys are alleged to excel because it supposedly demands hard, clear logic rather than fuzzy verbal ability, which underpins reputedly "soft" subjects such as language proficiency, art appreciation, and the social sciences, in which girls are thought to fare better. A second aspect of gender performance is Aomame's social isolation. As a child of Witness parents, she is required to recite a formulaic prayer of thanks over every meal she eats, and this means that nobody at school ever speaks to her. Aomame's religion makes her a social outcast, quite the opposite of stereotypes regarding girls' social abilities and facility with language. Religion is perceived as mystical, numinous and profoundly imbricated with power, in a way that mathematics, which prides itself on objectivity, is not. It is ironic that Aomame's religion (purportedly a system of connection between the deity and human beings) makes her a social pariah, in parallel with Tengo, who is exiled because of his mathematical prowess. In this early encounter, Murakami sets up what has by now become a signature dichotomy in his fiction between social conformity and social disjuncture. Strecher observes that "Murakami's central theme for most of his career has been that the concept of individual identity runs counter to the dominant social structure of post-1970 Japan" (Strecher 1999, 280).

The two protagonists are presented to the reader twenty years later, as thirty-year-old adults. By now, Aomame has become a gym instructor by day and a hardened killer in her secret life, while Tengo is a mathematics tutor at a cram school by day and an aspirant novelist in his spare time. They have both shifted away from their previous gender performances.

Aomame

In the novel's opening chapter, significantly entitled "Don't let appearances fool you" (with obvious resonances for demands that women conform to fixed ideas about attractiveness), the reader learns that Aomame tries to blend into every situation and consequently leaves no fixed impression on the minds of those who meet her. We are told that

> what she most wanted was to blend in with her background by changing color and shape, to remain inconspicuous and not easily remembered. This was how she had protected herself since childhood. (Murakami 2012, 35)

In this pointed remark about social conformity, Murakami suggests that Aomame (whose unusual name means "green peas" in Japanese), overtly, at least, conforms to social ideals of femininity as a cover for her subversive performance of gender. It is as though Aomame dare not openly reveal the extent of her disaffection with gender norms, and is driven to adopting a bland and featureless, gender-conforming persona as a survival mechanism. While Aomame is not in drag, she nevertheless manifests a similar drive towards invisibility as a sign of successful gender performance, concealing another persona within.

Aomame is a gym instructor and excels in physical fitness. In this way, she has adopted a masculine position *vis-à-vis* embodiment, cultivating the resilience, hair-trigger reflexes and nerves of steel that characterise the traditional male hero. This figure is described by science fiction critic, Joanna Russ, in terms that recall dragon-slayers in traditional fantasy tales: " 'invulnerable … super-potent … absolutely self-sufficient … never frightened [or] indecisive' and 'he always wins.' In short, she conclude[s], 'an alien monster' " (Kelso 2006, 247).

The traditional male hero's task is to right a social or global wrong, as Joseph Campbell notes in *The Hero with a Thousand Faces* (1972), and this is Aomame's quest, too. The victims of Aomame's deadly precision with her sharpened mini-ice pick are all men who have physically or emotionally abused women. In killing one male abuser after another, Aomame avenges the victims of male aggression and also channels social anger towards the perpetrators. Her choice of sexual partners also does not conform to stereotypes about women's fondness for emotional intimacy. In fact, these choices reveal masculine propensities. Her only close relationship as an adolescent was a lesbian encounter with Tamaki Otsuka. After Tamaki's suicide, provoked by her husband's abuse, Aomame develops a taste for casual, anonymous sexual encounters. In both these cases – first, in the lesbian encounter with Tamaki, and second, in the habit of anonymous sex – Aomame behaves more in keeping with what is expected from a man than a woman. Nevertheless, her aversion to emotional intimacy is revealed, as the plot unfolds, as the result her unshakeable attachment to her first love, Tengo Kawana, who stood up for her when they were both ten years old. In this way, although Aomame appears to challenge conventions regarding gendered behaviour in intimate relationships, in fact she complies with stereotypes of women's fidelity and emotional sensitivity.

Tengo

Tengo, like Aomame, also violates gender norms, and in particular, hegemonic masculinity, in a variety of ways. The first detail the reader learns about him is that he is susceptible to emotional flashbacks to an event in infancy, when he came upon a man who was not his father sucking his mother's breasts (Murakami 2012, 18–21). A hegemonic perspective on masculinity would see this behaviour as weakness, since rationality is the preserve of masculinity and its opposite, susceptibility to attacks of emotion, is perceived as equivalent to feminine hysteria. The corollary is that normative behaviour for men is emotionally distant: "For females, the cultural script for a romantic relationship dictates being sentimental, vulnerable, and submissive; for males, the cultural script dictates being cool, nonchalant, and in control" (Norona et al 2013, 440). Tengo's uncontrollable memory of his mother's breasts being adulterously sucked is a version of a primal Oedipal moment, when a highly susceptible child came upon his primary love object – his mother – engaged in adultery. Under the influence of this trauma, Tengo displays none of the attributes of normative masculinity: he is neither cool, nonchalant, nor in control, but seized by emotional excess beyond his control. This is in contrast with Tengo's usually passive, routine lifestyle, observed by the private investigator Ushikawa to be "a monotonous, simple lifestyle, easy to fathom" (Murakami 2012, 624). In contrast to conventional ideas of men as initiators of action, Tengo is slow to rouse and seldom engages either in decisive activity or in risk-taking.

His feminised gender attributes are possibly most clearly evident in the exercise of his creative aspirations. He spends days either writing an unsuccessful novel, or editing the work of others. His most important act in *1Q84* sees him reluctantly editing a novel entitled *Air Chrysalis* by the adolescent girl, Eriko Fukada, whose pseudonym is Fuka-Eri. In the resulting co-authorship, Fuka-Eri contributes the plot and main ideas of the book, while Tengo adds literary style and form. If we follow the conventional distinction between meaning and form in literature, meaning is prioritised as being closer to the notion of pure idea or mind (which is associated with men), while form is seen as less important and associated with women. In this act, Tengo is a far cry from the image of a male author as warrior or God-like creator, wielding his pen as a phallic weapon.[3] Rather, Tengo acts as a literary midwife, facilitating the completion and publication of a text whose driving ideas he has not authored (the gender connotations are intentional). Fuka-Eri is the originator of the text's meaning, while Tengo contributes as an editor or ghostwriter, working on the novel's form. The novel is published under Fuka-Eri's name, with no reference to Tengo, in an inversion of the more usual situation where women act as editors or ghostwriters for men, receiving no acknowledgement for their work.

Aomame and Tengo are brought together, after a twenty-year separation, by means of a complicated series of events involving supernatural forces (the Little People) and at least two sinister assassination plots. Overall, this resonates with the trope of a predestined union between lovers. At one point, in the playground where they will finally meet again, Aomame thinks:

> *I'm just following the plan that has already been laid out. Continuing to live, alone, in this unreasonable world – where there are two moons in the sky, one large, one small, where something called Little People control the destiny of others – what meaning could it have anyway?* (Murakami 2012, 675)

This quotation alludes to many layers of meaning, including the feeling of being controlled by others which is a feature of Murakami's representation of Japan in the late twentieth century, but is used here with ironic intent because Aomame does not realize the extent to which she is being controlled by Murakami and by the romantic narrative script.

3 See, for example, Gilbert and Gubar (2000, 6–8).

One of the most significant features of Tengo's and Aomame's reunion is that they come together in a different world from that of consensus reality. In that world, which Aomame dubs "1Q84" because it is insidiously, but qualitatively different from 1984, many factors coalesce to engineer their romance. The reader is led to conclude that huge ontological and representational shifts are required in order for the (re-)union of true lovers to occur.

The *Hunger Games* Trilogy

In a similar vein, the *Hunger Games* trilogy presents two adolescents, Katniss Everdeen and Peeta Mellark. The two of them combat sinister forces together in a dystopian society, where the forces of social control, centralised in the Capitol, conduct cruel "Games", modelled on the Roman Circus, where contestants fight to the death in a specially designed arena. The contestants are "reaped" by the Capitol's agents from the subservient Districts in order to reinforce state power. Katniss and Peeta are finally united as lovers after extensive and traumatic conflict, both in the Games as sacrifices to the power of the Capitol, which stages these deadly activities in order to reinforce its power over the populace, and in the rest of Panem. The series ends once the cruel regime has been defeated, and it is then that Katniss and Peeta are romantically united. It is also significant that the trilogy is structured as a love triangle, with Katniss being courted by both Gale and Peeta, and her eventual choice of Peeta is portrayed as inevitable or predestined. The proletarian anger against the Capitol that fuels a rebellion with Katniss as its figurehead is associated with fire, and this, she says, is not what she needs for healing:

> what I need to survive is not Gale's fire, kindled with rage and hatred .... What I need is ... [t]he promise that life can go on .... And only Peeta can give me that. (Collins 2010, 274)

Social media sites acclaim the *Hunger Games* trilogy as a prototypical romantic narrative: there are two entire Facebook pages entitled "I want somebody to love me like Peeta loves Katniss" (Facebook 2014a) and "I want someone like Peeta Mellark" (Facebook 2014b), testifying to the mass appeal of their story of mutual devotion and eventual romantic union. These popular romantic responses conveniently overlook the fact that the trilogy is shaped by the dominant concerns of the society that produced it. In fact, it manifests similar kinds of gender blurring to *1Q84*, with the two main protagonists diverging significantly from gender ideals. Despite this, they attain a conventional romantic union in which the once-ferocious hunter, Katniss, settles down to marriage and motherhood in the final chapter of the trilogy. This outcome is reminiscent of the opening line of *Jane Eyre*'s final chapter: "Reader, I married him" (Bronte 1969, 381), and has a similar disappointing effect on the reader. Collins attempts to create continuity with the dramatic events that have preceded this outcome by inserting the trope of a game, which has dominated the trilogy, into the incongruous domestic scene of Katniss as a mother of two anonymous children (a boy and a girl, in an echo of the statistically average heteronormative family with a father, a mother and 2.5 children (Collins 2010, 275)).

Katniss

Katniss is introduced to the reader, at the beginning of the trilogy, in hypermasculine terms:

> I … slide into my hunting boots. Supple leather that has moulded to my feet. I pull on trousers, a shirt, tuck my long dark braid up into a cap, and grab my forage bag. (Collins 2007, 4)

Katniss's boots and trousers appear to be simply functional and appropriate for a day of hunting for food in the woods. In fact, though, they are masculine (not unisex) items of clothing; their colours are bland and neutral; her long hair, which is an obvious signifier of femininity, is bound up beneath her cap; and importantly, she carries a bow and arrows with which to hunt prey for her family to eat. Since her father's death on the mines, Katniss has been the major food provider: a traditionally masculine family role. Her bow and arrows emphasise her physical prowess and masculinity. Her first interaction is with her sister's cat, and it is bristly and unaffectionate, quite the opposite of women's supposed fondness for pets: Katniss feeds the cat the entrails of her kills in return for him not hissing at her (Collins 2007, 4).

Later in the narrative, her hypermasculinity is replaced by hyperfemininity. Once Katniss has volunteered as tribute in her sister's place (an act motivated by stereotypical feminine concern for her family), she is subjected to a series of makeovers conducted by a "prep team" whose job is to prepare her for public appearances. The prep team removes Katniss's body hair (an act designed to emphasise "feminine" vulnerability) and engages in extended and systematic hair, make-up and clothing interventions. These makeovers present a highly contrived version of Katniss to the public of Panem, in an attempt to gain sympathy for a pretty girl who is destined to die. They are, in effect, devices that yoke together decorative femininity and death. Death is inevitable for all the tributes in the Hunger Games, while the Games themselves are an elaborate mass media production, aimed to drive home the Capitol's power to inflict death by violence or starvation on its hapless citizens.

As part of the makeovers, Katniss is clothed in three bespoke outfits: the unitard that she wears for the tributes' parade; her fire-coloured interview dress; and the wedding dress that she is sent, with considerable cynicism, by President Snow. While Katniss enjoys being "dressed up", in a textual reference to girls' fondness for clothing and fashion, all the dresses encode a variety of signifiers. For example, each of them changes to another outfit with a more sinister meaning than the original garment. The black unitard breaks into fake flames as Katniss and Peeta ride around the Capitol, reminding the viewers of their origin in the coal-mining district and also alluding to the deadly dangers of the Hunger Games. This appearance earns Katniss the moniker "Girl on Fire", which is borne out by the fire-coloured dress she wears for her television interview before the Games. This one makes Katniss appear "as radiant as the sun" (Collins 2007, 146), and also bursts into flames as she twirls. Finally, the wedding dress, although originally intended cynically as a public relations exercise to distract the citizens' attention from the uprising that is spreading, like wildfire, throughout the service districts, burns away entirely as she twirls. It leaves behind a black feathery mockingjay outfit that prefigures Katniss's role as the figurehead of the uprising that will eventually destroy the Capitol.

The mutability of the dresses signals Katniss's hybrid identity, as both a hypermasculine hunter and a hyperfeminine fashion icon. At the same time, her role as a mockingjay alludes to the jabberjays, birds that have been genetically manipulated to copy others' utterances. Mockingjays are mutations on the jabberjay prototype, and they also copy what is said or sung to them, but not on command. Katniss is a human version of a mockingjay: initially she behaves according to the Capitol's programming, but eventually turns it to revolutionary ends.

Peeta

The subplot of *The Hunger Games* trilogy concerns a love triangle in which Katniss's affections are divided between Gale and Peeta, and the narrative dénouement presents the final resolution between their competing suits. The opening chapter recounts Katniss' meeting with Gale in terms that emphasise their parity, both as hunters and as deprived citizens of District Twelve, where food is constantly in short supply and teenagers resort to hunting wild animals in order to feed their families. Katniss and Gale, dressed in similar brown outfits for camouflage, are presented as equally masculine in their ability to find their way in the woods and kill their prey. Peeta Mellark, who will later be the male tribute from District 12 and Katniss's eventual partner, is presented in contrasting, feminised terms: he is more at home indoors, in the bakery, than in the outdoor terrain of Katniss's hunting ground. He is also given to expressions of spontaneity and emotion which do not sit well with the stereotype of masculine rationality. For example, in the pre-Games interview with Caesar Flickerman, Peeta declares to the entire television audience that he is in love with Katniss. Radway explains that the romantic formula transforms the male protagonist from emotional distance and coldness to intimacy and expressiveness (1991, 216), but Peeta needs no such transformation. He does not display the same level of rationality in solving problems as Katniss; in the Games arena, his strategy is defensive rather than aggressive, and when wounded, he follows Katniss's lead without question. He easily adopts the feminised role of a follower in their relationship, rather than taking on the "strong" leadership role that characterises hegemonic masculinity.

Peeta is also cognitively feminised through his greater facility with language than Katniss possesses. Throughout the trilogy there are numerous references to his ability to use words persuasively and evocatively. Katniss reflects:

> I think of words and I think of Peeta. How people embrace everything he says. He could move a crowd to action, I bet, if he chose to. Would find the things to say. (Collins 2009, 124)

This contradicts the supposed division between science and mathematics as subjects in which boys excel, and languages as subjects where girls excel ("Gender Achievement and Motivation" 2014). Peeta's artistic talents – decorating confectionery and sketching – are also more in line with "decorative" skills, purportedly more suitable for women, than Katniss's hunting prowess. Finally, the cognitive difficulties he displays after being wounded in the special Hunger Games held every twenty-five years (known as the Quarter Quell) compromise his ability to serve as a beacon of rationality according to the masculine ideal. After this, Peeta relies on Katniss to help him distinguish between reality and his twisted mental version of it. It is significant that Collins chooses to illustrate the effects of post-traumatic stress disorder in a male victim, because this hints at emotional weakness that is usually associated with women, further feminising Peeta. In the final analysis, Katniss remains both emotionally and physically stronger than Peeta, and her superiority, together with his dependency, is portrayed as a central component in their union. She chooses Peeta, not only because he adopts a resolutely optimistic approach to life, but because he needs her.

Conclusion

The romantic unions of Aomame and Tengo in *1Q84*, and Katniss and Peeta in the *Hunger Games* trilogy, show each protagonist diverging from the socially constructed ideal of gender performance. Each of the female protagonists sports physical strength and prowess, which are necessary attributes for a male hero. In addition, they engage in aggressive and violent behaviour, although the texts portray these choices as morally motivated. Correspondingly, the male protagonists are feminised in a variety of ways. Tengo is revealed to be as passive as Aomame is active, while both he and Peeta are cognitively drawn to language and discursivity in ways that contradict boys' supposed greater facility with mathematics and science. (Tengo also displays genius in his talent for mathematics.) The result is that both couples' gender performance approach one another, with the men displaying more interest in emotional connection than is usually supposed to be masculine, and also demonstrating significant emotional weakness: Tengo through his susceptibility to Oedipal trauma, and Peeta through the psychic wounds inflicted on him by the Hunger Games. By contrast, the women behave, in many ways, as male heroes. Both Aomame and Katniss are motivated by a desire to right social wrongs, and they both adopt violence in order to achieve their goals.

The protagonists' gender-nonconformity may be interpreted as signifiers of a more egalitarian understanding of gender performance than the stereotypes that dominate mass media. However, this effect is mitigated by the fact that both of the love stories take place in unreal worlds. The world of 1Q84 is distinguished from 1984 by the presence of mysterious supernatural forces directing events, while the *Hunger Games* trilogy plays out in the alternate fantasy world of Panem. In this way, the authors locate their representations of true love outside the verisimilitude of social realist fiction. In this way, the novels diverge from what Lara calls "the stage in which life is experienced and conceived linguistically in the everyday world of fiction" (Lara 1998, 93). There are two possible interpretations of this. One is that the novels present traditional norms of gender performance as restricting individual identity. If we accept this explanation, then these works make valuable and liberating interventions into the way individual gendered identities are structured. In addition, the fact that the romantic unions take place between masculinised women and feminised men may be read as meaning that gender conformity is not (or is no longer) a prerequisite for romantic love. Another reading of the texts might hold that the authors view romantic love as impossible (an oft-recurring theme in Murakami's fiction) within the prescriptive bounds of contemporary society and hence choose to locate it in parallel worlds where different realities obtain. Whichever interpretation one prefers, neither text offers much hope for the conventional narrative of heterosexual romance along with the gender conformity that it requires and inscribes.

References

Bausells, Marta. 2015. "Everything You Need to Know about Svetlana Alexievich, Winner of the Nobel Prize in Literature". http://www.theguardian.com/books/booksblog/2015/oct/08/everything-you-need-to-know-about-svetlana-alexievich-winner-of-the-nobel-prize-in-literature.

Boonzaier, Floretta. 2006. "A Gendered Analysis of Woman Abuse". *The Gender of Psychology*, by Tamara Shefer, Floretta Boonzaier and Peace Kiguwa (eds), 135–150. Cape Town: UCT Press.

Brontë, Charlotte. 1969. *Jane Eyre*. London: Oxford University Press.

Burcher, Charlotte, Neil Hollands, Andrew Smith, Barry Trott and Jessica Zellers. 2009. "Core Collections in Genre Studies: Fantasy Fiction 101". *Reference & User Services Quarterly* 48: 226–231.

Butler, Judith. 2008. *Gender Trouble: Feminism and the Subversion of Identity*. New York: Routledge.

Campbell, Joseph. 1972. *The Hero with a Thousand Faces*. Princeton, N.J.: Princeton University Press.

Collins, Suzanne. 2009. *Catching Fire*. New York: Scholastic.

Collins, Suzanne. 2007. *The Hunger Games*. New York: Scholastic.

Collins, Suzanne. 2010. *Mockingjay*. New York: Scholastic.

Facebook. 2014a. "I Want Somebody to Love Me Like Peeta Loves Katniss". http://www.microsoft.com/isapi/redir.dll?prd=ie&clcid=&pver=&ar=Best.

Facebook. 2014b. "I Want Someone Like Peeta Mellark". https://www.facebook.com/IWantSomeoneLikePeetaMellark.

Gilbert, Sandra M. and Susan Gubar. 2000. *The Madwoman in the Attic: The Woman Writer and the Nineteenth-Century Literary Imagination*. London: Yale University Press.

Kelso, Sylvia. 2006. “Evolutions of the Fantasy Hero in Peter Jackson’s *The Lord of the Rings* and Lois McMaster Bujold’s *The Curse of Chalion*”. *Paradoxa: Studies in World Literary Genres* 20: 247–262.

Lara, Maria Pia. 1998. *Moral Textures: Feminist Narratives in the Public Sphere*. Cambridge: Polity Press.

Murakami, Haruki. 2012. *1Q84*. Translated by Jay Rubin and Philip Gabriel. London: Vintage Books.

Norona, Jerika C., Avril Thorne, Madeleine R. Kerrick, Halley B. Farwood and Neill Korobov. 2013. “Patterns of Intimacy and Distancing as Young Women (and Men) Friends Exchange Stories of Romantic Relationships”. *Sex Roles* 68: 439–453.

Plato. 2013. *Symposium*. Translated by B. Jowett. Project Gutenberg. http://www.gutenberg.org/ebooks/1600.

Radway, Janice. 1991. *Reading the Romance: Women, Patriarchy and Popular Literature*. Chapel Hill: University of North Carolina Press.

Shakespeare, William. 1999. *Romeo and Juliet*. Edited by Rex Gibson. Cambridge: Cambridge University Press.

Strecher, Matthew C. 1999. “Magical Realism and the Search for Identity in the Fiction of Murakami Haruki”. *Journal of Japanese Studies* 25: 263–298.

Suvin, Darko. 1979. *Metamorphoses of Science Fiction: On the Poetics and History of a Literary Genre*. New Haven and Connecticut: Yale University Press.

Tuchakinsky, Riva H. 2002. “Feminist and Postfeminist Readings of Romantic Narratives: Heterosexual Romantic Experiences Versus *Sex and the City*”. *Feminist Media Studies* 8: 181–196.

University of Michigan. 2014. “Gender Achievement and Motivation: Differences in Math, Science, and Reading”. http://sitemaker.umich.edu/356.ling/differences_in_math__science__and_reading.

Wood, Julia T. 2001. “The Normalization of Violence in Heterosexual Romantic Relationships: Women’s Narratives of Love and Violence”. *Journal of Social and Personal Relationships* 18(2): 239–261.

CHAPTER 11

Anne Fontaine's *Nathalie*: Ungendered Spaces and Fluid Desires

Angela Tumini

> A l'interieur, ou je suis,
> le sexe n'existe pas.
>
> JEFFERSON 2000, 32

∵

Reclaiming the Gaze

Willing and able to discard the gender-biased parameters of classical films, Anne Fontaine operates as a female director who is fundamentally at odds with the gender-biased tradition that has dominated the film world for generations. Her work, therefore, offers a critique of society's middle-class value system, to which film-making has been bound over the years. Fontaine articulates her distaste for canonical male-dominated mainstream cinema, not simply by distancing herself from female conditioning, but by going a step further into denaturalizing the sex/gender role divide in her narrative. Fontaine challenges how gender categorization and task assignment within society is constructed and attributed within a heteronormative social system, and she reacts to the way in which gender roles have always succeeded in imposing themselves on female subjects. Thus, in *Nathalie*, her objective is to deconstruct the social assumption about sex differentiation, the question of femininity and masculinity, as well as the effect on women produced by the power of representation of such tropes in cinema making. Evidently, one of the impulses generating this feminist film is also the state of mind that has conditioned, formed and consequently framed women, morally and psychologically, within society. In particular, the pervasiveness of disciplinary power inscribing femininity, which produces women's constant preoccupation with appearance, has come to be regarded as natural and voluntary. It is something that women have internalized and it is organized around pleasing the patriarchal ego.

 | DOI:10.1163/9789004380233_013

Where film is concerned, Fontaine argues for new cinematic rules that resist codification according to patriarchal powers. She defies those hierarchies that prevail in patriarchal narrative structure or forms of art that respond solely to a male-centred agenda. Most of all, Fontaine works against what has been understood throughout the years as "woman's film," which has been described by Molly Haskell as:

> A term of critical opprobrium, woman's film carries the implication that women, and therefore women's emotional problems, are of minor significance. A film that focuses on male relationships is not pejoratively dubbed a "man's film" [...] but a psychological drama. (Haskell 1973, 20)

Fontaine's frustration as an artist is related to the practice of gender codification that has been going on in cinema for many years, having many adverse effects. Female characters have been damaged and marked both on the fictional and the artistic levels in a way that serves the needs of patriarchal social rule. The labelling of women has always proliferated on screen, whether it served to titillate men's erotic or obsessional sensibilities, or whether it reflected the themes of patriarchal control through social rituals. The patriarchal imprint has effectively been instilled in classical film-making through repetitive narrative patterns that favour certain typical scenarios. Examples are scenarios where damsels in distress are rescued by men, or where virginal brides are proudly delivered by fathers to their future husbands along flower-adorned church aisles, or the usual domestic spaces where the wife as commodity takes on the husband's name. As a woman director, Fontaine shows a particular sensitivity to the question of whether cinema, in all its sophistication, has consistently reinforced a cultural attitude that sees women as being nothing more than a part of the world of men. In this respect, her work seeks to reconfigure women's positioning and experiences within film on a radical level. Indeed, this is a trope that had represented a strong point of concern for feminists in previous years. As pointed out by Rachel Ritterbusch

> In 1973 Claire Johnston called for a women's cinema that would provide a viable alternative to the repressive structures of male-dominated cinema. For Johnston, such a counter-cinema would embody the working through of female desire. (Ritterbusch 2008, 68)

Johnston also stated that "in order to counter our objectification in the cinema, our collective fantasies must be released" (1973, 39). The argument she makes is validated by years of androcentric practice that has characterized film-making in general. That is to say that there has been a deliberate exclusion of women's voices and agency onscreen, which reflects a subconscious sexual conservatism, typical of society rooted within patriarchal ideology. While gender roles and their definition within cinema has been largely re-negotiated due to the increasing appearance of female heroes – the Lisbeth Salander saga for example, or the hard-fighting female killer-model such as Kill Bill – the general perception of the stereotypical dominant role in film being male still largely exists. One of the explanations for the predominance of "maleness" in cinema-making is offered by Nalini Paul, who concludes that:

> Ann Kaplan in *Women and Film: Both Sides of the Camera,* takes this analysis a step further by explaining why, in her view, the cinematic arena itself is gendered. Although the process of filming may seem objective, it is not sexually "neutral", in that the technical process itself corresponds to male sexual fantasy. (Paul 2004, n.p.)

Paul aptly remarks that, as indicated by Kaplan, the process of film-making is masculine because in most cases of mainstream Hollywood cinema, a male director and/or producer is in control of the camera's gaze.

In 2003, though, a new film appeared on the European cinematic horizon, entitled *Nathalie,* directed by French film-maker Anne Fontaine. With this work, Fontaine countered classical cinema by avoiding some of its most rigid conventions. Not only is the film entirely shot from a woman's perspective; it actually emasculates the male gaze by excluding his point of view from the centre not long after the beginning of the film. During the course of the film, the male protagonist is deprived of his agency and the narrative is re-written by positioning a woman as the main subject, agent and possessor of the gaze. Fontaine, this way, creates a gynocentric melodrama and rejects the classical narrative that sees women as excluded from the domain of male language. Interestingly, this film counters the androcentric view of traditional filmmaking with an unprecedented onscreen triangle of husband/wife/lover that, while seemingly altogether conventional in its nature at the outset, becomes entirely re-invented by the end. *Nathalie* gradually questions, shakes and finally deconstructs the concepts of traditional gender roles and gendered patterns of desire to their foundations. Framing these themes within the context of western societies, and French society in particular, Fontaine, in her film, reflects the argument brought forward by Connell and Messerschmidt, who regard the idea of masculinity in itself as flawed because it essentializes the character of men and imposes a false unity on a fluid and contradictory reality (Connell and Messerschmidt 2005). The narrative in *Nathalie* is built precisely around the fluidity and interchangeability of identity and gender positions, and it is in accordance with Simone de Beauvoir's theory of fabricated rather than "inherent" female gender. As Judith Butler explains:

> When Simone de Beauvoir claims, "one is not born, but, rather, becomes a woman," she is appropriating and reinterpreting this doctrine of constituting acts from the phenomenological tradition. In this sense, gender is in no way a stable identity of locus of agency from which various acts proceed; rather, it is an identity tenuously constituted in time – an identity instituted through a stylized repetition of acts. Further, gender is instituted through the stylization of the body and, hence, must be understood as the mundane way in which bodily gestures, movements, and enactments of various kinds constitute the illusion of an abiding gendered self. (Butler 1986, 35)

At first glance, the "stylization" of the body in the film, to use Simone de Beauvoir's term, may appear encoded in a frequently-seen binary opposition of women's higher and lower social status. What we are presented with is, as in many conventional films, the classy and aloof upper-middle class wife who has to compete with the exotic allure of the blonde-haired and sultry-looking sex worker. Yet, Fontaine's two female protagonists co-exist within the narrative as completely non-troublesome non-rivals, in spite of the divergence of their social backgrounds, identities and sexual behaviours. The usual tension between the women, which would be expected in this particular situation, is replaced by a natural harmony and affinity between them that borders a suggested intimacy. Determined to undermine the scopophilic tendencies of classic male-oriented cinema, Fontaine avoids any such visual pleasures by denying importance to graphic sexual moments. She, therefore, chooses to restrict the intimacy between the women, or between man and woman, to either a vocal or a mnemonic level, both of which are ambiguous and intriguing. That is because Fontaine considers what is behind the camera to be as important as what is in front of it. What matters the most to her is the investigation of the character's psychology when freed of the restrictive boundaries of mainstream cinema, and when allowed to snatch femininity away from the prejudices of the male gaze.

In *Nathalie,* there are two parallel narrative processes: Fontaine progressively reveals the traits of her female characters to the audience, while the two characters themselves are in the process of exploring the dynamics of their own desires; desire in this film fluctuates outside of gender-normative privileges and boundaries. In *Nathalie's* narrative the stereotypical dramatic triangle of wife/husband/lover is substituted with a double *entendre* between Catherine and Marlène/Nathalie that leaves no room for dominant male-centred language, which is instead muted and excluded. The film's voice is entirely female and deconstructs the concept of love and desire, which is used as a utopian force perpetually to reaffirm a social ideology that positions women in a subordinate role to men. As Marianne Schleicher points out in her chapter entitled "Attitudes to Deviation from Gender Norms in Israelite and Early Jewish Religion" in this volume, "gender and love are two performances that are formed by, but also render the human being vulnerable to the disciplinary forces of culture" and, one could add, this has generally determined the way in which femininity has been artificially designed. It is evident that Fontaine's work is fuelled by anger directed at the way in which gender roles and sexual behaviour have been structured by the regulatory power of patriarchy, and to which she reacts as a female artist. By regaining the powers of language and the gaze, and by re-positioning them within a system that favours ungendered representation, she gives new meaning and interpretation to her female characters. They exist, therefore, as independent active agents, who cannot be categorized as idealized objects of male fantasy. At the same time, Fontaine exposes how, within the patriarchal social order "gender, specifically femininity, is a discipline that produces bodies and identities and operates as an effective form of social control" (King 2004, 30).

To return to my earlier quotation by Claire Johnston, in *Nathalie* female objectification is completely countered by the absence of a male point of view from the diegetic space. Fontaine is deeply aware that throughout western art, from painting to modern film and television, as well as advertising, there has been a general assumption that the viewer is male and heterosexual. Since the vast majority of works were indeed created by males and heterosexuals, they have sealed the fate of the unspoken and unrepresented female perspective and psyche. Consequently Fontaine is seen to upset the mould of sexual difference, which is encoded in classical narrative. The dramatic composition of rich light and heightened emotions in Fontaine's film comes from her compelling female-centred narrative. Like a filmic surgeon, she uses her camera as an operating tool, with which she dissects, modifies and sews back the parameters of film according to her own terms. The elements of her characters, such as psychology, sexuality and desire, exist outside of the ruling symbolic order. Each of these elements has a hybrid and fluid undertone that she reworks in a way that escapes the pervasive power of patriarchal imagery and the repeated patterns of societal situations. In other words, Fontaine manages to create a "viable alternative to the repressive structures of male-dominated cinema", which was earlier proposed by Johnston.

Ungendering Desire

Nathalie begins with a disruption that occurs in the bourgeois life of a Parisian couple when the wife accidentally becomes aware of her husband's infidelity. We are, therefore, immediately introduced to the couple formed by Catherine, a gynaecologist played by Fanny Ardant, a woman who seemingly has it all, and Bernard, a successful businessman played by Gérard Depardieu. Upon the casual reaction of Bernard, who dismisses the affair as being of no importance, Catherine decides to hire Marlène, an *entreneuse* whom she carefully selects. One only needs to take a glance at Marlène to realize that she is configured according to the sexual spectrum of women who perfectly fit into men's sexual fantasies, hence the pre-meditated choice of having Emmanuelle Béart playing that role. Renamed Nathalie, the woman is hired by Catherine to seduce her husband and report all intimate details of her sexual encounters with him. The deliberate re-naming of the hired prostitute is intended to call attention to how identity is erased whenever women are objectified, while their bodies are valued only as objects for use by others, and for which they are evaluated in terms of the male gaze.

As a female character, Catherine is unique, considering that her emotional reaction to the discovery of her husband's infidelity is – to say the least – unusual. Rather than allowing her distress to get the better of her, she decides to engage in a "didactical" experiment in order to learn what her husband needs from women and how sexual desire can intersect with his socio-cultural identity. At this point in the film, Catherine's reaction completely defies the norms of the "cheated wife". As seen in the majority of films, infidelity is usually managed by women as traumatic, or, at best, by repressing their emotions, which in this case would be more typical of Catherine's upper-middle class social milieu. The camera then begins to focus more and more on the developing relationship of the two co-conspirators, Catherine and Marlène/Nathalie, which becomes closer and closer. During the regular *rendez-vous* between the two women, Marlène/Nathalie recounts her erotic performances to Catherine, sparing no graphic details. At the same time, however, she disinhibits the dividing social platforms from which the two women normally operate. Gradually, the two of them grow fond of each other "and not just because," as Slavoj Žižek remarks, "Marlène is the woman Catherine has chosen to perform an unusual task" (Žižek 2006, 189–190).

As their attachment gains strength, Marlène/Nathalie confesses to Catherine that her husband had, in truth, rejected all her advances, thus revealing how all of her accounts were completely fabricated. "Why?" asks Zižek when discussing *Nathalie* in his book, *The Parallax View*. In this film, there is no hint or promise of a *ménage à trois*, or of a clear lesbian affair. "It is crucial," adds Žižek,

> that the narrative they share is heterosexual [...] there is no frustration in it, no sacrificial renunciation of consummating their relationship "in the flesh", their conversation is not a foreplay endlessly postponing full satisfaction. (Žižek 2006, 189–190)

What we witness, rather, is a re-dimensioning of sensuality and expression between the two women as they learn from each other's reality, fiction and imagination. When Anita Gates reviewed the film in the *New York Times*, she could not resist tainting her admiration for the film with an amusing speck of irony by saying "Ms. Béart, in her scenes with Ms. Ardant, is soft, slow and a little breathless, which might have made *Nathalie* one long dirty phone call if it weren't so intelligent" (2006, n.d.). Gates' statement serves as a warning that to view this film through a narrow sexualized lens is to miss the essence of its meaning and its message. The development of the relationship between Catherine and Marlène/Nathalie in this film is, if anything, rather de-sexualized. By this I mean that Fontaine remains ambiguous in her narrative about the trope of lesbian intimacy, which in some films contributes to arouse men's imagination by hyper-sexualizing the screen with overt Sapphic scenes.

Fontaine's purpose is to avoid the objectification of the female body because that is a *leitmotif* of classical cinema and one of the points that she is clearly contesting. Besides, the objectification of women's bodies is part of a larger discourse concerning the scrutiny of the female body, which has perennially been the site of political contestation. From abortion to prostitution to virginity, the female body has been both idealized and denigrated, as well as being the focus of policy-makers in shaping society. As suggested by Angela King,

> Association with body/nature is strengthened by biological essentialist and determinist paradigms which define woman according to her reproductive physiology. She is thus feeble and passive, literally a receptacle for the desires of the male and incubator for his offspring; a creature driven by emotion and instinct; Woman's a slave to her reproductive organs/hormones. Man may be able to transcend his biological materiality, but woman is entrenched in her physicality – [as described by de Beauvoir] "a thing sunk deeply in its own immanence". (2004, 31)

Fontaine recognises that women's bodies are also the sites through which communal male identities are formed. For this reason she purposely frustrates the erotic appetite of the male spectators who may expect the homoerotic subject-matter that underpins her film to develop into a graphic sexual representation. In addition, the film deprives the male spectator of a possible pleasure of identification given that, as Jackie Stacey remarks,

> …[identification] involves not only *visual* point of view, constructed by type of shot, editing sequences and so on, but also *narrative* point of view, produced through the sharing of knowledge, sympathy, or moral values with the protagonist. (1973, 197)

Instead, the male protagonist in *Nathalie* has his moral values re-assessed by the two women. In this process, Fontaine steers the audience towards another feminist trope that she wishes to refer to in her narrative, namely the question of female bonding. This phenomenon is better understood as disturbing the conceptualization of male bonding, which is fundamental to the patriarchal language and economy originating in structural anthropology and psychoanalysis.

In *Nathalie* there is a major concern with the ungendering of desire and sexuality. This cannot be contained within the construction of rigid heterosexual or homosexual binaries, but must be understood as a fluid emotion that mutates through the stages of life and the various levels of love experiences. This perspective clashes with traditional views of sexual desire as having fixed traits and distinguishing parameters. The contents of Marlène/Nathalie's personal accounts, interacting with Catherine's cognitive curiosity, form the pivotal motif of the entire film-text. Bernard's character is overshadowed by the incisive presence of the two women and becomes only minimally relevant. Slavoj Žižek has interpreted this point in the film as a lesson on

> "true" *jouissance* which is neither in the act itself nor in the thrill of the expectation to come, but in the melancholic remembrance of it. And the enigma is: is it possible to imagine a sexual act in which the participants, while "really doing it" already adopt the imagined position of remembering it from which they *now* enjoy it? Furthermore, can we say that this position of *futur anterieur* is feminine, while the *jouissance* engendered by the thrill of pleasures to come is masculine? (2006, 189)

Catherine's *jouissance* is derived from an artificially fabricated memory of *jouissance* that she inherits through Marlène/Nathalie's erotic accounts. Furthermore, her *jouissance* responds to an "epistemological" desire and is not erotically perverted or merely voyeuristic in its origin, as it may seem. Her character function in the film is devised purely to reinstate the female displaced subject as the social determinant of events, who is not subjugated by the male gaze. On the contrary, the women in the film re-possess the gaze and the agency to subvert and to de-legitimize patriarchal dominance by ridiculing the very hierarchy on which it is built. The enigmatic and disquieting aspect of female nature, for which women were long held in contempt, takes on a refreshingly positive aspect in this film as a harmonious balance between emotion and rationality.

For this reason, Rachel Ritterbusch points out that Fontaine is one of those women film-makers who, much like Catherine Breillat and Laetitia Masson, "portrays women who explore sexuality without fear of punishment or social sanction" (Ritterbusch 2008, 69). In *Nathalie*, the patriarchal norm, which is usually there to repossess the female body for the purposes of male pleasure and exchange, is effectively disregarded. As gender positions are transgressed, Fontaine proposes a type of female identity that is totally insubordinate to conventional divisions in dominant societies. By hiring a prostitute to seduce her husband, Catherine is not merely interested in testing her husband's infidelity; she also sets in place a cognitive process that has psychoanalytical undertones. The element of jealousy, if there, remains vague and quite untraceable; Catherine's emotions in response to her husband's affair are channelled into a guise that is both unique and extreme. Fontaine's subtext in this film is to underline and assess the role played by imagination in the individuals' lives and the tension it can create in relation to their sexuality. In conventional film scenarios portraying the disruption of married life by the husband's infidelity, the wife's reaction would involve a sudden damaging surge of emotions that could even require medical assistance and that would not be resolved by paying for the services of a prostitute. But Fontaine cleverly pilots her narrative away from the usual *ménage à trois* stereotype and creates a feminist *oeuvre* which addresses the question of an ungendered sexual identity stripped of social restrictions. This perspective clashes with traditional views of sexual orientation as being a stable and fixed trait. Sexual identity acts quite autonomously in this film, since it cannot be related to distinct socially classified categories such as wife or lover, which are mutually exclusive. Neither can sexual identity be restrictively defined in relation to the "archetypal" divide between heterosexual and homosexual desires. Fontaine amplifies a critical message in her narrative: the evolution of desire pivots on the solidarity and the bonding of two women whose feelings are divorced from gender. Her mission is to prevent the women's desire from being hijacked once more by the patriarchal camera gaze, which systematically re-proposes a filmic syntax that disregards women's point of view on the screen. As Catherine and Marlène/Nathalie move through the various stages and circumstances of their relationship in the film, gender becomes irrelevant. Fontaine, therefore, enables her characters to freely explore themselves as individuals worthy of love, longing and belonging. Fontaine configures a new understanding of women's psyche, based on an unbiased fluidity of sexuality and desires. She rejects any specific "queer" or heterosexual affiliation, proposing no affiliation at all. Moreover, by deconstructing the process of positioning an active subject versus a passive one, Fontaine challenges the basic assumptions of scopophilic pleasure that plague mainstream cinema. For this reason, she purposely avoids explicit sex scenes between the characters, as mentioned earlier, in order to frustrate the male spectator by depriving him of his dominant voyeuristic role, which is inherent in his phallocentric position.

Nathalie strongly recalls Laclos's *Les Liaisons Dangereuses – Dangerous Liaisons* (1782), adapted for the screen in 1988 by Stephen Frears. Here, the Marquise de Merteuil employs her former lover and confidant, the Vicomte de Valmont, in an intricate play of seduction in order to ridicule the concept of love. Whereas the accounts of the intrigue in *Nathalie* are all vocal, they are seen to be exclusively epistolary in *Dangerous Liaisons*. Interestingly, Kelly Gardiner, in her chapter in this volume entitled "Fictions of Love: Writing about 17th-Century Ideas of Love and Gender," asks: "in an era before Freud, before feminism, before notions of identity, how did a few transgressive women come to be celebrated, when others were punished?" The epistolary element that characterises *Dangerous Liaisons* partly relates to that question. Given that letter-writing in the eighteenth century was one of the principal vehicles for women to influence public opinion, it represented one of the ways in which some women were able to gain privileged access to a participatory social role over other women. Yet, while *Dangerous Liaisons* is a tale of seduction, but primarily a tale of complex moral ambiguities, in Fontaine's *Nathalie* the question of morality is of no importance. Catherine's deceitful enterprise represents an intellectual exercise that investigates the depths of human sexuality and desire; sex is not in the least romanticized, but it is mechanically recounted in time, while Bernard's point of view is completely silenced.

As already mentioned, the argument of feminist scholarship in several cases has been based on the evidence that classical Hollywood cinema was traditionally prone to favour active male protagonists gazing upon women displayed for their viewing pleasure. For example, Mary Anne Doane states that

> The cinema, in its alignment with the fantasies of the voyeur, has historically articulated its stories through a conflation of its central axis of seeing/being seen with the opposition male/female. So much so that in a classical instance such as *Humoresque*, when Joan Crawford almost violently attempts to appropriate the gaze for herself, she must be represented as myopic. (1988, 216)

Fontaine's intention in her film is to defy the laws of the patriarchal gaze, which are established as an omnipresent systemic structure of control, but, at the same time, she re-assesses the question of familiar theories such as those put forward by Laura Mulvey, where the male is identified as the active subject, while the female is considered as a passive object within the sexual framework (Mulvey 1988). In this film, Fontaine opposes the clear-cut assumptions made by Mulvey by developing fluid subject positions for her female characters. This way, she is able to enable them to transcend the rigid binary oppositions that shape and control conventional film plots. In other words, Fontaine alters Mulvey's binary model by reversing the role of women as objects of male desire and by purposely undermining the structure of the symbolic order. In Fontaine's cinematic universe, the gaze is not male by definition, nor is the passive female objectified over and over again. Fontaine's most evident thematic preoccupation in *Nathalie* is to rework the idea of subject self-creation by overtly avoiding the usual discourse based on established patriarchal sexual regimes. Essentially, she repudiates those connections that exist between inhibited individual choice and social determinants.

Evidence of that is given by Catherine, who symbolically crosses into a traditionally male space when she ventures into the "bowels" of a sleazy night club; this is a space populated by the spectacles of objectified women, namely the pole dancers and prostitutes, who are adorned and moulded to arouse the fantasies of libidinous men. It is worth noting that, in the official movie poster, Marlène/Nathalie is portrayed as sliding down a pole and bound in leather and black hosiery, as well wearing a corset-like bra. The corset is an object of scrutiny in the film because, as Susan Bordo observed, "[it] caused women actual physical incapacitation" but it also "served as an emblem of the power of culture to impose its designs on the female body" (King 2004, 34).

At first reaction, one would associate the image in the poster with the sadomasochistic tendencies found in the erotic rapports that feature in certain film narratives. Take for example Just Jaeckin's *Emmanuelle* (1974) and *Histoire d'O* (1975), which managed to rekindle curiosity about the notorious teachings of the Marquis De Sade amongst the younger generations of the 1970s. Yet, the poster of *Nathalie* is deceiving because, after viewing the film, we discover that the male need for "fetishistic scopophilia, [that] builds up the physical beauty of the [woman] object, transforming it into something satisfying in itself" (Mulvey 1988, 65), as defined by Laura Mulvey, will remain eventually unfulfilled. In truth, Fontaine's corseted heroine is never turned into a scopophilic object, but she is there to invite a reflection on the consequences produced by the structural parameters of femininity imposed on women through clothing.

Historically, the corset has bracketed ideal femininity, wavering between modesty and eroticism:

> [...] it conversely also had the effect of emphasising two erogenous zones: pushing up the breasts and flaring out over the hips and genital area. In fact, the pressure that the diaphragm and chest underwent due to the shape of the corset created the "peculiarly feminine heaving of bosoms so lovingly described in popular novels." This enhancement of feminine sexuality can also be seen in the connotations that having a slender, delicate waist would have. A slender waist suggests that the woman has not borne children yet, implying virginity and purity. (Aspinall 2012, n.p.)

At this point, it may also be useful to recall Simone de Beauvoir's theory of the "incapacitation" of females through male-originated fashion devices, as mentioned by King, which can easily apply to Fontaine's feminist discourse in the film:

> Paralysed by either too little or too much weight, by inconvenient attire or the "rules of propriety", woman's body could then "present the inert and passive qualities of an object" and "[seem]" to man to be his property, his thing". Thus containing the threat of the potentially unruly, too-physical female body. (King 2004, 34)

Fontaine creates a tension in her film between the "spatial illusion in which he [the male, Bernard] articulates the [his] look" (Mulvey 1988, 64) and her own personal mode of interpretation of femininity, female and gender dynamics. At the beginning of the film Bernard will appear as pivotal to the narrative and as the main event determinant. The position he holds, however, will become diminished and marginalized, while his perspective will be ignored. All the techniques that in cinema usually exalt voyeurism as an exclusively male privilege are avoided within this film to make sure that the man is denied the chance to assess and evaluate the body-object of women. On the subject of the gaze, Jaime Bihlmeyer explains that:

> In order for the female gaze to manifest itself, a re-evaluation/re-visioning of the Symbolic Order and its masking of femininity must occur, if only intuitively for the film-maker and the spectator [...] The female gaze is necessarily multiplex, problematic, ambivalent and progressive in terms of its potential for deconstructing the Symbolic Order. Furthermore, the female gaze poses a primal threat to phallocentric subjectivity, because

> it (re)asserts an uncanny and non-linear link to the repressed pre-(and extra-)lingual Imaginary Wholeness. (2013, n.p.)

This theory can be applied to Fontaine's filmic text, which is intended to advocate a refreshing female perspective that favours a fluid surge of desire unchained from socio-political demands, and that is not bound by a strict binary gender dynamics. After a brief encounter with the male protagonist Bernard, the spectators get to hear of him only through the erotic accounts reported by the hired *entreneuse* Marlène/Nathalie, which turn out to be entirely fabricated. As the film progresses, therefore, not only is the male voice completely effaced, but there is an ongoing alienation of the male figure: Bernard becomes a fictional character within the fiction that takes place in the diegetic space. His major purpose within the narrative is to facilitate Fontaine's deconstruction of accepted notions of female sexual subjectivity, which have conveniently been inscribed within the laws of patriarchy, and to challenge the conventional discourses that construct female sexuality. This revolutionary process of ungendering desire in *Nathalie* must be understood in terms of rational individual choice; a choice of style that sees fluidity of sexual identities as a tool to deny social constraints. Catherine's choice represents her quest for an identity *per se* which is ungendered and at odds within the inhibiting parameters of accepted collective social behaviour. Catherine's style reflects some of the insights mentioned by Ladelle McWhorter, who states that:

> The work of style is the artistry with which we live our lives. We can't just say no to sexual regimes; if we want to undermine the regimes of power and knowledge that oppress and threaten to dominate us, we have to cultivate a new way of life that stands counter to them and eventually that is just other to them. And that is a matter of the deliberate cultivation of style. (1999, 190)

Conclusion

The narrative of Anne Fontaine's *Nathalie* is determined by the "cultivation of style", in McWhorter's words, which implies shifting identities and tropes such as erotic energy and sexual fantasy dictated by female voices. Moreover, the film offers a sustained critique of the stereotypes put forward by classical cinema that has constructed and promoted the ideological image of woman according to sexual and psychological determinants, which exist entirely to serve patriarchy. Fontaine creates a scenario that destabilizes the structure of mainstream cinema, where the men control the gaze, emotions, events and their consequent reactions. The narrative of this film is, therefore, centred on women's agency and voice and aims at destabilizing the structures of mainstream cinema where the action, the gaze and vocal discourse usually belong to men. In other words, Fontaine opposes a cinema where the women characters are defined by their relationship to the already-established default of masculinity, whose authority and identity traits have been set in stone by cultural traditions. What makes the situation unusual within the discourse of distinctive gendered tasks is Catherine's pioneering of a gender position that implies a self-formulated use of her husband's desire in the service of her own cognitive investigation. Her husband's presupposed and manipulated seduction takes place thanks to a second woman, whom she chooses, instructs and finally bonds with. Moreover, Catherine's *jouissance* relates to an objectification of Bernard, which is dependent on his seduction by an "other" woman; someone whom she, herself, distracts from the typical masculine arena of the nightclub. Fontaine, therefore, reworks the idea of patriarchal sexual regimes by subverting those connections that exist between inhibited individual choice and socio-political and cultural determinants. Furthermore, not only does this eliminate the stereotypical masculine trait of sexual aggressiveness, but it also represents an ungendering of the male sexual authority when Bernard's desire is shaped and controlled by the bonding of two women.

References

Aspinall, Hanna. 2012. "The Fetishization and Objectification of the Female Body in Victorian Culture." *Brighton Online Student Literary Journal.* 10 August 2012. http://arts.brighton.ac.uk/study/literature/brightonline/issue-number-two/the-fetishization-and-objectification-of-the-female-body-in-victorian-culture.

Bihlmeyer, Jaimie. 2013. "Jane Campion's The Piano: The Female Gaze, the Speculum and the Chora within the H(y)st(e)rical Film." *Feminine Politics in Popular Culture: The Construction of Gender* 4 (I): n.p. http://commons.pacificu.edu/cgi/viewcontent.cgi?article=1064&context=eip.

Butler, Judith. 1986. "Sex and Gender in Simone de Beauvoir's Second Sex." *Simone de Beauvoir: Witness to a Century. Yale French Studies* 72, 35–49. Yale University Press.

Connell, W. R., and James W. Messerschmidt. 2005. "Hegemonic Masculinity: Rethinking the Concept." *Gender & Society*.19: 829–959. http://www.engagemen-me.org/sites/default/files/HegemonicMasculinity-RethinkingtheConcept(R.W.ConnellandJamesW.Messerschmidt).pdf.

Doane, Mary Anne. 1988. "Woman's Stake: Filming the Female Body." In *Feminism and Film Theory,* edited by Constance Penley, 216–228. New York: Routledge.

Gates, Anita. 2006. "French Star Power and Sex in Anne Fontaine's 'Nathalie'." *The New York Times.* April 14. http://www.nytimes.com/2006/04/14/movies/14nath.html?_r=0.

Haskell, Molly. 1973. "The Woman's Film." In *Feminist Film Theory*, edited by Sue Thornham, 20–30. New York: New York University Press.

King, Angela. 2004. "The Prisoner of Gender: Foucault and the Disciplining of the Female Body." *Journal of International Women's Studies* 5 (2): 29–39. http://vc.bridgew.edu/cgi/viewcontent.cgi?article=1532&context=jiws.

Jefferson, Anne. 2000. *Nathalie Sarraute, Fiction and Theory: Questions of Difference.* Cambridge: Cambridge University Press.

Johnston, Claire. 1973. "Women's Cinema as Counter-Cinema." In *Feminist Film Theory: A Reader*, edited by Sue Thornham, 31–40. New York: New York University Press.

McWorther, Ladelle. 1999. *Bodies and Pleasures: Foucault and Politics of Sexual Normalization.* Bloomington: Indiana University Press.

Mulvey, Laura. 1973. "Visual Pleasure and Narrative Cinema." In *Feminist Film Theory: A Reader,* edited by Sue Thornham, 58–69. New York: New York University Press.

Ritterbusch, Rachel. 2008. "Anne Fontaine and Contemporary Women's Cinema in France." *Rocky Mountain Review* 62 (1): 68–81.

Stacey, Jackie. 1999. "Feminine Fascinations: Forms of Identification in Star-Audience Relations." In *Feminist Film Theory: A Reader*, edited by Sue Thornham, 27–42. New York: New York University Press.

Žižek, Slavoj. 2006. *The Parallax View.* Cambridge MA: MIT Press.

Index

www.ingramcontent.com/pod-product-compliance
Lightning Source LLC
Chambersburg PA
CBHW071442230926
51846CB00001B/310
9789004378285